The European Community : Econoı

The European Community: Economic and Political Aspects

Valerio Lintner
School of Languages and European Studies
Polytechnic of North London

and

Sonia Mazey
Department of Government
Brunel, The University of West London

McGRAW-HILL BOOK COMPANY

London · New York · St Louis · San Francisco · Auckland
Bogotá · Caracas · Lisbon · Madrid · Mexico
Milan · Montreal · New Delhi · Panama · Paris · San Juan
São Paulo · Singapore · Sydney · Tokyo · Toronto

Published by
McGRAW-HILL Book Company Europe
Shoppenhangers Road, Maidenhead, Berkshire, SL6 2QL, England
Telephone 0628 23432
Fax 0628 770224

British Library Cataloguing in Publication Data
Lintner, Valerio
   The European Community : economic and political aspects.
   1. European Community
   I. Title II. Mazey, Sonia
   341.2422

   ISBN 0-07-707231-6

Library of Congress Cataloging-in-Publication Data
Lintner, Valerio.
   The European Community : economic and political aspects / Valerio Lintner and Sonia Mazey.
      p.   cm.
   Includes bibliographical references and index.
   ISBN 0-07-707231-6 :
   1. European Economic Community. 2. European Economic Community countries--Economic policy.
   3. Europe 1992. I. Mazey. Sonia.
   II. Title.
   HC241.2.L554 1991
      337.1'42--dc20   90-24723
                                                                          CIP

45 CL 93

Typeset by BookEns Limited. Baldock. Herts.
and printed and bound in Great Britain by Clays Limited. St Ives plc.

To our Parents

CONTENTS

Preface   xi

Acknowledgements   xiv

Selected abbreviations relevant to the European Community   xv

1.   THE EUROPEAN COMMUNITY: THEORY AND HISTORY   1
1.1   Introduction   1
1.2   Federalism and European integration   1
1.3   Pragmatic federalism: the establishment of the ECSC, EEC, and Euratom 4
1.4   Functionalism and neo-functionalism: 'spillover' as a means of integration   7
1.5   Community development and neo-functionalism: reappraisal and evaluation   8
1.6   Conclusion   11
       References   11

2.   EUROPEAN COMMUNITY POLICY-MAKING: THE INSTITUTIONAL
     CONTEXT   12
2.1   Introduction   12
2.2   The institutional parameters of Community policy-making   12
2.3   European Community institutions and policy-making: the impact of the
       Luxembourg Compromise   19
2.4   European Union and institutional reform   20
2.5   Conclusion   27
       Notes   28
       References   29

3.   THE CUSTOMS UNION AND THE COMMON MARKET: THEORETICAL
     BASIS   30
3.1   Introduction   30
3.2   Customs union theory   31
3.3   The theory of common markets: effect of factor mobility   38
       References   40

4.   '1992': THE COMMON MARKET IN PRACTICE   42
4.1   Introduction   42
4.2   The customs union: trade aspects of the common market   42
4.3   Labour and capital mobility aspects of the common market   47

4.4	'1992': the completion of the EC internal market?	48
4.5	1992: prospects	51
4.6	Conclusions	53
	References/further reading	53

5. MONETARY INTEGRATION IN THE EUROPEAN COMMUNITY — 55

5.1	Introduction	55
5.2	The theory of monetary integration	55
5.3	Monetary integration in practice: the European Monetary System	60
	References	71

6. THE BUDGET OF THE EUROPEAN COMMUNITY — 72

6.1	Introduction	72
6.2	The budget at present: size and limitations	73
6.3	Financing the Community	75
6.4	Community expenditure	76
6.5	Equity issues and the British problem: budgetary crisis	82
6.6	The budget in the future	86
6.7	EC budgetary politics	87
6.8	The budgetary procedure	88
6.9	Budgetary conflicts	90
6.10	The politics of budgetary reform	91
6.11	Conclusion	92
	References/further reading	92

7. THE COMMON AGRICULTURAL POLICY — 94

7.1	Introduction	94
7.2	The nature and functioning of the CAP	94
7.3	The benefits of the CAP	97
7.4	The disadvantages of the CAP	98
7.5	How the CAP might be improved	105
7.6	Obstacles to change	107
7.7	Recent reforms	108
	References	109

8. EUROPEAN COMMUNITY SOCIAL POLICY — 111

8.1	Introduction	111
8.2	The social provisions of the treaties establishing the communities	111
8.3	The evolution of Community social policy	112
8.4	The 1980s, European Union, and the social dimension of the internal market	122
8.5	Conclusion: towards a social Europe?	126
	References	126

9. MULTINATIONAL ENTERPRISES AND COMPETITION POLICIES — 128
   Nadia Tempini

9.1	Introduction	128
9.2	MNE: a definition	128
9.3	Economic consequences of MNE operations: the theory	129

9.4	Foreign direct investment and world trade	131
9.5	The need to establish countervailing power	133
9.6	International initiatives	134
9.7	EC policy on multinational enterprises	135
9.8	The Spinelli proposal	137
9.9	Multinational enterprises and merger control policies in the single market	140
9.10	A final assessment	142
	References	143
	List of relevant EC Directives	144
10.	BRITAIN AND THE EUROPEAN COMMUNITY: THE IMPACT OF MEMBERSHIP	146
	Michael Newman	
10.1	Introduction	146
10.2	Continuing controversy	146
10.3	The economic impact	147
10.4	Constitutional/political aspects	154
10.5	Conclusion	161
	References	164
Appendix A.	THE 1989 EURO-ELECTIONS IN PERSPECTIVE	165
A.1	The electoral system	165
A.2	The electoral campaign	167
A.3	The election results	168
A.4	Conclusion: the European Parliament—more than a sum of its parts?	170
Appendix B.	EC RELATIONS WITH THE THIRD WORLD: THE LOMÉ CONVENTIONS	173
B.1	Introduction	173
B.2	The Lomé Conventions	174
B.3	Trade provisions	176
B.4	Aid provisions	176
B.5	Prospects for Lomé IV	178
	Summary	179
	References/further reading	180
Appendix C.	FURTHER READING	181
Index		183

To use a well-worn expression, the European Community is a topic whose time has very much come. Public interest and debate in the whole area of European integration have been intense in the wake of the 1986 Single European Act, the ensuing '1992' programme for completing the internal market, the momentum towards monetary union that has been created by the Delors Report, and the momentous changes that have taken place in Eastern Europe in recent months. Public attention has been focused upon the growing importance and relevance of the European Community; government, business, financial organizations, educational establishments, professional associations, and consumers will all be affected by the developments mentioned above. In the United Kingdom the debate has been intensified by controversy over Britain's role in an increasingly integrated Europe in the context of considerable national economic difficulties. Everywhere, extra spice is provided to the issue of European integration by the remarkable changes taking place in Eastern Europe which will undoubtedly affect the future development of the European Community. German reunification will dramatically alter the internal balance of power within the Community, impose strains on Community resources and policies, and increase the political and economic importance of the Community *vis-à-vis* the rest of the world. Clearly, any attempt to analyse these ongoing developments would be both premature and thus doomed to failure. Instead, our primary intention is to produce a book on the European Community that will be both an accessible 'core text' for undergraduate students and a primary teaching aid for those involved in teaching subjects related to the European Community at a variety of levels. We also hope that the book will be attractive to general readers whose interest in European integration has been recently awakened by current events.

Our own experience of teaching the economics and politics of the European Community within the framework of an interdisciplinary social science degree has convinced us of the need for an up-to-date, accessible, informative, interesting, but analytical and critical, interdisciplinary (or at least multidisciplinary) evaluation of the nature and functioning of the European Community. We hope that the book offers some insights into the complex reality of Community economics, politics, and policy-making.
economics, politics, and policy-making.

The book can be seen as dealing with three aspects of the European Community: the explanatory theories of European integration that have been invoked to explain the historical evolution of the Community; the institutional framework of the Community; and detailed analyses of key policies and issues. Case studies of Community policy formulation and implementation are used throughout the book, partly in response to the growing popularity of policy studies courses in educational establishments. The policy areas singled out for specific attention have been chosen because they appear on a wide range of course syllabuses and/or because they are central to the European Community, and/or because they are issues of widespread concern within the Community. Our initial intention was to include a section on EC external relations. However, as events in Eastern Europe began to unfold, it became clear that any attempt to evaluate the implications of these changes for the European Community would at the present time be presumptuous. Instead, we decided to focus upon the internal structures and policies of the Community.

Running through the following chapters are several common themes. Primary among them is the dynamic and dialectical relationship between nationalism and supranationalism that is reflected in the political discourse, the institutional framework, and policy-making processes of the Community. A second closely related theme is the waning power of individual nation-states as a result of growing international interdependence (e.g. a trend clearly illustrated by the long-running debate in Britain on the impact of EC membership on parliamentary sovereignty). A third general theme that emerges from the following studies is the incremental development of EC policies and institutions since 1958. Federalist aspirations notwithstanding, European integration has not been imposed in accordance with some grand design. In practice, diverse motivational forces—economic and political—have combined to edge the Community further along the path towards European Union in a somewhat haphazard and erratic fashion. Finally, the arguments presented in the following studies are premised upon the belief that in order to understand fully EC policy-making it is necessary to appreciate the close interrelationship between politics and economics.

The first three chapters of the book deal with the framework of the European Community. Chapter 1 considers the historical development of the Community in the context of explanatory models of integration. The second chapter outlines the institutional framework of the Community and evaluates the importance of recent institutional reforms designed to facilitate speedier and more 'European' policy-making. As a case-study of Community decision-making, culminating in the Single European Act of 1986, institutional reform highlights the functions and powers of the various Community institutions, illustrates national differences in attitudes towards European Union, and introduces the institutional framework for following chapters. Chapter 3 then outlines the fundamental economic basis of the Community as a customs union and a common market, discussing the costs and benefits of these arrangements. The insights that the existing body of theory in this area can give us into the nature of the Community are explored, as well as the limitations of this theory. The objective of this chapter is to present the theory of customs unions and common markets in a way that is both rigorous and accessible to non-economists. Chapters 4, 5, and 6 straddle the division between the framework of the Community and its policies. Chapter 4 looks at the operation of the Common Market in practice, discussing the impediments that have existed to the free movement of goods, services, capital, and people, and analysing the nature and prospects of the '1992' programme. The instigation and progress of the latter especially yields interesting insights into the nature of policy-making and implementation, and admirably illustrates some of the central themes of the book. The same can be said for Chapter 5 on monetary integration, which represents a further development of the economic framework of the Community. This chapter discusses the theory of monetary integration, discussing its precise nature and implications, as well as its costs and benefits. The European Monetary System is evaluated in detail, together with the United Kingdom's reluctance to join the System's Exchange Rate Mechanism. The future of monetary integration and the EMS are then discussed in the light of the Delors Report. Chapter 6 then deals with the Community budget, the issues surrounding which again give us important insights into the essential nature and functioning of the Community. The chapter examines the nature, development, and limitations of current budgetary income and expenditure. The budgetary crises of the 1980s and the

'British problem' are analysed, and the 1988 reforms are closely scrutinized. More speculatively, the future role of the budget in European integration is discussed, along with some aspects of budgetary politics.

Chapters 7, 8 and 9 focus upon specific Community policies. No book on the European Community could fail to include a section on the Common Agricultural Policy, which is the aspect of the Community that perhaps most directly affects the majority of people's lives, as well as being arguably the most important and also the most controversial of the Community's joint policies. Chapter 7 duly presents what is hopefully a lucid and accessible exposition of the mechanisms of the CAP. The chapter then presents an evaluation of its costs and benefits, and in addition it includes a critical and up-to-the-moment survey of proposals for, attempts at, and obstacles to reform of the present system. The latter point illustrates one of the central themes of the book as a whole, i.e. the problems involved in decision-making in international and supranational institutions. Chapter 8 examines Community social policy, which has taken on an especially high profile in the light of the debate on the 1992 'social charter'. Chapter 9 then examines the Community's relationship with multinational enterprises, an issue of continuing importance and interest, especially in the context of the 1992 programme. The chapter deals with the theory of multinational corporations (MNCs) and their influence on nation-states and, particularly, international institutions. It involves an examination of some essential features of MNCs, and their impact on integration in Western Europe. A discussion of the Community's role in this area is included, as well as an evaluation of Community policies towards multinationals. A central theme of the chapter is the impact of interdependence on national sovereignty.

The final chapter of the book presents a case-study of the impact of Community membership on the United Kingdom, which of course is very pertinent at a time when Britain's attitude to European integration has moved to the very centre of national political and economic debate. This analysis combines an evaluation of the economic benefits/costs of membership with a critical evaluation of the political debate in Britain surrounding the issues of Community membership. The chapter highlights in a direct fashion both the importance of nationalism within the Community and the motivating factors behind the development of the European Community. Finally, the appendices provide valuable up-to-date information on the 1989 Euro-elections and the latest Lomé agreements.

V.L. and S.M.
London, 1990

ACKNOWLEDGEMENTS

We would like to thank the staff and students on BA Contemporary European Studies at the Polytechnic of North London for providing suggestions, encouragement, and patience (as well as two chapters!), and for providing a useful sounding board for our ideas. In particular our thanks go to Elmarie McCarthy in the PNL European Documentation Centre for helping us locate relevant primary sources on the Community.

SELECTED ABBREVIATIONS RELEVANT TO THE EUROPEAN COMMUNITY

AASM	Associated African States and Malagassy
ACP	African Caribbean and Pacific Ocean Countries
BRITE	Basic Research in Industrial Technologies for Europe
CAP	Common Agricultural Policy
CBI	Confederation of British Industry
CCP	Common Commercial Policy
CEDEFOP	European Centre for the Development of Vocational Training
CET	Common External Tariff
CFP	Common Fisheries Policy
COMETT	Community Programme in Education and Training for Technology
COPA	Committee of Professional Agricultural Organizations (Comité des Organisations Professionnelles Agricoles de la CEE)
COREPER	Committee of Permanent Representatives (Comité des Représentants Permanents de la CEE)
COST	Committee on European Cooperation in the Field of Scientific and Technical Research
EAGGF (FEOGA)	European Agricultural Guidance and Guarantee Fund
EC	European Community
EC 6	European Community: Belgium, France, German Federal Republic, Italy, Luxembourg, the Netherlands
EC 9	EC 6 plus the United Kingdom, Eire and Denmark
EC 10	EC 9 plus Greece
EC 12	EC 10 plus Spain and Portugal
ECC	European Community Commission
ECSC	European Coal and Steel Community
ECTS	European Credit Transfer System
ECU	European Currency Unit
EDC	European Defence Community
EDF	European Development Fund
EEC	European Economic Community
EFTA	European Free Trade Area
EIB	European Investment Bank
EMCF	European Monetary Cooperation Fund
EMF	European Monetary Fund
EMPC	European Monetary Policy Committee
EMS	European Monetary System
EMU (a)	Economic and Monetary Union

EMU (b)	European Monetary Union
EP	European Parliament
EPC	European Political Community
EPU	European Payments Union
ERB	European Reserve Board
ERDF	European Regional Development Fund
ERM	Exchange Rate Mechanism (of the EMS)
ESC	Economic and Social Committee
ESCB	European System of Central Banks
ESF	European Social Fund
ERASMUS	European Action Scheme for the Mobility of University Students (and staff)
ESPRIT	European Strategic Programme for Research and Development and Information Technology
ETUC	European Trade Union Confederation
EUA	European Unit of Account
Euratom	European Atomic Energy Community
EUREKA	European Research Coordination Agency
EUT	European Union Treaty
FAST	Forecasting and Assessment in Science and Technology
GATT	General Agreement on Tariffs and Trade
GDP	Gross Domestic Product
GMP	Global Mediterranean Policy
GNP	Gross National Product
GSP	Generalized System of Preferences
IGC	Inter-governmental Conference
IMF	International Monetary Fund
Lingua	European Community Language Training Programme
LDC	Less Developed Country
MCA	Monetary Compensation Amount
MEP	Member of European Parliament
MFA	Multi-fibre Agreement
MNE	Multinational Enterprise
NATO	North Atlantic Treaty Organization
NCI	New Community Instrument
NFU	National Farmers Union (UK)
NIC	Newly Industrialized Country
NTB	Non-tariff Barrier
OCA	Optimum Currency Area
OECD	Organization for Economic Cooperation and Development
OEEC	Organization for European Economic Cooperation
OPEC	Organization of Petroleum Exporting Countries
RACE	Research into Advanced Communications Technologies for Europe
R and D	Research and Development
SAP	Social Action Programme
SEA	Single European Act

SEDOC	European System for the Diffusion of Registered Unemployment Offers and Demands
SPRINT	Strategic Programme for Innovation and Technology Transfer in Europe
STABEX	Stabilization of Export Earnings Scheme
SYSMIN	Scheme for Mineral Products (in Lomé Conventions)
UA	Unit of Account
UEF	Union of European Federalists
UN	United Nations
UNCTAD	United Nations Conference on Trade and Development
UNICE	Industrial Confederation of the European Community (Union des Industries de la Communauté Européenne)
VAT (TVA)	Value Added Tax
VER	Voluntary Export Restraint
WEU	Western European Union
YES	Youth for Europe Scheme

THE EUROPEAN COMMUNITY: THEORY AND HISTORY

1.1 INTRODUCTION

The public disagreement between the former UK Prime Minister, Margaret Thatcher, and other Community heads of government over the proper meaning of European Union is, in many respects, reminiscent of the post-war debate on European integration. Then, as now, the key issues were what kind of community—economic or political? What kind of institutional framework? And how might European integration be achieved? The creation of the European Communities in 1957 provided no unambiguous answers to these questions. At one level, the European Coal and Steel Community (ECSC), the European Economic Community (EEC) and the European Atomic Energy Community (Euratom) originated as functional agencies, whose purpose was to coordinate national strategies in specified policy areas. However, European federalists, impressed by the supranational nature of these authorities, hoped they would serve as the basis for more comprehensive integration.

In practice, the development of the European Community since 1957 has been uneven and erratic; nationalism, economic recession and enlargement of the Community have served to delay and divert the process of European integration. Yet, as illustrated in subsequent chapters, significant changes have occurred which have served to consolidate and strengthen the legal basis, institutional framework, and policy-competence of the European Community. The result has been a complex intermeshing of the Community's and the member-states' economic, legal, and political systems. Explaining how and why this process has occurred is far from easy. Indeed, it might be argued that the establishment and subsequent development of the European Community is a unique phenomenon that can be understood only in terms of traditional national interests and the particular circumstances of the day. Nevertheless, a number of more general, explanatory theories of integration have been developed in the context of European integration. Among the various approaches suggested, two have dominated European Community studies—federalism and neo-functionalism. This chapter highlights the interrelationship between these theoretical approaches to the study of integration and the actual development of the European Community.

1.2 FEDERALISM AND EUROPEAN INTEGRATION

Federalist thought comprises two distinct, but obviously related elements. First, the term federal describes a *form* of government in which power is divided between a central authority and several regional authorities (as in the United States of America). Each level and type of

1

authority performs those tasks most appropriate to it. The principal, alleged advantages of federal (as opposed to unitary) political systems are the limitations imposed upon the powers of the central government and the degree of political, social, and economic pluralism that federalism permits. Secondly, however, federalism is concerned with the *process* of achieving political union within a federal (i.e. supranational) organization. The emphasis here is upon political commitment and constitutional development.

An unashamedly normative doctrine, federalism is based upon a particular view of human nature. Underlying all federalist thought is the fundamental assumption that human society is composed of diverse ethnic, cultural, economic, and regional groupings whose interests inevitably conflict. Since all interests are equally valid, their peaceful reconciliation is the only justifiable course of action. A federal system of government is thus defended as the best institutional framework for combining local diversity with overall social harmony and a central authority capable of defending common interests. Though desirable, the establishment of a federal organization cannot—according to federalist theory—be taken for granted since the economic and political rivalry between states that makes federalism necessary, also makes it difficult to achieve. The only way forward, according to so-called radical federalists is to create, from the outset, a federal institutional and political framework (Héraud, 1968). Such a step requires a major commitment on the part of the constitutent states who are required to surrender their sovereignty in key policy areas (notably defence and foreign policy) to a supranational authority.

Clearly, the federalist position in its most radical form is incompatible with confederal associations, international functional agencies, and economic incrementalism as a means of integration since all such arrangements are dependent upon the voluntary cooperation of sovereign states. But more moderate federalists are less dismissive of such organizations as a means of integration. While accepting the federalist goals of their more radical colleagues, so-called 'functional federalists' nevertheless accept that it may well be necessary to adopt an evolutionary path to integration. In the context of European integration, the battle between the radical and evolutionary federalists during the 1940s and 1950s was finally won by the latter.

The basis of post-war federalism was the belief that the establishment of a federal European government would put an end to the long-established dismal pattern of wars between European sovereign states. The idea was, of course, not a new one. In the aftermath of the First World War the idea of a 'United States of Europe' had been propounded by the Austrian count, Koudenhove-Kalergi, leader of the Pan-Europa movement, as well as by leading politicians such as Aristide Briand, French Foreign Minister, 1925–32, and Gustav Streseman, his German counterpart from 1923 to 1929 (Morgan, 1972). The Second World War gave fresh impetus to this debate. After 1939, federalist movements and publications proliferated, particularly among national resistance organizations in Italy, France, Spain, Belgium, and Luxembourg. The Italian federalist, Altiero Spinelli, author of the 1985 Draft Treaty on European Union (which culminated in the 1986 Single European Act) in 1941 set out a framework for a federal Europe in the Manifesto of Ventotene. It was also the Italian federalists who organized a series of meetings in Geneva with other European resistance federalists, which resulted in the 1944 international federalist Draft Declaration of the European Resistance Movements. This document proposed the creation of a post-war federal union with a supranational government, single federal army, and a supreme federal court.

The immediate post-war period witnessed a further upsurge of public opinion in favour of European integration. From the outset, however, the debate was ambiguous; while the general idea of European cooperation attracted widespread support, no such consensus existed regarding the precise nature of any such arrangement. Federalist movements from the Netherlands, the United Kingdom, Belgium, Italy, Luxembourg, Switzerland, and France came together in December 1946 in the Union of European Federalists (UEF) which campaigned for a federal Europe. But not all 'European' movements established during this period shared the federalist aspirations of the UEF. In September 1946, for instance, the International Committee for the Study of European Questions was formed. Composed mainly of parliamentary delegates from Belgium, Britain, Denmark, France, the Netherlands, and Norway, the Committee published a report recommending the creation of a loose, confederal type of European Union as a means of facilitating economic recovery and as a bulwark against Soviet Communism. The latter model of European cooperation was also the one that the British Prime Minister, Winston Churchill, had in mind when he called for the establishment of 'some kind of United States of Europe' while visiting Zurich in September 1946.

The momentum created by the diverse European and federalist movements culminated in the European Congress held in the Hague in May 1948. The meeting was organized jointly by the International Committee of the Movement for European Unity (established in Paris in 1947 by the UEF), Churchill's United Europe Movement, the French Council for a United Europe, the European League for Economic Cooperation, and an international association of Christian Democratic and Centre parties called Nouvelles Equipes Internationales, founded in June 1947. The Hague Congress brought together 713 delegates from 13 countries. Among those present were Konrad Adenauer, the West German Chancellor from 1949 to 1963; some twenty ex-prime ministers including Winston Churchill, Paul Reynaud, and Paul van Zeeland; famous writers and academics such as the English philosopher Bertrand Russell; and leading federalists like Hendrik Brugmans, Alexandre Marc, and Denis de Rougemont (Vaughan, 1979).

On the key issue of what kind of European organization should be created there emerged at the Hague Congress a clear divide between the federalist UEF and the more moderate United Europe Movement which, backed by other conservative groupings, advocated a confederal association. In the event, the latter view prevailed; the Congress approved a vaguely worded communiqué demanding 'a United Europe throughout whose area the free movement of persons, ideas and goods is restored', a Charter of Human Rights, a Court of Justice, and a 'European Assembly where the live forces of all our nations shall be represented'. In October 1948 the broad-based European Movement headed by four presidents—Leon Blum, Winston Churchill, Alcide de Gasperi and Paul Henri Spaak—was founded to implement the recommendations of the Hague Congress. Subsequent negotiations were marked by disagreement between the French, Belgian, and Italian governments, which wanted to establish a supranational European organization, and the UK government (backed by the Scandinavian governments), which favoured an intergovernmental arrangement along similar lines to the Organization for European Economic Cooperation (OEEC). Once again, the federalists were defeated. The Council of Europe, established in May 1949, provided a forum for voluntary cooperation between national governments in the Committee of Ministers and between members of national parliaments in the Consultative Assembly. Moreover, even this weakened form of European organization was regarded with extreme suspicion by the British (Labour) government whose members shared Winston Churchill's opposition to European federalism.

Undeterred, the European federalists launched a further attempt in 1952 to establish a European Political Community with federal institutions as part of a proposal for a European Defence Community (EDC). The EDC idea was the French government's response to US demands that West Germany be permitted to rearm in order that it might contribute to the defence of Western Europe. As outlined by the French Prime Minister, René Pleven, the EDC would involve the creation of a single European army to which West Germany would commit all of its troops and to which other participants would devote a proportion of their armed forces. Though controversial, the proposal was supported by both the West German Chancellor, Konrad Adenauer, and the US government. Since the existence of an EDC would require institutionalized coordination of member-states' foreign and defence policies, the federalists also submitted an accompanying proposal for a European Political Community. In fact, the whole project collapsed in August 1954 with the refusal of the French National Assembly to ratify the project.

The failure of the EDC project marked an important turning-point within the post-war European federalist debate. Clearly, as has been illustrated above, the origins of European integration are bound up with the post-war debate on European federalism. In the immediate post-war period, the social, economic, and political situation in Europe was so fluid that it was just conceivable that the radical federalist strategy might have succeeded. In reality, as demonstrated by the intergovernmental structure of the Council of Europe and the rejection of the EDC project, nationalism and the nation-state proved an insurmountable barrier to such a development.

1.3   PRAGMATIC FEDERALISM: THE ESTABLISHMENT OF THE ECSC, EEC, AND EURATOM

During this period, so-called evolutionary federalists—notably the founding fathers of the European Community, Jean Monnet, French Commissaire au Plan, and Robert Schuman, French Foreign Minister—sought to achieve federalist objectives by a different route. Although they shared the ideals of their more radical colleagues, they disagreed with their head-on approach, believing instead that the best way to move towards European integration was by small, incremental steps in sectors where the issue of national sovereignty was less contentious than in the areas of defence and foreign policy. This strategy formed the basis of the so-called Schuman Plan which resulted in the creation of the European Coal and Steel Community (ECSC) in 1951.

The ECSC proposal was drafted by Jean Monnet in April 1950 and presented to the French Council of Ministers by Robert Schuman the following month. To Schuman's relief, the proposals were adopted without much discussion. The Schuman Plan recommended that all aspects of Franco-German steel production be placed under a common High Authority in an organization open to other European countries. Undoubtedly, a major reason for the initiative was French concern at the possible threat to French interests posed by the steady post-war increase in German industrial productivity. Equally, for the West German Christian Democratic government, the ECSC offered a means of re-establishing its international position while at the same time demonstrating its commitment to Europeanism. However, in defending the ECSC proposal to the French Council of Ministers, Robert Schuman clearly stated that, in his view, this was only the first step towards a much more far-reaching objective, declaring that: 'This proposal will build the first concrete foundation of a European federation which is indispensable to the preservation of peace' (R. Schuman, quoted in Pryce, 1973, p. 1).

Six countries—Belgium, the Netherlands, Italy, Luxembourg, West Germany, and France—signed the Paris Treaty in April 1951, establishing the ECSC. Significantly, the UK government, though invited to participate, refused to join the ECSC. Three reasons help to explain the British position during this period. First, the British wartime experience had strengthened rather than weakened the UK government's (and people's) sense of national pride. Secondly, UK foreign policy was based upon the Churchillian concept of British influence resting upon three overlapping circles—with the United States, the Commonwealth, and—finally—Europe. In Winston Churchill's words, Britain was with Europe, but not part of it. Thirdly, British politicians—Conservative and Labour—were united in their opposition towards the establishment of a supranational European authority, which they believed would constrain British policy-makers and undermine the sovereignty of Parliament.

As Haas (1968) points out, though the ECSC was clearly not truly federal in nature, its supranational character and legal powers distinguished it from all other international organizations. The basic task of the ECSC was to establish a common market for coal and steel among the member-states, implying the abolition of all tariffs, quantitative restrictions, exchange controls, and double-pricing practices. Although limited to a particular sector, the role of the ECSC was thus federal in scope since implementation of the common market would entail harmonization and coordination of national industrial policies. The institutional framework of the ECSC also contained federal elements. Five ECSC institutions were created by the 1951 Treaty, the High Authority, the Consultative Committee, the Common Assembly, the Court of Justice, and the Council of Ministers. The High Authority, comprising nine persons, was the supranational motive force of the ECSC and the executive organ. It was also responsible for maintaining and policing the competitive common market. To the extent that a parliamentary check upon the High Authority existed, this role was played by the Common Assembly. Composed of 78 members chosen from the six national parliaments, the Assembly scrutinized the activities of the High Authority and had the power to force the entire High Authority to resign by means of a censure motion. A crucial innovation and essential element of a 'supranational' body was the Court of Justice, described by Haas (1968, p. 44) as 'a mixture of arbitral tribunal, dispenser of constitutional interpretation, and . . . an administrative court on the model of the French *Conseil d'Etat'*. Alongside the 'federal' institutions of the ECSC was the 'intergovernmental' Council of Ministers, composed of national ministers. Its role, briefly stated, was to approve or forbid policy measures proposed by the High Authority voting either by simple majority, two-thirds majority, or unanimity depending on the issue under discussion. Once adopted by the Council of Ministers, ECSC decisions and recommendations were binding upon those governments and/or firms/individuals to which they were directed.

Spurred on by the successful establishment of the ECSC, Monnet (President of the High Authority from 1952 to 1955) campaigned for further sectoral integration. At the Messina Conference in June 1955 the foreign ministers of the six set up an intergovernmental committee under the leadership of the Belgian Foreign Minister, Paul Henri Spaak, to study ways in which 'a fresh advance to the building of Europe' could be made. The Spaak Report, published in 1956, recommended further sectoral integration in two areas—nuclear energy production and the creation of a general common market. Although once again invited to participate in the European Atomic Energy Community (Euratom) and common market initiatives, the UK government again declined. A medium-ranking Board of Trade official sent as an observer to the Messina Conference was withdrawn from the Spaak committee in November 1955. The UK government's opposition centred upon the impact of a customs union upon trade with the Commonwealth and the supranational implications of the proposals.

Monnet's own preference was for the extension of sectoral integration in the field of nuclear power on the grounds that here was an expanding policy sector which was apparently free from national interests. Euratom was duly established by the Rome Treaties in

March 1957. Its purpose was to encourage research, industrial development, and supervision of fissile materials. Although Monnet expected Euratom to become the most important of the three European Communities, it has, in fact, proved less significant than either the ECSC or the European Economic Community (EEC). Two reasons help to explain this. First, Euratom research and training programmes required the unanimous support of the Council of Ministers, and secondly, member governments refused to renounce their right to undertake their own national programmes into nuclear energy (and weapons) research (Vaughan, 1979).

At the Messina Conference, the six also agreed to the establishment of a general common market, namely the EEC. More specifically, member-governments committed themselves to the joint study of plans for European transport, consideration of an overall policy for (non-nuclear) energy, creation of a common market involving the removal of obstacles to trade and the harmonization of economic policies, the establishment of a European investment fund, and the harmonization of social regulations governing working hours, overtime rates, and paid holidays. The Treaty of Rome establishing the EEC was signed along with the Euratom Treaty in March 1957. The general objectives of the EEC are defined as follows in Article 2 of the Treaty:

> By establishing a Common Market and progressively approximating the economic policies of Member States to promote throughout the Community a harmonious development of economic activities, a continuous and balanced expansion, an increase in stability, an accelerated raising of the standard of living and closer relations between the States belonging to it.

In the first instance, the common market meant the abolition of internal duties and quotas on trade as well as any other measures having an equivalent effect. The establishment of a Common External Tariff (CET) was to be established gradually over a 12–15 year transition period. More ambitiously, the treaty also committed the signatories to the establishment of a Common Agricultural Policy (CAP), the coordination of member-states' economic and monetary policies, and the partial harmonization of their fiscal and social policies. Finally, the EEC Treaty created three funds: the European Social Fund (ESF) 'to improve employment opportunities for workers and to contribute to the raising of their standard of living'; the European Investment Bank (EIB) to facilitate the economic expansion of the Community through a system of loans and guarantees; and the European Development Fund (EDF) to assist associated overseas territories (Vaughan, 1979).

The institutional framework created by the Rome Treaties to administer the EEC and Euratom resembled that of the ECSC. The new executive authority created was the nine-member Commission, whose powers were, however, far more circumscribed than those of the High Authority. Its role was to see that the other Community institutions and the member-states observe and implement the Treaty, to submit proposals to the Council of Ministers for decision, and to enforce the rules laid down by the Council.

Article 145 of the Treaty clearly gave decision-making power to the Council of Ministers, which was to consist of a minister from each government. Decisions were to be reached either by a simple or qualified majority. On important matters unanimity was required. The influence of national governments was further increased by the creation of the Committee of Permanent Representatives (COREPER), made up of ambassadorial-ranking officials from the member-states permanently located in Brussels. Besides these two new institutions, the EEC and Euratom were served by the ECSC Common Assembly (with an increased membership of 142 representatives) and Court of Justice. In 1965, the institutions of the three separate European Communities were merged with the Commission taking over the powers and responsibilities of the High Authority.

1.4 FUNCTIONALISM AND NEO-FUNCTIONALISM: 'SPILLOVER' AS A MEANS OF INTEGRATION

The piecemeal approach to European integration adopted by Monnet and Schuman fits neatly into the 'neo-functionalist' theory of regional integration developed by Haas (1968) and Lindberg (1963) in the context of post-war European integration. This theory is itself based upon a sympathetic critique of an earlier functionalist theory of international integration developed by David Mitrany (1966), who was not concerned with regional integration, but with creating conditions that would prevent war. In fact, Mitrany was opposed to regional government, believing that it would merely reproduce national rivalries on a larger scale. Instead, he advocated the linking of authority to a specific activity, thereby breaking the traditional link between authority and a definite territory. The functionalist approach is essentially non-political. It avoids the areas of conflict and focuses instead upon the common needs of nation-states. National governments, argued Mitrany, would surrender control over technical policy sectors such as transport, communications, or health research because they would appreciate the net advantages of such tasks being coordinated at a higher level. The process, as Mitrany saw it, was already underway in the activity of the International Labour Organization (Harrison, 1975).

The premises of the theory are those of a very simple utilitarianism in which the calculation of welfare interest is the ultimate determinant of behaviour. According to functionalist theory, the natural community of interest, identified and exploited, becomes the basis of a community of feeling and a socio-psychological entity. Technological and economic developments serve as important catalysts in this process, since they render international cooperation both necessary and possible in an increasing range of policy sectors. As more and more areas of control are surrendered, individual states become less and less capable of independent action until they find themselves enmeshed in a 'spreading web of international activities and agencies' (Mitrany, 1966, p. 35) from which they cannot easily extricate themselves. Opposed to the creation of permanent regional or world government, functionalists believed the institutional framework of the various international agencies would vary according to the function in hand:

> The functional *dimensions* . . . determine themselves. In a like manner the function determines its appropriate *organs*. It also reveals through practice the nature of the action required under the given conditions, and in that way the *powers* needed by the respective authority. (Mitrany, 1966, p. 27)

Functionalist theory attracted critical support from Ernst Haas and Leon Lindberg, who further developed the thesis in the context of the ECSC experience. In contrast to functionalist theory, which stressed the importance of an underlying social consensus as the primary source of stability, the neo-functionalists argued that social life was dominated by competition among interests. Thus, whereas functionalism saw integration as being primarily about consensus building, neo-functionalism saw the best chance of achieving international integration in the efficient management of conflict in a pluralist society (Taylor, 1983).

This shift in emphasis marks an important theoretical development in that it introduces politics and political conflict as part of the integrative process. Indeed, neo-functionalists argue that the activities of national governments, political parties, and interest groups are influential in bringing about integration. As sectors are brought under supranational control, organized interest groups, parties, and politicians are drawn into the regional (i.e. European) policy-making process. As central regional institutions are given more power and functions by the member-governments the theory is that the demands, expectations, and (to varying degrees) the loyalties of groups and parties will gradually shift to the new centre of decision-making (Harrison, 1975).

Central to the neo-functionalist thesis is the concept of 'spillover' which has two aspects. 'Functional spillover' refers to the process whereby 'a given action, related to a specific goal, creates a situation in which the original goal can be assured only by taking further actions, which in turn create a further condition and a need for more action, and so forth' (Lindberg, 1963, p. 10). Because modern industrial economies are composed of interdependent parts, it is impossible to isolate any particular policy sector; integration of one sector will succeed only if other contiguous areas are also integrated. For example, monetary union logically implies full economic union including fiscal harmonization, while a common transport policy has implications for energy policy. Alongside this technical version of spillover, neo-functionalists also identified 'political spillover'. This process involves the build-up of political pressures in favour of further integration in the member-states. Briefly, the argument is as follows: once the ECSC assumed responsibility for coal and steel production, national representatives associated with these industries (employers, trade unions, and consumer groups) switched at least part of their lobbying activities to the High Authority. Once aware of the advantages available to them from the ECSC, these organizations became advocates of further sectoral integration (George, 1985). In addition, national politicians and bureaucrats would come under pressure from interest groups to participate fully in European policy-making. As Haas concluded from his observations of the ECSC:

> The 'good Europeans' are not the main creators of the regional community that is growing up; the process of community formation is dominated by nationally constituted groups with specific interests and aims, willing and able to adjust their aspirations by turning to supranational means when this course appears profitable. (Haas, 1968, p. xxxiv)

This conception of group activity does not necessitate the assumption of a common good or common interest. Apart from the acceptance of a general commitment to certain procedures for conflict resolution, there is rarely a consensus on the content of policies (Harrison, 1975, p. 78).

An important corollary of the acceptance of interest group competition is the recognition by neo-functionalists that central institutions with policy-making powers have a crucial role to play in the determination of common policies. Whereas functionalist theory was only marginally concerned with the institutional aspects of integration, neo-functionalists recognize the importance of regional structures and legislation in the integrative process. Central institutions—the High Authority and Commission—must play not merely a passive, but a promotional role in the integration process, providing solutions that resolve conflict while at the same time promoting further integration.

1.5   COMMUNITY DEVELOPMENT AND NEO-FUNCTIONALISM: REAPPRAISAL AND EVALUATION

The neo-functionalist explanatory theory—revised in the light of subsequent developments—has dominated analyses of European integration. We should, therefore, conclude with a brief consideration of its value as an explanatory theory of EC development. On the one hand, there is considerable evidence of functional spillover within the Community. As illustrated in subsequent chapters, the European Community has gradually extended its activities into an increasing range of related policy areas. The CAP has since its establishment in the 1960s gradually become more extensive, embracing an increasing range of products and activities. The development of the CAP has also affected EC budgetary policy and—in the Commission's view at least—demonstrated the need for monetary union (in order to overcome the need for Green exchange rates). This and other pressures towards monetary integration lie behind the present debate on the Delors package (see Chapter 5). Similarly, the planned completion of the single market has persuaded the Commission and most member-states of the need to extend further Community social policy (in order to harmonize labour market conditions throughout the Community). Perhaps the most significant example of functional spillover has been the recognition since the early 1970s of the foreign policy connotations of external trade relations. Realization of this fact led to the institutional spillover establishing European Political Cooperation, a development that was incorporated into the Treaties of the European Community by the 1986 Single European Act. The financing of the Community has also undergone important changes. As Taylor (1983) points out, the European Community made some progress towards the establishment of supranational authority with the introduction of its 'own resources' in 1970. Finally, the 1986 Single European Act has extended the Community's sphere of competence to include new policy areas such as the environment and research and development.

However, as George (1985) argues, the record of political spillover has been much slower and uneven. While the transition from the ECSC to the EEC was supported by industrial pressure groups, they did not initiate the change. Nor did they pressurize national governments to participate. The attitude of other groups towards the EEC varied from positive support (especially in West Germany) to widespread opposition, notably in France. As indicated above, the EEC initiative came from national politicians (supported by the US government) who believed a common market would bring national benefits. The predicted increase in pressure group activity at the European level *has* occurred, but it has been far from uniform. Peak associations have, of course, for many years been represented within the Community in the Economic and Social Committee. Here, some 500 Euro-groups comprising affiliated national groups examine Community proposals. Broadly speaking, those Euro-groups that are most prominent at the European level are those most affected by Community policies. Thus, the agriculture lobby, composed of some 150 groups, is predictably by far the most influential of the Euro-lobbies. Other prominent lobbies include industrial employers, along with representatives from commerce and the service industries (banking, insurance, transport, liberal professions) and trade unions. However, as Nugent (1989) points out, most non-producer groups (e.g. those representing consumer interests, women's rights, environmental issues) are poorly organized, underfunded, and often internally divided over policy objectives. Nevertheless, in recent years there has been a discernible increase in interest group activity at the Community level, a trend that has been given a further boost by the '1992' programme. In addition to the Euro-groups, private corporations and local and regional authorities have also begun to take a greater interest in Community policy-making. The chemical industry, for example, has been prompted into action by the Community's growing interest in environmental protection. The West German *Lander*—which enjoy considerable autonomy within the federal political system—have established contact with the Commission as well as with MEPs. Similarly, most French and UK regional authorities are represented in Brussels.

National political parties within the Community have adopted a wide range of attitudes towards European integration. The neo-functionalist thesis that parties would become more Community oriented has been only partially borne out in practice. On the one hand, it is true that MEPs from all parties actively campaigned for the introduction of direct elections to the Parliament and have, since then, continued to campaign for increased legislative powers for the Parliament. Yet while virtually all national parties now participate in the European elections, several have reservations about all or some aspects of European integration (e.g. the French and Greek Communist Parties, the Danish anti-Common Market Movement, the French National Front, and the British Conservative Party). Furthermore, as Pridham and Pridham (1981), Lodge (1985), and Bourguignon-Wittke *et al.* (1985) have shown, the introduction of direct elections to the European Parliament has not resulted in the establishment of cohesive, well-organized transnational parties inside the European Parliament. Euro-elections continue to be dominated by national parties and national issues (see Appendix A), while the transnational party groupings in the European Parliament are often internally divided along ideological and/or national lines. However, in view of the recent increase in the Parliament's legislative powers (see Chapter 2) and present discussions about further institutional reform it is possible that this situation may change in the future.

General de Gaulle's veto on British membership of the Community in 1963 followed by the 1965 French boycott of the Community and the 1966 Luxembourg Compromise (for details of the Luxembourg Compromise, see Chapter 2) prompted Haas and Lindberg to revise their thesis in two respects: they acknowledged that they had neglected the importance of national political leaders in the integration process and underestimated the strength of nationalism. In fact, as George (1985) argues, neo-functionalist theory had assumed too much homogeneity of interests and placed too much emphasis on the role of pressure groups in influencing government policy. In consequence, the neo-functionalists had failed to appreciate the need for and difficulties of coalition-building within the Community between governments of different political doctrines. As several commentators have observed (Wallace, Wallace, and Webb, 1979; Wallace, 1985; George, 1989), European Community policy-making invariably involves coalitions and compromises in which national interests are a primary concern for national politicians sensitive to domestic political pressures.

These two areas—leadership and nationalism—have attracted much critical attention. Taking up the issue of nationalism, Stanley Hoffmann (1965) argued that as soon as integration attempted to pass from low politics (economic and welfare issues) to high politics (foreign policy and defence), nationalism would come into its own, presenting an insurmountable barrier. In fact, the establishment of EPC in the 1970s seems to challenge—though given the limited nature of EPC, not disprove—this view. What *is* clear, however, is that key national leaders with very distinctive views of European integration have to varying degrees influenced both the pace and direction of European integration. Alongside General de Gaulle, both the French Socialist President François Mitterrand and the former British Prime Minister Margaret Thatcher have played an important role in shaping the development of the Community. The former played a critical role in extending the definition of the '1992' programme to include economic and monetary union and the social dimension. Meanwhile, the latter will be remembered for her opposition to European federalism, though as George (1989) argues, this does not necessarily mean that Mrs Thatcher is a narrow-minded nationalist. While the political rhetoric that emanated from 10 Downing Street may have been nationalist in tone (for reasons relating to domestic party politics), it might be argued that Mrs Thatcher's conception of 1992 (as being about the opening up of European markets) was, in fact, more internationalist and more consistent with UK economic interests than the Delors vision of a regionalist bloc.

1.6   CONCLUSION

Federalist and neo-functionalist theories of integration have dominated academic analyses of European integration. As illustrated above, federalist movements played a vital role in the early post-war period in opening up the whole debate on European integration. Furthermore, even after the collapse of the EDC project had demonstrated the unrealistic nature of the federalist strategy, federalist aspirations continued to motivate more pragmatic 'functional-federalists' such as Monnet and Schuman. The incremental development of the European community can, to some extent be explained by the neo-functionalist model of integration. However, as argued above, it is necessary also to take into account the role played by key political leaders and diverse national interests, which have, inevitably, resulted in 'intergovernmental' policy compromises within the Council of Ministers. In addition, it is also necessary to consider the impact of external factors such as the prolonged economic recession of the 1970s and 1980s and, more recently, developments in Eastern Europe that impinge upon Western European politics. In short, the evolution of the European Community does not fit neatly into any single explanatory model. Furthermore, as illustrated by the present debate on the implications of the Single European Act and the '1992' programme, the very meaning of European Union remains unclear. In consequence, when trying to explain and understand the development of Community policies and institutions it is necessary to bear in mind both federalist and neo-functionalist approaches. In addition, however, one should not lose sight of the continuing importance of external pressures or of national political and economic interests which continue to determine the limits of European integration.

REFERENCES

Bourguignon-Wittke, R., Grabitz, E., Schmuck, O., Steppat S., and Wessels, W. (1985), 'Five years of the directly elected European Parliament: performance and prospects', *Journal of Common Market Studies*, **24**.

George, S. (1985), *Politics and Policy in the European Community*, Clarendon Press, Oxford.

George, S. (1989), 'Nationalism, liberalism and the national interest: Britain, France and the European community', *Strathclyde Papers on Government and Politics*, no. 67, Strathclyde University, Glasgow.

Haas, E. (1968), *The Uniting of Europe*, 2nd Edn, Stanford University Press, Stanford, Calif.

Harrison, R. J. (1975), *Europe in Question*, 2nd Edn, George Allen & Unwin, London.

Héraud, G. (1968), *Les Principes du Fédéralisme et la Fédération Européene*, Presses D'Europe, Paris.

Hoffmann, S. (1965), 'The European process at Atlantic cross-purposes', *Journal of Common Market Studies*, **3**, 85–101.

Lindberg, L. N. (1963) *The Political Dynamics of European Economic Integration*, Stanford University Press, Stanford, Calif.

Lindberg, L. N. (1966) 'Integration as a source of stress on the European Community system', *International Organisation*, **20**, no. 2, Spring.

Lodge, J. (1985), 'Euro-elections and the European Parliament: the dilemma over turnout and powers', *Parliamentary Affairs*, **38**, 40–55.

Mitrany, D. (1966), *A Working Peace System*, Quadrangle Books, Chicago, Ill.

Morgan, R. (1972), *West European Politics since 1945*, B. T. Batsford, London.

Nugent, N. (1989), *The Government and Politics of the European Community*, Macmillan, London.

Pridham, G. and Pridham, P. (1981), *Transnational Party Cooperation and European Integration*, George Allen & Unwin, London.

Pryce, R. (1973), *The Politics of the European Community*, Butterworths, London.

Taylor, P. (1983), *The Limits of European Integration*, Croom Helm, London.

Vaughan, R. (1979), *Twentieth Century Europe*, Croom Helm, London.

Wallace, H. (1985), 'Negotiations and coalition formation in the European Community', *Government and Opposition*, **20**, 453–472.

Wallace, A., Wallace, H., and Webb, C. (1979) *Policy-making in the European Communities*, Wiley, London.

TWO

EUROPEAN COMMUNITY POLICY-MAKING: THE INSTITUTIONAL CONTEXT

2.1 INTRODUCTION

'Cumbersome' and 'bureaucratic' are two words commonly used to describe the way in which the European Community goes about its business; when it comes to establishing common policies, the Community seems to be incapable of going at more than a snail's pace. One major obstacle to faster, 'European' decision-making and further integration has been the institutional framework of the Community. Neither the Commission nor the European Parliament—the intended catalysts for European integration—have the power ultimately to determine EC policy. Instead, decision-making power in the Community has become concentrated in the Council of Ministers whose function is to represent the interests of individual member-states rather than the Community as a whole. Since the early 1970s, the Community has thus been preoccupied with the subject of EC institutional reform and its implications for European integration. The 1986 Single European Act marks the latest stage in this debate.

Section 2.2 of this chapter explains the impact of the institutional framework of the Community upon the decision-making process—in theory and in practice. In this respect, the discussion forms an important introduction to subsequent chapters which focus upon particular policy areas and which assume a basic knowledge of the Community's decision-making process. Section 2.3 outlines the way in which national interests came to dominate European policy-making during the 1960s and 1970s following the 1966 Luxembourg Compromise. Section 2.4 focuses upon two related issues—European Union and institutional reform—which have dominated the Community's own agenda in the 1980s. Underlying this debate are two key questions—what exactly is meant by European Union and what kind of institutional arrangements does it require? At present there are no simple answers to these questions. While the 1986 Single European Act has pushed the Community in the direction of further economic, social and political integration, European federalism remains some way off.

2.2 THE INSTITUTIONAL PARAMETERS OF COMMUNITY POLICY-MAKING

The institutional framework established by the Treaties of Paris and Rome was designed to facilitate cooperation between member-states in these policy areas. As indicated below, while this was not a federalist structure, the founders hoped that it would form a basis for closer integration.

2.2.1   The European Commission

Based in Brussels, the Commission is the Community's executive. There are 17 commissioners: two each from the five largest states—the United Kingdom, France, Italy, Spain and West Germany; and one from each of the other states—the Netherlands, Belgium, Luxembourg, Greece, Ireland, Denmark, and Portugal. The commissioners are appointed by their government for a four-year (renewable) period, but once appointed swear an oath of allegiance to the European Community in which they promise not to put national interests before those of the Community. Nevertheless, governments do expect loyalty from their commissioners. Mrs Thatcher's decision in 1988, for instance, to dismiss the UK Conservative commissioner, Lord Cockfield, after just one term of office was openly defended by the government on the grounds that he had 'gone native', i.e. he had become far too enthusiastic a supporter of European integration for the Prime Minister's liking.[1]

The commissioners are assisted by a permanent staff of some 15 000 people (including translators and interpreters) who are grouped into 23 Directorates General, each of which is responsible for a specific policy area.[2] The Commission is formally accountable to the European Parliament, which by a vote of censure passed by a two-thirds majority could force all the commissioners collectively to resign. Individual commissioners, however, are not accountable and cannot be dismissed either by the European Parliament or by their national governments during their period of office. The Commission President is elected— by a system likened to that used for papal elections—for a four-year (renewable) period by the College of Commissioners. The President of the Commission enjoys high political status both within and, increasingly, beyond the Community. At EC summits he or she ranks with prime ministers and presidents of the member-states and represents the Community in other international arenas.

Powers   As guardian of the Treaties, the Commission is responsible for taking to the European Court of Justice (see below) any individual, organization, or government that contravenes the Treaties, regulations, or decisions made by the Community. The Commission also has the power to impose fines on any organization or individual found to be in breach of Community competition rules.

As the executive arm of the European Community, the Commission is responsible for ensuring the implementation of Community policies, whether based upon decisions of the Council of Ministers or Treaty provisions.

The Commission implements Community policies on a day-to-day basis and manages the structural funds, i.e. the European Agricultural Guidance and Guarantee Fund (EAGGF), the European Regional Development Fund (ERDF), the European Development Fund (EDF), and the European Social Fund (ESF).

The Commission is responsible for initiating Community policy. All Community proposals and legislation must originate in the Commission. Once a proposal has been drafted it is passed to the European Parliament and the Economic and Social Committee for consultation and to the Council of Ministers for adoption.

2.2.2   The Council of Ministers

The Council is the Community's legislature; its principal function is to accept or reject proposals put to it by the Commission, taking into account the views of the Parliament and the Economic and Social Committee. It does not have a permanent membership; participants change according to the subject under discussion. Agriculture ministers from the member-states, for instance, meet to discuss farm prices, while transport ministers discuss European transport policy, and so on. Meetings of foreign ministers are known as 'General Councils' and are widely believed to be 'higher status' than the other so-called 'Technical Councils', though there is no formal basis for this view. The presidency of the Council of Ministers rotates among the member-countries every six months in alphabetical order.

In fact, the bulk of the work within the Council is undertaken not by ministers, but by the Committee of Permanent Representatives (COREPER). Established in 1958, COREPER comprises civil servants of ambassadorial rank who act as gatekeepers, examining Commission proposals and liaising between national officials, other COREPER officials, and the Commission bureaucracy. In theory, COREPER officials promote the views of national ministries, but as several commentators have observed (see, for instance, Lodge, 1989) the reality is more complex. Interaction between Commission officials and COREPER members has resulted in the growth of 'bureaucratic interpenetration' or *engrenage*—within which the division between Community and national interests becomes blurred in the search for a proposal acceptable to all participants.

Nevertheless, in contrast to the Commission, the Council of Ministers is essentially an 'intergovernmental' body, which means that the primary objective of each participant is to get the best deal for his or her government. Similarly, each member-state uses its six-month presidency to push to the front of the agenda those policies it wishes to see adopted. In this way, the conflicting ideologies and policy aims of member-governments help to determine the Community's own policy agenda. Under the West German presidency in the first half of 1988, for instance, EC–Comecon links were strengthened. Since 1988, Greece, Spain, France, Ireland, and now Italy have each, in turn, controlled the Council Presidency. All of these member-states regard themselves as being pro-European and have used their presidencies to push forward plans for monetary and political union. Furthermore, the first three heads of government–Andreas Papandreou, Felipe González and François Mitterrand—are members of socialist parties and so gave priority during their presidencies to the promotion of the social dimension of 1992 (health and safety at work, and most controversial of all, the European Social Charter). Mrs Thatcher strongly opposed these trends; had the UK government controlled the Council presidency during this period, the policy agenda would undoubtedly have been somewhat different.

National electoral considerations and general elections also affect Community policy-making. A major obstacle to the much-needed reform of the CAP, for instance, has been the reluctance of French and German agriculture ministers over the years to offend the farming constituency, which in both countries forms a significant portion of the electorate. The ongoing cycle of national elections and cabinet reshuffles in the twelve member-states also results in frequent changes of membership in the Council of Ministers. These changes often disrupt the decision-making process as new participants make new demands. The replacement of the British Foreign Secretary, Sir Geoffrey Howe, with John Major in the July 1989 Cabinet reshuffle provides a good illustration of this point. Whereas Howe had opposed Mrs Thatcher by supporting greater European economic and monetary integration, his successor indicated that he shared Mrs Thatcher's opposition to such a step.

The Treaties state that voting in the Council of Ministers may be by a unanimous vote or by either an absolute or qualified majority. In a vote by an absolute majority each member-state has one vote and a simple majority is binding. In a qualified majority vote each member-state has a number of votes proportionate to its size: Britain, France, West Germany, and Italy have ten each; Spain has eight; Belgium, Greece, Portugal, and the Netherlands have five each; Denmark and Ireland three each and Luxembourg has two. Fifty-four votes out of the total of 76 constitutes a qualified majority. Under the Treaties, majority voting was to come into force automatically in January 1966 in specified areas, although unanimity would always be required for decisions considered crucial to the future development of the Community. As explained below, until the adoption of the Single European Act, majority voting in the Council was used only for technical and administrative decisions and for decisions relating to the budget and the Agricultural Management Committees, which must be taken within a fixed time limit.

2.2.3   The European Council (summits)

In 1974 it was agreed (on the suggestion of the French President, Giscard d'Estaing) to hold regular summit meetings of the heads of state and government to plan the long-term future of the Community and to discuss international developments affecting member-states. Summit meetings—known as European Councils—are held three times a year (once in each of the countries holding the presidency of the Council and once in Brussels) and whenever 'crisis management' requires it. Not mentioned in the original Treaties, the European Council was given formal recognition by the 1986 Single European Act. There is considerable debate about the integrative significance of the European Council. Some view the establishment of the European Council as a device invoked by national governments to divert the Community along an intergovernmental as opposed to a supranational road. However, functionalists have argued that the summits provide a valuable safety-valve on those occasions when the normal decision-making procedures break down (Haas, 1976). As always, there is evidence to support both views. On the one hand, it is true that many items are now dealt with by the heads of government which were formerly resolved by the Commission and the Council. However, major Community developments have also been instigated by the European Council including institutional reform, economic and monetary union, and European Union (Lodge, 1989).

2.2.4   The European Parliament

The Treaty of Rome established a European Assembly composed of delegates from the national parliaments of member-states. Since 1979, this body has been elected by direct universal suffrage, since which time it has been known as the European Parliament (a title that was formalized by the Single European Act). Following the entry of Spain and Portugal into the European Community in January 1986, the European Parliament comprises 518 members, elected for a period of five years. The four most populous member-states—France, the United Kingdom, Italy, and West Germany—each have 81 members. Spain has 60, the Netherlands 25, Belgium, Greece and Portugal 24, Denmark 16, Ireland 15, and Luxembourg 6. Plenary sessions are held in Strasbourg where members sit in political rather than national groups. (For details of Euro-election results and transnational party groupings, see Chapter 3).

Powers
Powers of censure   The European Parliament has the power (as yet never used) to dismiss *en bloc* the Commission by means of a vote of censure passed by a two-thirds majority. It is unlikely that this power will ever be used; not only would such a decision bring chaos, but the Parliament would have no influence over the appointment of a new Commission.

Budgetary powers   Since 1975, the Parliament has shared the Community's budgetary powers with the Council. While the latter has the last word on the 'compulsory' expenditure (i.e. on policies specified in the Treaties, notably the CAP) which accounts for around 75 per cent of the budget, the Parliament determines 'non-compulsory' expenditure (i.e. the structural funds—ERDF, EAGGF, EDF, and ESF) which accounts for the remaining 25 per cent of the budget. Amendments to this category of expenditure adopted by the Parliament cannot be rejected by the Council. However, Parliament can only increase non-compulsory expenditure up to a maximum level that is set annually by the Commission. This maximum rate can only be increased by common agreement between the Parliament and the Council (acting by qualified majority). In addition, since 1975 the Parliament has had the power to reject the entire budget by means of majority vote of its members and two-thirds of the votes cast. The Parliament has exercised this right to reject the 1980 budget, the 1982 supplementary budget, and the 1985 budget. On each occasion the Parliament deemed the budget to be insufficient, thereby forcing the Commission and the Council to agree an amended budget. (For further details on EC budgetary politics see Chapter 6.)

Legislative powers   The policy-making role of the Parliament prior to the Single European Act was wholly advisory. Commission proposals were scrutinized by Parliamentary Committees, debated, and voted on in plenary session and the Parliament's opinion (i.e. the version of the proposal as amended by the Parliament) then forwarded to the Council. In 1980, the European Court of Justice ruled that the Council could not take a decision until the Parliament had given its opinion on the proposal in question. Yet Parliament's opinion was in no sense binding upon the Council, which could, if it so wished, ignore totally the views of the MEPs. The 1986 Single European Act has increased the legislative role of the Parliament in two ways. First, the Act established a formal Cooperation Procedure whereby the Parliament is given a further opportunity in a second reading to amend the Council's views on all policies relating to the internal market, social policy, social and economic cohesion, and research. Secondly, the Act granted the Parliament joint decision-making power with the Council in relation to Accession Treaties (i.e. negotiations with states wishing to join the Community) and Association Agreements with non-EC countries, including the Lomé Conventions. These changes, their impact on Community policy-making and their significance with regard to European Union are discussed in detail below (p.20).

The European Parliament, due to its somewhat limited constitutional powers, has often been dismissed as being of little significance in Community policy-making. In recent years, however, the Parliament has consciously sought to extend its influence by actively campaigning for additional powers and stretching to the limit its existing powers. It has, for instance, become involved in a wide range of topical issues (e.g. AIDS and violence against women) and monitors international developments such as human rights and apartheid. MEPs have also drafted their own rules of procedure in such a way as to enable them to put issues on to the Community's policy agenda. The Parliament drafts its 'own initative' reports on matters and passes resolutions asking the Commission to submit policy proposals to the Council reflecting the MEPs 'own initative' report within a time limit fixed by the Parliament. This relatively straightforward mechanism was the foundation for the draft Treaty on European Union which led ultimately to the Single European Act (Lodge, 1983, 1989).

Nevertheless, the title 'European Parliament' is in many respects a misleading one. Certainly, the European Parliament performs the traditional parliamentary functions of scrutiny, representation, and public debate. The Parliament also enjoys limited budgetary powers, the power to delay the adoption of legislation, the means to initiate legislation, and, since 1987, increased legislative powers. Yet, constitutionally speaking, the European Parliament is an anomalous institution. Unlike national parliaments in Western democracies, it does not sustain an executive, it is not elected to carry out a comprehensive political programme, and it has no effective control over either the Commission or the Council of Ministers. The Community's only directly elected body wields least authority and, as highlighted in Section 2.4, disquiet over the Community's 'democratic deficit' is a major theme of the present debate on institutional reform and European Union. The prospect of monetary union, the reunification of Germany, and widespread speculation concerning future eastern enlargement of the Community have prompted widespread demands for further institutional reform to increase the democratic legitimacy of the Community.

2.2.5 The Economic and Social Committee

Corporatist interests are represented in the Economic and Social Committee, which is an advisory body comprising 189 representatives drawn from three groups: employers, workers, and 'various' (professional bodies, consumers, environmentalists, etc.). All Commission proposals are considered by the Committee, which also publishes its own detailed reports and recommendations on issues. In practice, its influence is greatest in those highly technical areas in which representatives have specialist knowledge.

2.2.6 Pressure groups

Alongside the Economic and Social Committee there are some 700 pressure groups organized into European umbrella pressure groups, based mainly in Brussels. Among the most important European groups are the employers' group, the Industrial Confederation of the European Community (UNICE), the European Trade Union Confederation (ETUC), and the Committee of Professional Agricultural Organizations (COPA). Of the officially recognized groups in 1980, 40 per cent represented industrial employer interests and a third were from the food and agriculture sectors, reflecting the importance of the prominent position of the CAP within the Community (Lodge, 1989). The planned completion of the internal market has prompted the arrival of a fresh wave of lobbyists, including representatives from internal organizations and foreign corporations. The close links maintained by the Commission with the major groups have given rise to fears in some quarters (notably on the part of consumers and trade unions) that Community decision-making is becoming excessively dominated by corporatist interests.

2.2.7 The European Court of Justice

The European Court of Justice (not to be confused with the European Court of Human Rights in Strasbourg, which is a Council of Europe body, or the International Court of Justice in the Hague) sits in Luxembourg and comprises 13 judges (assisted by six advocates-general), including at least one from each member-state who are appointed for a period of six years. The Court is an appellate court whose task is to interpret and enforce the application of Community law in cases of dispute and to ensure that national laws are compatible with those of the EC. Community legislation takes one of the following forms:

1. *The Treaties of the European Community* (primary legislation): these have 'direct effect'—i.e. are immediately binding upon the member-states and may be relied upon in national courts.

2. *Regulations*: these are binding and have direct effect in member-states.
3. *Directives*: these are also binding, but the method of achieving the end result is left to the individual states.
4. *Decisions*: these are obligatory on the government, organization, or individual concerned.
5. In addition, policies may be adopted in the form of *Recommendations*, *Resolutions*, and *Opinions*. These are *not* legally binding.

Indirectly, the Court plays an important role in the EC policy-making process since its judgments not only settle the particular matter at issue, but also spell out the construction to be placed on disputed passages of legislation. Since European Court rulings in the field of EC law override those of the national courts, governments and lawyers in all member-states must abide by them. (In these respects the European Court of Justice is similar to the US Supreme Court.) The extension of Community law into more and more policy areas has thus steadily eroded the degree of legislative autonomy previously enjoyed by member-states.[3] One consequence of this development has been an increase in the number of requests from national courts for the European Court to give preliminary rulings on possible areas of conflict between national and EC legislation.

Within the United Kingdom especially, there has been much debate over the *de facto* legislative powers of the Court, which, it is argued, undermine a central principle of British government, namely that of parliamentary sovereignty (for further details of this debate see below, Chapter 10). The debate has been given fresh impetus by a recent ruling of the European Court in June 1990 which granted British courts the power to suspend Acts of Parliament alleged to be in breach of EC law until the Luxembourg court is able to determine whether or not the legislation in question is compatible with EC law. The judgment was in relation to a claim by Spanish fishermen that the 1988 Merchant Shipping Act cannot prevent 'quota hopping'. UK fishing quotas have been circumvented by Spanish-owned vessels flying the British flag. The European Court of Justice will probably not decide for several months the substantive issue of whether or not the UK statute is in breach of EC law. Meanwhile, however, the Luxembourg court has ruled that the UK statute be suspended. This decision has served to underline the fact that not only must British legislation comply with EC legislation, but British courts must enforce EC law. Furthermore, Community law forms part of national law and can be used to win British court cases which would otherwise be lost, or indeed to lose cases which were winners under UK law.

Yet, while the Court has played an important role in prompting member-states to comply with Community law, its power is not unlimited. First, it cannot intervene in a dispute unless requested to do so. Secondly, many individuals and organizations are put off by the length of time it takes to obtain a judgment from the Court (up to two years). Thirdly, the Court 'lacks teeth' in that it has no sanction beyond public reprimand and humiliation. In consequence, the Court's views have not always been respected by member-states.

2.2.8   European Political Cooperation

At the 1969 Hague Summit member-states agreed to consult each other regularly on important foreign policy issues and to attempt to reach common positions on key issues of common interest (e.g. South Africa, the Middle East). Thus at each summit meeting time is set aside for the foreign ministers of the Twelve to meet as the European Political Community (EPC). These meetings have become increasingly institutionalized and in 1986 the EPC was finally incorporated into the Treaties in the Single European Act. Potentially, this represents an important institutional and political development since Title III of the SEA states that 'The High Contracting Parties (i.e. the member-states) being members of the European Communities shall endeavour jointly to formulate and implement a common foreign policy' (Nugent, 1989, p. 225).

2.3   EUROPEAN COMMUNITY INSTITUTIONS AND POLICY-MAKING: THE IMPACT OF THE LUXEMBOURG COMPROMISE

The founders of the Community intended that the Commission—as the European executive—would become the most powerful of the Community institutions. Between 1957 and 1965, an assertive Commission under the presidency of the ardent federalist Walter Hallstein set about realizing this aim. During this period the Commission publicly declared itself to be the motor of European integration and clearly perceived itself as an embryonic European government; Walter Hallstein, talking to American journalists, proudly declared that he could be considered as 'a kind of Prime Minister of Europe'. In fact, there were no grounds for such optimism since the authority of the Commission had never really been put to the test. The Luxembourg Compromise in 1966 revealed just how unrealistic Hallstein's vision of the Community was.

2.3.1   The Luxembourg Compromise

In the spring of 1965 the Commission announced a 'package-deal' linking increases in farm prices to two further policies designed to strengthen the Community insititutions: the introduction of import levies to be paid directly to the Community; and the granting of greater budgetary powers to the European Assembly (Parliament). The effect of these measures would have been to enhance the powers of the Commission and the Assembly *vis-à-vis* those of the Council. The French government, which was at that time hostile to the idea of supranationalism, opposed the measures. After just one day of negotiations, the French Foreign Minister, M. Couve de Murville, walked out of the Council of Ministers on 30 June 1965. The following day the French government issued a statement declaring the Community to be in a state of crisis, withdrew its permanent representative from Brussels and for the next seven months boycotted the Community—the so-called 'empty-chair' policy. At the centre of the dispute lay the executive ambitions of the Commission and the fact that plans (outlined in the Treaties) to extend majority voting in the Council to a range of new policy areas were about to come into effect. The French President, General de Gaulle, declared that majority voting would 'put France under duress' and demanded that the Commission—'a technocracy'—abandon its 'present mistaken ideas' about its role and cease its attempt 'to evade the Council's authority'.

The crisis was resolved by the Luxembourg Compromise which shifted the institutional balance of power away from the Commission in favour of the Council. While the Commission's right to initiate policy was confirmed, it was agreed that it should, in future, consult more closely with member-states' governments before issuing new proposals. With regard to majority voting in the Council of Ministers, the document states:

> Where in the case of decisions which may be taken by majority vote . . . very important interests of one or more partners are at stake, the Members of the Council will endeavour, within a reasonable time, to reach solutions which can be adopted by all the Members of the Council.

This agreement put an end to the Commission's pretensions to be a European government in the making and pushed the Community in the direction of intergovernmentalism. With every country in effect able to veto important legislation, a complex system of consultation developed between member-states, and this meant there was a shift of decision-making power from the Commission to the Council. While the Commission continued to play a major role in the policy process, it was forced after 1966 to tailor its proposals to accommodate the interests of member-states. The principal way in which it has sought to secure adoption of its proposals in the Council of Ministers has been through the preparation of 'package-deals' which offer all member-states a favourable deal in one area in return for their support on another issue.

This institutional development has slowed down the policy-making process. It has also hindered the establishment of 'European' policies, because the primary objective of government ministers attending the Council of Ministers is to get the best deal for their country—or at least for their government—even if that means an unsatisfactory policy for the Community as a whole. Mrs Thatcher's insistence in the early 1980s upon Britain's right to a substantial reduction in its Community budget contributions was a clear example of this. But Britain is not the only culprit. In 1985, the German government, anxious to protect Bavarian farmers, vetoed a proposed reduction in the level of subsidy paid to cereal farmers—despite the Community's massive grain surplus and the desperate need to reduce the cost of the Common Agricultural Policy. Later that year, Greece insisted that the accession of Spain and Portugal to the Community be linked to a £1200 million aid package for Greece. Even when national interests are not at stake, agreement is often difficult to achieve since the twelve member-states have different political outlooks. Council meetings invariably bring together conservative, liberal, and socialist ministers who, because of their different values, usually disagree over what constitutes a 'desirable' policy. The worsening economic climate during the 1970s and early 1980s and the piecemeal enlargement of the Community from six to twelve member-states (not all of whom were equally committed to European integration) served only to compound the difficulties of policy-making. Protracted negotiations between member-states, crisis meetings at European summits, and unsatisfactory policy compromises thus became the characteristic hallmarks of the European Community.

2.4   EUROPEAN UNION AND INSTITUTIONAL REFORM

Institutional reform of the Community has been a constant subject of discussion among the member-states since the early 1970s. Underlying this debate, however, has been the extremely contentious issue of the future direction of European integration. At the Paris Summit in 1972 the heads of government publicly declared their commitment to the development of 'European Union'. What they meant by 'European Union' and how it was to be achieved has preoccupied the Community ever since.

In fact, the Community is deeply divided on the matter. On the one hand there are the 'maximalists' who interpret 'European Union' to mean a Federal Europe. In order to achieve this, they favour amending the Treaties to establish a powerful Commission, accountable to a far more powerful Parliament, and restrictions on the use of the national veto. The 'minimalists', on the other hand, are opposed to further social and political integration, which they perceive to be at odds with the Community's basic economic role. They regard the term 'European Union' to mean the establishment of a common market and believe major institutional reform to be both unnecessary and a threat to national sovereignty. Among the member-states Italy and the Benelux countries have consistently been the keenest advocates of a Federal Europe. West Germany and—since the mid-1970s—France, have also generally been in favour of greater European integration. Most firmly opposed to such a development has been the United Kingdom, supported by Greece and Denmark (Tugendhat, 1987). Predictably, the European Parliament and the Commission have favoured the federalist proposals for institutional reform, while the Council of Ministers has defended the status quo.

Throughout the 1970s and early 1980s institutional reform was rarely absent from the Community's agenda. But circumstances during the 1970s were not conducive to any such changes. The entry of the United Kingdom, Ireland, and Denmark into the community in 1973, the onset of world-wide economic recession in 1974, and the protracted row over British EC budget contributions (see Chapter 11) placed considerable strains upon the Community, which underwent a period of stagnation in the 1970s. But though the reform proposals of the 1970s came to nothing, they did serve to keep the issue of institutional reform on the Community's agenda until the mid-1980s, by which time the prospects for institutional reform were considerably improved. The European economies had begun to recover, the UK budget rebate had finally been resolved, Spain and Portugal were about to enter the Community, and key figures within the EC (notably the French President, François Mitterrand, and the new Commission President, Jacques Delors) were intent on pushing ahead with European Union. And by linking institutional reform to a British objective—completion of the internal market—it was possible to secure the support of the UK government for the institutional reforms contained in the 1986 Single European Act. The major stages in the debate on European Union and institutional reform during this period were are follows:

The Paris Summit (1974) A communiqué issued at the end of the Summit reiterated the earlier commitment to the establishment of European Union. As a first step to relaunching the Community it was agreed that the first European elections should take place in 1979, though the powers of the Parliament were—largely at Britain's insistence—to remain unchanged. The Belgian Prime Minister, Leo Tindemans, was also asked to prepare a report on how the Community's institutions should be reformed to achieve European Union.

The Tindemans Report (1975) This report, published in 1975, was unmistakably federalist in tone, and with regard to institutional reform recommended the establishment of a powerful executive Commission and a bicameral legislature comprising a Chamber of the People (similar to the existing Parliament) and a Chamber of States appointed by national governments. Despite appearing regularly on European Council agendas between 1975 and 1978, the Tindemans Report was never discussed by the heads of government.

The Report of the Three Wise Men (1979) At the December Summit in 1978, the heads of government agreed to follow up the suggestion of the French President, Valery Giscard d'Estaing, that a 'number of eminent persons' consider what 'adjustments' in the Community's institutional machinery and procedures might be necessary for their effective operation, and whether progress could be made towards European Union. The so-called 'Three Wise Men' chosen by the European Council (Mr Barend Biesheuvel, former Prime Minister of the Netherlands 1971–3; Mr Edmund Dell, former British Secretary of State for Trade 1976–8; and Mr Robert Marjolin, former vice-president of the EEC Commission 1958–67) identified the cumbersome nature of policy-making as the principal weakness of the Community. Their report was particularly critical of the Council of Ministers, which it held to be responsible for the weakening of the 'supranational' Commission. To improve the situation the

Committee proposed there should be more majority voting in the Council and a reorganization and strengthening of the Commission.

The Genscher-Colombo Initiative (1981)   In November 1981 the German and Italian governments presented the draft of a European Act and draft declaration on economic integration. This was unmistakenly federalist in tone. It proposed the extension of common policies, increased cultural and legal cooperation, and the introduction of a common foreign policy.

The Spinelli Initiative (1981–4)   In 1980, Altiero Spinelli, the former Italian MEP (an independent Italian Communist and member of the Communist group in the European Parliament) and firm federalist, founded with eight colleagues the Crocodile Club (named after the restaurant in Strasbourg in which they met). In 1981 the group put forward a comprehensive plan for a federal European Union. Existing institutions formed the basis of Spinelli's reforms. Both the Commission and Parliament would enjoy enhanced roles within this scheme. The Commission would have the powers to prepare and implement the budget, initiate policy, supervise the implementation of the Treaty guaranteeing European Union, and represent the Union in external relations. The Parliament would acquire a joint legislative power with the new Council of the Union (the former Council of Ministers). This would include the power to ratify treaties and agreements. As one arm of this joint legislative body, the Parliament would also have independent revenue-raising powers and joint powers over the adoption of the budget and a say in the appointment of the Commission. In the Council, time limits and majority voting were proposed as two further means of preventing long delays. These proposals formed the basis of a Draft Treaty on European Union which was endorsed by the European Parliament in February 1984 by 237 votes to 31 with 43 abstentions (Bieber and Weiler, 1985).

The Solemn Declaration on European Union (1983)   The Genscher–Colombo initiative was finally discussed at the Stuttgart meeting of the European Council in 1983. While rejecting the proposals, member-states adopted a Solemn Declaration on European Union, yet a further declaration of their commitment to—an as yet undefined—objective.

The Dooge Committee (1984)   At the Fontainebleau Council (chaired by the pro-European French President, François Mitterrand), European Union and institutional reform were once again on the agenda. Two committees were set up to establish practical means of moving towards European Union: the Committee for a People's Europe which considered measures intended to promote a sense of common identity and a People's Europe; and the Ad Hoc Committee (known as the Dooge Committee after the name of its chairman, the President of the Irish Senate). The first committee listed as priority objectives the creation of a genuine internal market, economic convergence (i.e. common economic policies such as the European Monetary System), social and economic cohesion, the promotion of common values of civilization (social policies, culture), development of an external identity (representation at international meetings), and increased cooperation on foreign policy. The overall aim of the Dooge Report was to establish a 'true political entity' for the European Community 'with the power to take decisions in the name of all citizens by a democratic process'. In order to achieve these goals, the Dooge Committee proposed the following practical measures:

Easier decision-making in the Council   The Committee proposed that the only decisions that must be unanimous were those concerning new areas of action or new accessions. Other decisions were to be taken by qualified or simple majorities.

Strategic role for European Council   Summit meetings should be held only twice a year and should not be concerned with the day-to-day business of the Community, but with diplomatic and external affairs.

Strengthening of the Commission   The Commission should be a powerful and independent body, and to this end, while the President of the Commission should be designated by the European Council, other commissioners should be appointed by common accord of the governments of member-countries acting on a proposal from the President designate. The Commission must be acknowledged as an organ with full powers of initiative, implementation, and administration. It should also consist of no more than one commissioner from each country.

Enhanced powers for the Parliament   The Parliament should be given joint decision-making power with the Council, increased supervisory power over the Union's policies, political control over the Commission, cooperation in external policies, and more powers over the Community's revenue.

The Committee recommended that an intergovernmental conference be established to formulate a reform package on the basis of its report, the *acquis communautaire* (the existing Treaties and policy achievements of the Community), and the Stuttgart Solemn Declaration on European Union.

The Milan Summit (June 1985)   Community reform was the major subject of discussion at the Milan Summit. The meeting was marked by discord and deadlock. Mrs Thatcher infuriated the Italian Foreign Minister, Mr Giulio Andreotti, when she dismissed the Italian proposals for European Union as 'airy fairy' and put forward an alternative set of 'pragmatic' measures for the establishment of a common economic and financial market. A Franco-German initiative unveiled on the eve of the summit (relating principally to European Political Cooperation), which closely resembled the much-maligned British initiative, in turn irritated Mrs Thatcher and added to the confusion. Arguments over the meaning of the term 'European Union' inevitably affected discussions on institutional reform. Disagreement centred on whether or not the Treaties should be amended, what additional powers the European Parliament should have, and the extent to which the power of veto in the Council of Ministers ought to be diminished. Eventually, in an unprecedented European Council vote, it was agreed that an Intergovernmental Conference should be set up to establish a reform package on the basis of all existing reports and initiatives. The United Kingdom, Greece, and Denmark, who had consistently opposed all proposals to change the present institutional arrangement, voted against the setting up of the Conference, which Mrs Thatcher dismissed as 'a waste of time'.

The Luxembourg Summit (December 1985)   The Intergovernmental Conference met in October 1985 and prepared a modest reform package, which was presented to heads of state and government at the Luxembourg Summit in December. Several of the proposals were adopted in principle by member-states, though many were qualified by reservations on the part of individual governments. The United Kingdom entered a reservation against the social dimension of European Union, France opposed further European Political Cooperation (the harmonization of foreign policies), Italy declared the proposals relating to the European Parliament to be inadequate, and Denmark maintained a blanket reservation on all proposals. Nevertheless, the summit agreed in principle on texts that were incorporated into a Single

European Act, which amends the Treaties. The Act was signed by the heads of government in February 1986 and, following ratification by the national parliaments of the member-states, came into force in July 1987. The agreements covered the internal economic market (to be completed by 1992), monetary integration, regional inequalities, social policy, environmental policy, research and technological development, European Political Cooperation, and institutional reform. Our concern here is confined to the latter.

2.4.1 The Single European Act: institutional provisions

The institutional reforms introduced by the Single European Act may be summarized as follows:

Majority voting in the Council of Ministers In order to facilitate the completion of the internal market by the end of 1992, Article 100A of the Single European Act states that policies relating to the establishment or functioning of the internal market may be adopted by a qualified majority in the Council of Ministers.

The legislative role of the European Parliament The Single European Act increased the legislative powers of the European Parliament in two respects:

The cooperation procedure established by the Act in effect gives the Parliament the opportunity for a second reading of Community legislation related to the internal market, social policy, research, or social and economic cohesion (i.e. that category of legislation which may be adopted in the Council by a majority vote). The cooperation procedure is outlined in Figure 2.1 and may be summarized as follows:

1. At the end of the first reading, the Council adopts by a qualified majority a 'common position' which it must justify to Parliament, stating the reasons that led it to adopt the position. Parliament then has three months to decide whether to adopt the common position without amendment, or to amend or reject it. In order to amend or reject a common position, Parliament must act by an absolute majority of its membership (260). This is, in fact, no easy task, requiring the construction of alliances between the various transnational party groupings (see Chapter 3).
2. If the text has been amended, the Commission has one month in which to re-examine the common position on the basis of the amendments proposed by Parliament and to modify the proposal accordingly. Parliamentary amendments that are not accepted by the Commission must also be forwarded to the Council, which may adopt them, acting unanimously.
3. The Council then has three months in which to respond. It can adopt the proposal as modified by the Commission by a qualified majority. However, if the Council wishes to amend the revised proposal in any way (i.e. adopt its original common position or adopt Parliamentary amendments that were rejected by the Commission) it may do so only by acting unanimously. If the Council fails to act within the time limit, the proposal lapses.

Joint decision-making in respect of Accession Treaties and Association Agreements The Single European Act grants the European Parliament joint decision-making power with regard to the accession of third countries to the Community and Association Agreements negotiated by the Community (including the Lomé Conventions). The Parliament must act by an absolute majority of its membership (260 MEPs).

COOPERATION PROCEDURE

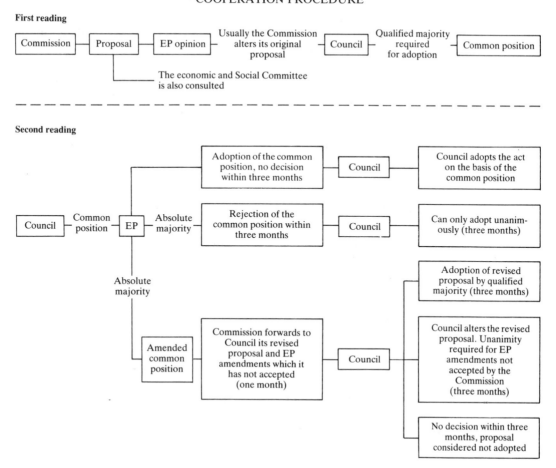

Figure 2.1 Cooperation procedure. (*Source: Ten Years that Changed Europe, 1979–1989.* European Parliament, Luxembourg, 1989)

2.4.2 The impact of the Single European Act

It is now possible to make some tentative comments about the actual impact these reforms upon Community policy-making and European Union. Taken together, the extension of majority voting in the Council and the new cooperation procedure have facilitated the adoption of policies relating to the single market and increased significantly the legislative powers of the Parliament. Since the Act came into force in July 1987, for instance, no member-state has used its veto at ministerial level. This marks a departure from previous practice. The Parliament has also used its new powers in relation to Association Agreements: in December 1987, it postponed consideration of two draft agreements with Turkey involving financial protocols, and in March 1988 rejected three protocols with Israel (Bogdanor, 1989).

Most attention, however, has focused upon the impact of the new cooperation procedure. Although it attracted little attention back in 1986, it is now clear that this procedure—in conjunction with majority voting in the Council of Ministers—does give the Parliament considerable leverage over the content of Community legislation. Paradoxically, the introduction of the second reading has served to increase the incentives for all parties to negotiate a compromise at the first reading stage. It is, for instance, in the Commission's interest to draft a proposal that is acceptable to both the Council and the Parliament, thereby avoiding the need to modify it significantly at a later stage. The Council must also take account of the Parliament's views on legislation from the outset or else risk having its common position rejected by the MEPs. However, MEPs must also maintain a dialogue with the Commission and Council from the outset since parliamentary amendments become increasingly difficult to accommodate as legislative proposals are 'firmed up' in package deals negotiated between the Commission and the Council (Fitzmaurice, 1988). As indicated in Table 2.1, EP amendments are more likely to be accepted by the Commission than the Council of Ministers and at the first rather than the second reading stage.

Table 2.1   Impact of the cooperation procedure (July 1987–December 1988)

Amendments adopted	Amendments accepted *	
By Parliament	By Commission	By Council
First reading	294 (60%)	212 (44%)
Second reading	62 (58%)	19† (23%)

* In whole or in part.
† Council accepted 19 out of 84.
Source: Ten Years that Changed Europe, 1979–1989, European Parliament, Luxembourg, 1989.

The cooperation procedure also has important implications for the interinstitutional balance within the Community. In the past, EC policy-making has been characterized by a Commission–Council dialogue. The insertion of the Parliament into the process marks an important change. Under the cooperation procedure, the Commission acts as mediator by deciding whether or not to support parliamentary amendments. In the past, the Parliament has been regarded as an ally of the Commission and it is therefore possible that the position of the latter *vis-à-vis* the Council of Ministers may be strengthened by the support of Parliament in the legislative process. Though the Council of Ministers ultimately has the last say on Community policies, its dominant position within the Community has been challenged by the procedure.

But what are the implications of these changes for European Union? There can be no doubt that the extension of majority voting in the Council of Ministers has further eroded the degree of national sovereignty enjoyed by the member-states. It is simply no longer possible for any member-government to block Community legislation that relates to the establishment or functioning of the single market. To the immense irritation of the UK government, such legislation embraces an extremely wide range of issues including the wording of health warnings on cigarette packets. Nevertheless, majority voting is not a panacea for all the Community's problems. It applies only to specified policy areas, and disputes over whether or not proposals fall within this category have already become commonplace. Furthermore, while majority voting may facilitate the introduction of Community legislation, it does not guarantee its successful *implementation*.

European policy-making has been rendered marginally more democratic by the increased legislative powers granted to the Parliament, but these reforms fall far short of the Spinelli proposals outlined in the 1984 Draft Treaty on European Union for a citizens' Europe. A major limitation of the Single European Act is its failure to remedy the Community's 'demo-cratic deficit'. Despite the changes outlined above, European policies continue to be ulti-mately determined by appointed officials (within the Commission and the COREPER) and national politicians who are not accountable to a democratically elected body. Predictably, federalists and intergovernmentalists disagree on the best means of resolving this problem. The former group (i.e. most MEPs, the Commission, and a clear majority of member-govern-ments) believe the solution lies in strengthening the powers of the Commission and the European Parliament. More specifically, it is argued that the Commission should become a political executive accountable to a strengthened European Parliament. The latter should, according to the pro-integrationists, be given joint legislative powers with the Council, the right to initiate legislation, greater financial powers, a bigger say in the appointment of com-missioners, and the right to dismiss individual commissioners. However, opponents of this view, led by the former British Conservative Prime Minister Mrs Thatcher, oppose such measures, which they claim would lead to excessive centralization of power. Instead, they favour decentralizing powers wherever possible (in accordance with the federalist principle of subsidiarity), consolidating the executive powers of the Council of Ministers, and granting national parliaments a greater role in EC policy-making.

2.5   CONCLUSION

As illustrated in the above analysis there is an intimate link between the interpretation given to the term European Union, the institutional balance of power, and the nature of the decision-making process within the Community. Since the European Community was set up in 1957, it has passed through a number of phases. During the 1950s and early 1960s, the federal-functionalist aspirations of the founders prevailed. The 1966 Luxembourg Compromise heralded the beginning of a more difficult period for the Community, characterized by dis-agreement over the objectives of European integration, a shift in the institutional balance of power away from the Commission, and a reluctance on the part of some member-states to 'pool their sovereignty'. Since the mid-1980s the situation has changed yet again and the Community is, once again, in a state of flux. The Single European Act has unblocked the Community's decision-making process and given fresh impetus to the completion of the internal market—a necessary first step towards further union.

There are also new external pressures for further EC institutional reform. The dramatic collapse of Communist regimes throughout Eastern Europe, the reunification of Germany, and the apparent ending of the Cold War have prompted major questions about the future dimensions, structure, status, and international responsibilities of the European Community. Thus far, the cumulative effect of these developments has been to accelerate the timetable for monetary and political union (much to the annoyance of the then British Prime Minister, Margaret Thatcher). Having declared their commitment to establishing political union, the heads of government had until the December 1990 summit to work out what this will mean in terms of further EC institutional reform. Nevertheless, it would be naïve to assume that these developments will lead inevitably to the establishment of a supranational 'United

States of Europe'. While all member-states support the completion of the internal market, no such consensus exists with regard to further integration, as was clearly illustrated by Mrs Thatcher's notorious Bruges speech in October 1988 (see Chapter 10). A minority of member-states have already begun to question whether the Single European Act requires full monetary union and implementation of the social charter. Such disagreements highlight the fragility of the commitment on the part of member-states to European Union and have prompted the Commission (particularly in the light of EC membership applications from East European and EFTA states) to raise the possibility of a 'two-tier' Community within which member-states could choose to play a less than full role. The future direction and composition of the European Community thus remains impossible to predict.

NOTES

1. The two British Commissioners appointed in 1989 are Mr Leon Brittan (former Conservative Minister for Trade and Industry) and Mr Bruce Millan (former Labour MP for Govan).
2. The European Commission Directorates General are:

DG I   External Relations
DG II   Economic and Financial Affairs
DG III   Internal Market and Industry
DG IV   Competition
DG V   Employment, Social Affairs and Education
DG VI   Agriculture
DG VII   Transport
DG VIII   Development
DG IX   Personnel and Administration
DG X   Information and Culture
DG XI   Environment, Consumer Protection and Nuclear Safety
DG XII   Science and Research
DG XIII   Telecommunications, Information Industries and Innovation
DG XIV   Fisheries
DG XV   Financial Institutions and Company Law
DG XVI   Regional Policy
DG XVII   Energy
DG XVIII   Credits and Investments
DG XIX   Budgets
DG XX   Financial Control
DG XXI   Customs Union and Indirect Taxation
DG XXII   Coordination of Structural Instruments
DG XXIII   Enterprise, Business, and Tourism.

3. The Commission President, Jacques Delors, recently predicted that by the mid-1990s some 80 per cent of all economic and social legislation in the EC would be determined by the Community and not nationally.
4. The SEA leaves intact the Luxembourg Compromise. In practice, however, member-governments have refrained from invoking it since the adoption of the SEA.

REFERENCES

Bieber, R. and Weiler, J. (1985), *An Ever Closer Union: a critical analysis of the Draft Treaty establishing the European Union*, Commission of the European Communities, Brussels.

Bogdanor, V. (1989) 'The June 1989 European elections and the institutions of the Community', *Government and Opposition*, **24**, 199–214.

European Commission (1984), Ad Hoc Committee for Institutional Affairs (1984) *Interim Report to the European Council*, Brussels.

European Commission (1985), 'The European Community and European Union', *Background Report*, 30 January, Luxembourg.

European Commission (1986), 'Single European Act', *Bulletin of the European Communities*, Supplement 2/86, Luxembourg.

European Commission (1989), *Forging Ahead: European Parliament 1952–1988*, 3rd Edn, Luxembourg.

Fitzmaurice, J. (1988) 'An analysis of the European Community's co-operation procedure', *Journal of Common Market Studies*, **26**, 389–400.

Haas, E. (1976), *The Obsolescence of Regional Integration Theory*, Berkeley University Press, Berkeley, Calif.

Lodge, J. (Ed.) (1983), *Institutions and Policies of the European Community*, Francis Pinter, London.

Lodge, J. (1986), 'The Single European Act: towards a new Euro-dynamism?', *Journal of Common Market Studies*, **24**, March, 203–223.

Lodge, J. (Ed.) (1989), *The European Community and the Challenge of the Future*, Frances Pinter, London.

Noel, E. (1989), 'The Single European Act: meaning and perspectives', *Contemporary European Affairs*, **1**, 93–108.

Nugent, N. (1989), *The Government and Politics of the European Community*, Macmillan, London.

Tugendhat, C. (1987), *Making Sense of Europe*, Pelican Books, London.

THREE

THE CUSTOMS UNION AND THE COMMON MARKET: THEORETICAL BASIS

3.1 INTRODUCTION

We now turn to the economic arrangements within the Community. At the very heart of these lie the customs union and the common market. These will be examined in the next two chapters: this chapter will outline the theory of customs unions and common markets, while Chapter 4 will look at how the attempt by the European Community to establish a customs union and a common market has actually functioned in practice, and what impact the ambition of completing the market by the end of 1992 is likely to have.

It would appear that there is widespread confusion about what the Community's economic arrangements precisely consist of. The terms common market, customs union, and free trade area are liberally and loosely used by the media and others, often seemingly without too much idea of their real meaning. It therefore seems useful to begin this survey with some definitions for clarification.

A *free trade area* is the most basic form of international economic integration (apart from, perhaps, single commodity agreements such as the European Coal and Steel Communities). It consists of an arrangement whereby participating countries agree to: (i) practice free trade amongst themselves by dismantling all tariffs and other impediments to internal trade within the area; and (ii) retain independence over their trade policies *vis-à-vis* the rest of the world, i.e. each country decides what tariffs it should charge on imports from countries outside the free trade area, subject of course to other international agreements such as the General Agreement on Tariffs and Trade (GATT). The best known example of a free trade area is the European Free Trade Area (EFTA), of which the United Kingdom was a member before joining the European Community, and which now consists mainly of Scandinavian bloc countries.

A *customs union* involves a greater surrender of economic sovereignty. It is an arrangement whereby countries agree to: (i) get rid of all internal tariffs and other trade impediments, as in the case of the free trade area; but (ii) additionally agree to practice a common and coordinated trade policy towards the rest of the world. In the European Community this takes the form of the Common External Tariff (or, for agriculture, the Variable Levy) on all imports into the Community from non-member countries. Thus a customs union concerns solely trade in goods and services, and involves changes that represent both an enhancement of free trade and (potentially) a retreat from it. On the latter point, it is interesting to note that customs unions in fact infringe the 'most favoured nation' clause of the GATT, which forbids discriminatory tariff changes. The clause had in fact to be amended to accommodate the creation of customs unions.

A *common market* implies still greater integration. It is a situation whereby members agree to take the customs union a step further by additionally promoting the free movement of labour and capital between the participating countries, i.e. the right for people and money to move at will throughout the area concerned. Thus a common market is an area of internal mobility for goods, services, and factors of production. Entry from the rest of the world is restricted: for goods and services by the Common External Tariff, and for factors of production by any prevailing exchange and immigration controls.

Beyond a common market, economic integration may take the form of monetary and economic union, which is likely to involve establishing a single currency for the area, as well as substantial joint determination of macro- and micro-economic policies (see Chapter 5).

3.2 CUSTOMS UNION THEORY

We begin our analysis by examining the theory of customs unions. Customs union theory, as this body of arguments has come to be referred to by economists, essentially consists of an evaluation of the effects of forming a customs union. The arguments can be divided into two categories, often referred to as static and dynamic theory.

3.2.1 Static customs union theory

Static customs union theory seeks to examine the 'once and for all' effects of the customs union on trade flows, economic welfare, and the international distribution of production. It does so by comparing the position 'before' and 'after' the formation of the union. It is thus what economists would usually refer to as 'comparative static' analysis.

What is now seen as mainstream static customs union theory was developed in the 1950s, principally by Jacob Viner and Richard Lipsey. Previous views suggested that customs unions were unambiguously a step towards free trade and therefore necessarily desirable in their effects, because of the internal tariff elimination to which they lead (economists can show that under certain conditions free trade optimizes economic welfare—see Begg *et al.*, 1987, or any other basic economics textbook). Viner's analysis shows that this view is simplistic since a customs union with its discriminatory tariff changes represents both a move towards free trade (the removal of internal trade barriers) and a move towards potentially greater protectionism (the common external trade policy). This leads to two separate effects: trade creation and trade diversion. The former improves the international allocation of resources and increases economic welfare. The latter has the opposite effect. Thus one can evaluate the trade effects of a customs union by comparing the relative dimension of the two effects.

Trade creation occurs when changes in tariffs and other trade impediments that result from the formation of a customs union lead to consumers purchasing relatively more efficiently and cheaply produced goods and services provided by other members of the union instead of less efficiently produced and more expensive products made domestically. How this can happen can be demonstrated with a simple numerical example. Table 3.1 shows the hypothetical production costs of a washing machine in three countries, the United Kingdom, Italy, and the United States, and the impact on consumer prices in the United Kingdom of different levels of UK tariffs on washing machines. It is assumed that the United Kingdom and Italy form a customs union together, while the United States remains outside.

Table 3.1   Numerical example of trade creation and trade diversion

	Before union			After union		
	UK	Italy	USA	UK	Italy	USA
(A) Costs of production (£)	400	250	220	400	250	220
(B) Price (£) in UK with 100% UK tariff (A × 2)	400	500	440	400	250	440
(C) Price (£) in UK with 50% UK tariff (A × 1.5)	400	375	330	400	250	330

We can see that in absolute terms, the United States is the most efficient and cheapest producer of washing machines, followed by Italy and then the United Kingdom. In a situation of world free trade, the United States would thus specialize in washing machine production and would export to both the United Kingdom and Italy. Tariffs change all this. If we first of all consider the case depicted in rows A and B, we can see that before the union is formed, the 100 per cent tariff on all imports into the United Kingdom renders domestically produced washing machines the cheapest for UK consumers, and, on the assumption that price is the sole factor that determines consumption, they will 'buy British' and there will be no imports. After the union, Italian washing machines enter the United Kingdom tariff free, while US machines are still charged the 100 per cent tariff. The result is that Italian machines become the cheapest on the UK market, and UK 'rational' consumers will buy them instead of British ones. This is trade creation—the positive trade and welfare effect of customs union formation. It consists of a production effect, in that production of a quantity of washing machines is switched from the United Kingdom to more efficient sources in Italy (but, it is important to note, not to the most efficient source of all, i.e. the United States), thereby saving resources. This change towards a more rational pattern of international specialization increases economic welfare since some washing machines are now produced more cheaply and efficiently. In addition, it will also have a consumption effect since consumers in the United Kingdom can buy washing machines more cheaply (£250 instead of £400) and will therefore probably purchase more of them.

Trade diversion, on the other hand, occurs when the tariff changes that follow the creation of a customs union result in prices changing in such a way as to lead consumers to buy goods and services produced relatively less efficiently in partner countries in place of those produced more efficiently and cheaply in other non-member countries. Again, the simple numerical example set out in Table 3.1 can illustrate this.

If we now consider the case depicted in rows A and C of Table 3.1, we can see that before the union consumers in the United Kingdom could be expected to buy washing machines imported from the United States, since these are the cheapest on the market, despite the tariff of 50 per cent. The domestic industry cannot compete with imports at this level of tariff. After the union is formed, Italian machines enter the United Kingdom duty free, while US machines are still charged the 50 per cent tariff. The result is that Italian machines become the cheapest on the market, and UK consumers buy these instead of US machines. The source of imports is thus shifted from a more efficient source to a less efficient one. This is trade diversion—the negative trade and welfare effect of a customs union. It is interesting to note that there is also a consumption effect with trade diversion, since prices also fall and consumers also buy more in this case. However, in this instance the consumption effect works in the opposite direction to the production effect. It is conceivable that in some cases the gains from the consumption effect might outweigh the production side losses, and thus on balance render trade diversion beneficial.

The above effects can also be illustrated in diagrammatic form. The simplest way of doing this is shown in Figure 3.1 (for fuller, but sometimes unnecessarily complex and complicated models, see texts such as Robson, 1987; Hine, 1985; or El-Agraa, 1985).

Figure 3.1 represents a simple model of the market for washing machines in the United Kingdom. It relies on all the restrictive assumptions that economists usually make in this type of model (see any basic economics textbook). Their price is measured along the vertical axis, and the quantity bought and sold is measured along the horizontal axis. P_w–S_w represents the world supply curve for washing machines—this is drawn as perfectly elastic, i.e. on the assumption that the United Kingdom can buy as many machines as it wants at the world market price 0–P_w (this is sometimes referred to as the 'small country model'—the consumption of large countries would affect the world market price). S_{UK} is the supply curve for washing machines in the United Kingdom, showing how many machines UK firms will produce at various prices, while $S_{UK + It}$ represents the aggregation of the UK and Italian supply curves—Italy and the United Kingdom are, to follow the earlier example, assumed to be the countries that form the customs union. Both supply curves are assumed to be of a standard nature, i.e. upward sloping with no scale economies. The way they are drawn assumes that

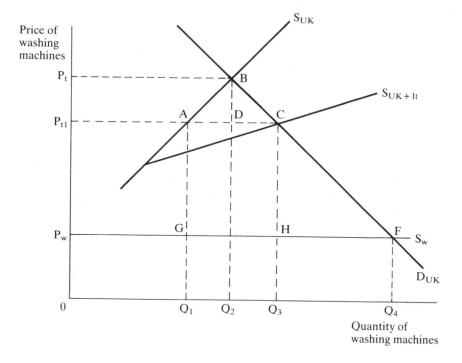

Figure 3.1 Diagrammatic illustration of trade creation and trade diversion.

on the whole the Italians are more efficient at producing washing machines than the British, although both are considerably less efficient than lowest cost producers elsewhere in the world. D_{UK} is the demand curve for washing machines in Britain, showing how many domestic consumers are prepared to buy at different prices. This is assumed to slope downwards from left to right, in line with usual assumptions about consumer behaviour.

With non-discriminatory free trade, domestic equilibrium would be at F, where consumers would buy $0-Q_4$ machines at a price $0-P_w$. All would be imported from the lowest cost world producer, and the UK market price would be too low to sustain a domestic industry.

If, however, before the customs union the United Kingdom wished completely to isolate the domestic industry from external competition, it would impose a tariff equivalent to P_w-P_t. Starting with this assumption, we can use the model to illustrate trade creation. A tariff P_w-P_t would result in equilibrium at B, at which $0-Q_2$ machines, all domestically produced, would be bought and sold at a market price of $0-P_t$. After the customs union, Italian goods enter the United Kingdom tariff free, while we can assume that the common external tariff remains at its previous level. Now UK and Italian firms operate in the same unified market, and we can represent this by adding together the supply curves in the two countries to give us the joint supply curve S_{UK+It}. Equilibrium shifts to C, where UK consumers buy $0-Q_3$ washing machines at price $0-P_{t1}$. $0-Q_1$ of these are produced at home, the remainder Q_1-Q_3 being imported from Italy. Imports from the rest of the world are still excluded.

This is an example of trade creation, since the customs union has resulted in production of some washing machines being shifted from higher cost sources in the United Kingdom to relatively lower cost and therefore more efficient sources in the new partner. There is a production effect equivalent to Q_1-Q_2, and a consumption effect equivalent to Q_2-Q_3 extra consumption at the lower price.

In terms of basic welfare economics, there is an increase in consumer surplus equivalent to area $P_t-B-C-P_{t1}$. Of this $P_t-B-A-P_{t1}$ represents a transfer from producers' surplus, while the remainder A-B-C is new welfare not transferred from another part of the population. This is the unambiguous welfare gain from trade creation, and it consists of a production effect A-B-D which arises from the more efficient allocation of resources in production, and a consumption effect B-D-C which arises from higher consumption at the the lower market price.

In this example trade creation results in the UK consumers enjoying welfare gains, some of them at the expense of domestic producers (with possible implications for the distribution of income in the United Kingdom). Italian producers gain from increased production worth Q_1-Q_3-C-A, although the position of Italian consumers would depend on other factors such as demand conditions in Italy. The rest of the world's position is unchanged: they were excluded from the UK market before the customs union, and they remain so. All in all, trade creation is considered to be beneficial.

We can also use the above model to illustrate trade diversion. If we assume that before the customs union the UK government wanted to protect its industry, but was also prepared to allow some imports, it might have levied a tariff of, say P_w-P_{t1} on imports of washing machines. In this case the domestic market price would be $0-P_{t1}$, at which consumers would buy $0-Q_3$ machines. $0-Q_1$ of these would be produced at home, the rest Q_1-Q_3 would be imported from lowest cost world producers. The UK government would enjoy tariff revenue equivalent to A-C-H-G. After the customs union, if we assume a common external tariff of at least P_w-P_{t1}, equilibrium in the United Kingdom will still be at C, consumption and market price will remain unchanged, as will the quantity of imports. What changes, however, is the source of the imports Q_1–Q_3. They no longer come from low-cost efficient rest-of-the-world producers, but from Italy, the new partner whose goods now enter the United Kingdom duty free.

This is trade diversion, since the customs union has resulted in production of a quantity of goods being transferred from low-cost producers elsewhere to a higher cost partner, and therefore in a worse allocation of world resources.

In this simplified example there is no consumption effect. Consumers and producers in the United Kingdom are unaffected, since price and domestic output remain the same. However, the UK government suffers the loss of its tariff revenue. Italian producers benefit from increased production worth A–C–Q_3–Q_1. The real losers, however, are washing machine producers in the rest of the world, who are forced to forego production and exports worth G–H–Q_3–Q_1.

Empirical studies of trade creation and trade diversion are reviewed in Chapter 4. Before we leave static customs union theory, however, it is important to note the following points:

1 Whether a particular customs union is on balance trade-creating or trade-diverting will depend principally on the following:

(a) The structure of production in the traded goods and services sector of member countries' economies prior to the union. Competitive, or overlapping productive structures offer greater opportunities for trade creation, whereas complementary, or dissimilar structures increase the possibility of trade diversion. Similar patterns of consumption and resource availability would clearly increase the probability of competitiveness. This has sometimes led to the conclusion that customs unions are most beneficial between similar countries at comparable stages of economic development.

(b) Differences in costs of production. It follows from the above that where countries do produce similar products, the greater the differences in costs of production, which may result from factors such as differing levels of productivity, the more scope there is for trade creation, and vice versa.

(c) The effect of the union on the height of tariffs. If on average the union leads to an increase in tariff levels, then it is more likely to be trade-diverting. If, on the other hand, the union on average leads to a reduction in tariffs, then it is more likely to be trade-creating.

2 Although mainstream static customs union theory gives us some important insights into the economic effects of a customs union, it should be treated with a certain amount of caution for various reasons, including the following:

(a) The assumptions on which the model is based are clearly somewhat less than totally realistic. Factors such as monopoly power, scale economies, transport costs, information deficiencies, unemployment, adjustment costs, and non-tariff barriers are conveniently ignored.

(b) The model is rooted very firmly in neoclassical trade theory. This seeks to explain trade in terms of 'comparative advantage' and 'factor endowments' (economists refer to this as the Hecksher–Ohlin model), i.e. trade takes place because there are gains to be had when countries specialize in making what they are good at, which in turn is determined by the quantity and quality of labour and capital available in each country. Countries with abundant labour will have an advantage in producing labour-intensive goods, for example. It is generally accepted that this approach ignores factors such as intra-industry trade and the technological determinants of trade, and therefore at best it explains only a proportion of international trade. This has obvious implications for the validity of our customs union model.

(c) The model assumes that tariffs and other barriers in practice constitute important impediments to trade, and that their removal will therefore have a significant effect. There must be some doubt about this given the large tariff cuts that have resulted from the various rounds of negotiations under the GATT. Furthermore, the growth of multinational enterprises (MNEs—see Chapter 9) has meant that international investment can increasingly replace trade when the latter faces obstacles—why ship goods around the world, pay tariffs, and face other barriers, when you can manufacture or assemble directly in the country in which you wish to sell? This may account for the increased volume of, for example, Japanese investment in EC countries in the run up to 1992.

(d) The approach ignores issues of distribution. Trade creation, for example, is always regarded as beneficial as it improves efficiency in the customs union as a whole. However, it can be a two-edged sword. Changes in the location of production can lead to unemployment, or at the very least, what economists refer to as 'adjustment costs'. If, to return to our previous example, Italian washing machines replace British ones in the UK market because they are cheaper, people working in the UK industry will lose their jobs, and it is probably small consolation to them that they are suffering for the common good. In theory, this is seen as not being of great importance. It is assumed that if people lose their jobs in declining sectors, they can then find new ones in other sectors which will be expanding at the expense of one's partners. If the distribution of trade creation between countries is more or less evenly balanced, then this may indeed be the case. However, even in this circumstance, structural unemployment could arise as there are serious obstacles to labour mobility—consider, for example regional differences in house prices in the United Kingdom. Even when people do move to find jobs, costs such as personal dislocation and retraining will be involved in migration. However, if changes in the international distribution of production favour some countries at the expense of others, then the resources rendered unemployed in weaker countries by the formation of the customs union are likely to remain unemployed. There is a view, largely substantiated by the admittedly often less than convincing empirical studies which are available, that the United Kingdom may be in this position *vis-à-vis* the European Community (see Winters, 1987, for example). This would suggest the imperative of an effective redistribution mechanism at the supranational level, perhaps in the form of regional policy, within customs unions. Economic theory assumes that customs unions are beneficial when 'gainers gain more than losers lose', since compensation is then a matter for the political process. Unfortunately, in the real world gainers rarely compensate losers, so this is a real issue for customs unions.

(e) Perhaps the most fundamental problem with customs union theory is that it does not really explain why customs unions are formed. If improvements in efficiency and consumer welfare were really the objectives, the best way of achieving these would be through a policy of universal non-discriminatory free trade. This would offer all the advantages of trade creation, with none of the drawbacks involved in trade diversion. To discover the rationale behind the formation of the European Community and other customs unions one perhaps has therefore to look beyond the model presented above. Some possible alternative explanations include the following:

(i) The 'pragmatic' view that although free trade would be the best solution, it is in fact politically impossible. Thus customs unions, however imperfect, represent the free trader's best realistic way forward.

(ii) The 'conspiratorial view', developed by Harry Johnson and Cooper and Massell in the 1960s and sometimes known as the 'public goods' approach to customs union theory. This points out that customs unions can be seen as an economical means of protecting industries that are threatened by competition, especially from the 'newly industrialized countries' such as Japan, Taiwan, and Korea. Countries operating together in a customs union can do this more cheaply and efficiently than on their own. Additionally, because the price of protecting industry is reduced, there is an income and a substitution effect that permits more of it to be protected. Thus the real rationale for their formation is protectionism.

(iii) The view that political integration is the principal objective of many customs unions. This would regard economic integration as an essential prerequisite for, and a stimulus towards, political integration, rather than a purely separate end in itself. Thus customs unions are formed to facilitate the achievement of political goals. Any economic advantages that may result are welcome extras rather than the central motivation.

3.2.2 Dynamic customs union theory

This area of customs union theory concentrates on the effects of a customs union over time, rather than on the once-and-for-all effects outlined above. There is some debate among economists as to what exactly constitutes a true dynamic effect; however, the following are usually mentioned in this context:

Economies of scale The increased internal specialization that results from the formation of a customs union leads to efficient firms and industries in a union expanding production and growing in size as they service a larger market. In many cases this allows unit costs of production to fall, thus increasing the welfare of consumers who can enjoy lower prices as a result. This process occurs as a result of the following:

1. Internal economies, which are advantages that result from the growth of firms. Examples of this might be the more efficient use of machinery with large production runs, and increased scope for the division of labour.
2. External economies, which result from the growth of industries as a whole. For example, large industries can be serviced by specialist and efficient manufacturers of components.

It is very difficult to quantify scale economies, but the EC Commission has recently estimated, perhaps rather optimistically, that the potential welfare gains available from the fuller exploitation of scale economies in the Community may amount to as much as 61 billion ECUs, or 2.1 per cent of Community GDP (Cecchini, 1988). Earlier studies (e.g. Owen, 1976) are less conclusive. However, the quest for scale economies is one of the factors that have influenced the spate of cross-frontier mergers which has occurred in the run up to 1992.

Increased competition The opening up of internal markets that results from the formation of a customs union can expose firms to increased competition from rivals in partner countries—national monopolies may become Community oligopolies. This may force firms to improve techniques, cut costs, and generally increase efficiency in order to remain or become competitive. This process will in the long run increase welfare and benefit all. Economists often refer to this as increasing 'X-efficiency'. Politicians have referred to it as 'the bracing cold shower'. It is a phenomenon that is very difficult to verify empirically.

Improvements in the terms of trade   A country's or an area's terms of trade can broadly be seen as the price at which it buys its imports in relation to the price it obtains for its exports. If the formation of a customs union leads to a fall in demand for imports from the rest of the world as a result of trade diversion, then the international price of these imports will tend to fall and the union's terms of trade will improve. In other words, the union can exert monopoly power in world markets. This effect may mitigate or even outweigh the negative effects of trade diversion, but it is important to note that any gains are made at the expense of the rest of the world. Petith (1977) suggests that terms of trade gains may be substantially more significant than static gains in the EC customs union.

Increased growth   It follows from the static and dynamic gains outlined above that, overall, the effect of a customs union should be to increase the rate of economic growth in the area concerned. This extra growth might in turn precipitate greater investment spending and stimulate growth further still. Empirical studies in this area should be treated with a good deal of caution. Nevertheless, in the case of the European Community, the growth effect has been traditionally estimated to be, overall, equivalent to about an extra 1 per cent GNP (see Lipsey, 1960; Balassa, 1975). A more recent estimate (Marques-Mendes, 1986) is more optimistic, suggesting that in 1972 the Community's GDP had been increased by 2.2 per cent by the European integration process, and that by 1981 the GDP of the enlarged Community was as much as 6.9 per cent higher than it would have been without any integration.

3.3   THE THEORY OF COMMON MARKETS: EFFECT OF FACTOR MOBILITY

A common market, as we have seen, involves the free movement of labour and capital between member-states, as well as the free movement of goods and services. In comparative static terms, the free movement of the factors of production can, under certain albeit restrictive assumptions, be shown to lead to improved resource allocation and welfare gains for the participants.

An accessible way of illustrating this is shown in Figure 3.2. For convenience, this example relates to the impact of the free movement of capital—a similar analysis could be applied to the effects of the free movement of labour. Here we assume that the hypothetical customs union we discussed above between the United Kingdom and Italy is extended into a common market, with capital able to move completely freely between the two countries. The impact of the common market on labour movements is disregarded, and the usual assumptions about full employment and so on are made. The marginal productivity of capital in the United Kingdom with a given amount of labour, is shown by the curve MPK_{UK}. The pre-common market quantity of labour available in the United Kingdom is assumed to be 0–B. It is assumed that this capital is owned by UK nationals, and that it is completely internationally immobile at this point. Furthermore, all foreign capital is excluded from the United Kingdom. In this situation, the UK's total national product will be equivalent to the area $a + b + c + d + e$. Since the return to capital (profit) is taken, in line with neoclassical assumptions, to be equal to its marginal product, the return to each unit of capital in the United Kingdom is equivalent to 0–X. Total profits in the United Kingdom are thus $d + e$, while the remainder of national product, $a + b + c$, accrues to the owners of labour. Similarly, MPK_{It} shows the (higher) marginal productivity of capital in Italy, which in the pre-

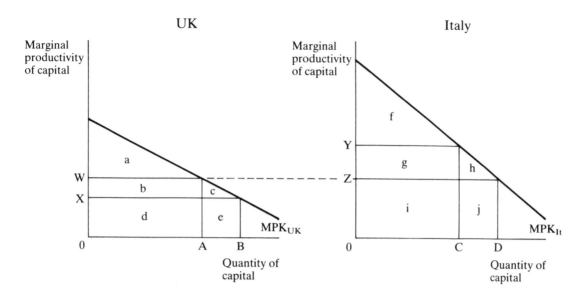

Figure 3.2 Welfare effects of the free movement of capital.

common market situation possesses an amount of capital 0–C, the return to each unit of which is 0–Y. Total pre-common market output in Italy is f + g + i, g + i of which accrues to the owners of capital, with the rest (f) going to labour.

When the common market between the two countries is completed, and capital becomes perfectly mobile between them, then capital will flow from the United Kingdom, where its return is lower, to Italy, where it can earn more. It is assumed that exclusive capital controls *vis-à-vis* the rest of the world are maintained. This process continues until the return to capital in both countries is equalized, i.e. 0–W = 0–Z. In total an amount A–B (which is equal to C–D) of capital moves from the United Kingdom to Italy. The result of this process is that the domestic product of the United Kingdom is reduced to a + b + d because of the capital outflow, i.e. domestic output equivalent to c + e is lost. However, national product, including the remitted profits from the capital that was exported to Italy (j) increase, since j is greater than the lost domestic output c + e. The return to each unit of capital in the United Kingdom increases to 0–W. The share of domestic product that accrues to capital is now b + d, with the rest (a) going to labour. Thus the establishment of the common market alters the functional distribution of income in the capital-exporting country in favour of capital and to the detriment of labour. In Italy, total product increases by h + j as a result of the capital inflow from the United Kingdom. However, some of this (j) is remitted to the UK, leaving a net gain to Italians equal to the triangle h. All of this accrues to the owners of labour. The return to capital falls to 0–Z, and the functional distribution of income changes in favour of labour (which now receives f + g + h) and against capital (which now receives i + j, of which j is remitted to the United Kingdom).

Thus we conclude that income in both the United Kingdom and Italy increases, and that both countries gain by the creation of the common market and the free movement of capital that it entails. There is, however, a change in the distribution of income in both countries, and a change in the international location of production. The impact of multinational enterprises is discussed in Chapter 9. The establishment of the free movement of labour between Italy and the United Kingdom can similarly be shown to result in welfare gains and changes in the distribution of income. There may also be dynamic gains to be had from the free movement of the factors of production. These are extremely difficult to analyse, but what literature does exist very tentatively suggests that they may broadly work in the same direction as the static effects discussed above. We thus have the broad theoretical rationale for promoting the free movement of labour and capital and creating and completing a common market, although one should bear in mind the familiar health warnings relating to the assumptions on which the model is based.

One of the conclusions from the above analysis is that the free movement of capital tends to equalize factor earnings between participating countries or regions, and thus leads to economic convergence in the common market. Before we leave this subject, however, it is salutary to point out that the radical critique of neo-classical theory in this area suggests that no such convergence will take place, but that instead the free movement of capital, in particular, will tend to lead to the exacerbation of national and regional differences in real income and welfare, with well-off areas gaining at the expense of less well-off countries and regions. This critique is largely based on the work of the Swedish economist Gunnar Myrdal (see Myrdal, 1957), who developed his theories in the context of development economics. He essentially held that the free movement of capital leads to 'polarization' effects through a process of 'cumulative causation'. Broadly, the inflow of capital into areas where its marginal productivity is greatest sets in motion dynamic processes that reinforce the attractiveness of these host areas, which grow in prosperity, and thus attract more and more capital from the source areas, which are gradually relatively pauperized. The free movement of labour may lead to similar effects, since it may drain source areas of the workers with the greatest amount of human capital and enterprise. There may be limited flow of capital from the prosperous economic centre to the less well-off periphery as a result of factors such as low labour costs, congestion, etc., but this is unlikely to be sufficient to compensate for the polarization effects referred to above. It is very difficult to test this hypothesis empirically, although it is arguable that the United Kingdom may be suffering from it in the context of the European Community. To the extent that it does exist, it at the very least provides a strong case for an active and well-resourced regional policy within a common market.

REFERENCES

Balassa, B. (1975), 'Trade creation and trade diversion in the European Common Market: an appraisal of the evidence', in B. Balassa (Ed.), *European Economic Integration*, North Holland, Amsterdam.

Begg, D., Fischer, S. and Dornbusch, R. (1987), *Economics*, 2nd Edn. McGraw-Hill, London.

Cecchini, P. (1988), 'The European challenge 1992, the benefits of a single market', Report of the 'Cost of Non-Europe Steering Committee', Wildwood House, Aldershot.

Cooper, R.C. and Massell, B.F. (1965), 'A new look at customs union theory', *Economic Journal*, **75**, December, 461–476.

El-Agraa, A.M. (Ed.) (1985), *The Economics of the Common Market*, 2nd Edn, Philip Allan, Deddington.

Hine, R.C. (1985), *The Political Economy of European Trade*, Wheatsheaf, Brighton.

Johnson, H.G. (1965), 'An economic theory of protectionism, tariff bargaining and the formation of customs unions', *Journal of Political Economy*, **73**, 256–283.

Lipsey, R. (1960), 'The theory of customs unions: a general survey', *Economic Journal*, **70**, 496–513.

Marques-Mendes, A.J. (1986), 'The contribution of the European Community to economic growth', *Journal of Common Market Studies*, **XXIV**, June, 261–277.

Myrdal, G. (1957), *Economic Theory and Underdeveloped Regions*, Duckworth, London.

Owen, N. (1976), 'Scale economies in the EEC', *European Economic Review*, **7**, February, 143–163.

Petith, H. (1977), 'European integration and the terms of trade', *Economic Journal*, **87**, June, 262–272.

Robson, P. (1987), *The Economics of International Integration*, 3rd Edn, George Allen & Unwin, London.

Winters, L.A. (1987), 'Britain in Europe: a survey of quantitative trade studies', *Journal of Common Market Studies*, **XXV**, no. 4, June, 315–335.

FOUR

'1992': THE COMMON MARKET IN PRACTICE

4.1 INTRODUCTION

Having examined the theory behind the EC common market in the previous chapter, we can now look at how it has operated in practice. The Treaty of Rome, which came into effect in 1958, and which of course provides the legal basis for the European Community, clearly establishes the Community as common market. The establishment of the internal market has always been one of the central aims of the European Community. However, although important steps towards this ambitious objective were undoubtedly taken during the first thirty years or so of the Community's existence, there was clearly a big difference between theory and practice, and much was left undone. Indeed a considerable amount still remains to be done despite the undoubted success of the '1992' programme.

In this chapter, taking the customs union aspect (free internal movement of goods and services) and then the common market aspect (free movement of labour and capital) in turn, we will briefly examine the empirical work that has been carried out into the effects of integration, then look at the extent to which the free movement of goods, services, labour, and capital are in fact a reality in the Community's common market, and finally we will critically evaluate the content and prospects of the '1992' programme for completing the market.

4.2 THE CUSTOMS UNION: TRADE ASPECTS OF THE COMMON MARKET

4.2.1 Effects so far

From one perspective, one might be tempted to regard the EC customs union as being complete already. By July 1968 the original six members had completed the elimination of tariffs and quota restrictions among themselves, and had also completed the establishment of the Common External Tariff. All this was achieved a year and a half ahead of the schedule laid down in the Treaty of Rome. When in 1973 the 'Six' became the 'Nine' with the accession of the United Kingdom, Ireland and Denmark, progress was equally swift: internal tariff and quota elimination and the adoption of the CET had all taken place in July 1977. Following the southern enlargements to include Greece (1981), and Spain and Portugal (1986), the adjustment of tariffs and quotas has been similarly satisfactory. What Kreinin (1989) refers to as 'first-stage integration' was thus completed by the mid-1980s.

These tariff and quota changes have clearly had some effect. Empirical investigation of the economic consequences of the EC customs union is extremely difficult and problematic. Apart from anything else, it is virtually impossible to separate out the impact of the Community from the plethora of other factors that influence trade flows. Nevertheless, the studies that have been carried out (notably by Truman, 1969, 1975; Williamson and Bottrill, 1971; Kreinin, 1972, 1981; Aitken, 1973; Balassa, 1975; Mayes, 1978, 1983) do suggest that the EC customs union has significantly altered trade flows and has on the whole been trade creating. Trade creation has been greatest in manufacturing, and has outweighed the trade diversion that has occurred, particularly in agriculture. The best estimates suggest that net trade creation may have increased national income in the European Community by something like 0.1 per cent—a small amount and certainly less than the estimated impact of dynamic factors. Estimates of the impact of integration on growth have, as we have seen in Chapter 3, traditionally held this to be in the region of 1 per cent (Balassa, 1975). A more recent study (Marques-Mendes, 1986) is more optimistic in its conclusions, estimating the impact of integration as a whole to have increased Community GDP by 2.2 per cent in 1972, and by 1981 to have increased the GDP of the enlarged Community by as much as 5.9 per cent more than it would otherwise have been.

It is clear, however, that in practice the EC customs union has been far from complete. The convergence of consumer prices that one would expect in EC countries if the customs union were in fact complete simply has not materialized. Just to take one example, there have been the much-publicized difference in new car prices between the United Kingdom and the Continent. This type of 'discriminating monopoly' could not have occurred in a complete customs union.

4.2.2   The incomplete customs union: non-tariff barriers to trade

In the 'real world', other factors apart from tariffs and quotas act as serious impediments to trade. These impediments are generally referred to as non-tariff barriers to trade (NTBs), many of which arguably have a more serious effect on trade flows than tariffs, since they directly displace trade rather than distort prices. Some are also less obvious than tariffs, and are thus more difficult to deal with. Despite some considerable progress over the years, the Community had, at least prior to the instigation of the '1992' programme, failed to deal effectively with NTBs in the customs union. In fact, the evidence is that in the 1980s NTBs have increased in scope and severity as countries have made attempts to protect domestic industries in the face of high unemployment. In principle an almost infinite number of factors can distort trade and thus act as NTBs. However, the most important ones relevant to the European Community are the following:

National preference in public procurement   Governments, for a variety of fairly obvious economic and political reasons, are very reluctant to award procurement contracts to foreign firms if a domestic producer is available. There is little statistical information about public procurement in the European Community as most governments have not bothered to collect information. However, the EC Commission suggests (Cecchini, 1988) that the value of member government contracts that might have been deemed suitable for competitive allocation in 1986 was between 240 and 340 billion ECUs (7–10 per cent of GDP), and of these only a tiny fraction (0.14 per cent of GDP) were placed abroad. Regardless of its exact dimensions, it is clear that this particular NTB acts as a serious distortion to trade. The same Cecchini Report, which incidentally was commissioned by the EC Commission itself and should thus be seen as, if anything, likely to overestimate the benefits of the completed internal market, suggests that telecommunications, power generation, railways, and defence are the sectors worst hit by these discriminatory practices. Opening up public procurement to Community-wide competition would result, the Commission and Cecchini suggest, in a saving of around 17.5 billion ECUs (0.5 per cent of 1986 Community GDP).

National preference in private purchasing Many private individuals buy domestically produced goods, even though they may be more expensive and of a lower quality than foreign substitutes, in order to 'keep jobs at home'. This is often encouraged by governments—think, for example, of the 'Buy British' campaigns of the 1960s and 1970s. The impact of this is clearly impossible to estimate, but it must be considerable, even though it also seems that it is a practice that is probably on the wane as European economies become more integrated. In the case of the United Kingdom, the particularly rapid decline of manufacturing industry (de-industrialization) during the 1980s has often left consumers without the option of 'buying British' even if they wanted to. In any case, it is difficult to envisage a way in which the EC authorities could realistically become involved in this area, even if they felt that it was desirable.

Differences in indirect taxation The European Community has introduced a common value added tax (VAT). This does not discriminate between goods and services according to where they are produced within the Community, and ensures that the turnover tax accrues to the country where final consumption takes place. As such, a major potential source of trade distortion has been eliminated. However, rates and coverage of VAT still differ considerably in EC countries (see Table 4.1). The exact importance of this as an NTB is the subject of some debate, but it does undoubtedly distort prices and requires elaborate bureaucratic procedures at frontiers. Additionally, there are even wider differences in excise duties in the Community, often discriminating according to country of origin. For example, despite Community action and some changes in recent Budgets, in the United Kingdom excise duty is greater on wine than it is on beer; and the Italians charge higher rates of duty on imported spirits than on the domestic varieties.

Table 4.1 Rates of VAT in the Community member-states*
(situation as of January 1986)

	Lower	Standard	Higher
Belgium	6 and 17	19	25 and 33
Denmark	–	22	–
Germany	7	14	–
Spain	6	12	33
France	5.5 and 7	18.6	33.3
Ireland	0 and 10	23	–
Italy	2 and 9	18	38
Luxembourg	3 and 6	12	–
Netherlands	5	19	–
Portugal	8	16	30
United Kingdom	0	15	–

*Greece has not yet introduced VAT.
Source: EC Commission.

Monopolies and restrictive practices   Large dominant firms or firms acting in collusion can distort trade by indulging in unfair practices such as price fixing or market sharing. Examples of this include the high UK car prices mentioned above, and the airline industry, which arguably operates a route-sharing and fare-fixing cartel. Interestingly enough, the European Community itself operates such cartel arrangements, for example in the steel industry.

Differences in technical regulations and standards   These have varied considerably across the Community, and specifically they have included differences in the following areas (Cecchini, 1988). First, technical regulations, which usually consist of legal requirements introduced by national governments to protect health and safety and the environment. Secondly, standards, which are devised and monitored by national organizations such as the BSI in the United Kingdom, AFNOR in France and DIN in Germany. They are not usually legally binding, but are almost invariably extremely important in the eyes of consumers and are often the basis for technical regulations. Thirdly, testing and certification procedures, which involve duplication or even exclusion from a national market. There were in 1983 an estimated 100 000 different specifications operating in the Community, a figure that is likely to have increased in the light of technical progress and increased concern about health and safety and the environment. These differences have clearly acted as a major impediment to EC intra-trade and increase costs. Their effects are very difficult to quantify, but they are identified by European companies as one of the most serious aspects of the incomplete customs union (Cecchini, 1988). Examples of their impact include different definitions of what exactly constitutes chocolate, which have prevented British chocolate from being sold in various Community countries; German 'purity laws' which have prohibited the sale in Germany of beers produced in other countries; and many goods such as forklift trucks and electrical goods which have had to be expensively modified for export to meet different national standards.

Significantly, particularly from the United Kingdom's point of view, there are often severe obstacles to trade in services, and in particular insurance, banking, and other financial services. Services are a central and growing sector of the European economy, credit and insurance alone accounting for over 6.5 per cent of the Community's GDP. They are often closely related to capital movements which are discussed below, but the wide price differentials which exist between EC countries in this area (divergences of almost 50 per cent of more are not uncommon) give an indication of the severity of the barriers that exist. Apart from exchange controls, the most serious obstacles to trade in financial services have been national regulations preventing foreign banks and insurance companies from soliciting for business, national rules preventing foreigners from being licensed as brokers, discriminatory tax regimes, and restrictions on the acquisition of banks by foreigners. The Cecchini Report estimates that the gains from the integration of banking, insurance and securities brokerage could amount to 22 billion ECUs. The countries that have most to gain in terms of price falls for financial services are Spain (around 21 per cent), Italy (14 per cent), and France (12 per cent), while the United kingdom is expected by the Commission to experience price falls of around 7 per cent, the lowest proportion apart from the Netherlands' 4 per cent. The United Kingdom is expected to gain most from integration, however, in terms of overall economic welfare (an estimated gain in consumer surplus of 5.1 per cent), given the size of its financial services sector.

A further problem has been posed by separate national systems of accounting and corporate law and taxation, as well as differences in industrial policies between member-states, which have naturally acted as impediments to the establishment of firms in other Community countries. Additionally, differences in transport policies are significant here. Apart from different national requirements for hauliers and vehicles, most EC countries have operated quotas limiting the number of journeys that can be made by foreign hauliers.

Frontier formalities   These have abounded in the Community. The bureaucracy at borders has existed because of a number of factors, including the need to enforce VAT and excise duty differentials, the operation of Monetary Compensation Amounts to agriculture (MCAs—see Chapter 7), the enforcement of bilateral trade quotas for goods such as textiles and cars imported from outside the Community, and transport and veterinary checks to enforce different regulations and standards in these areas. Bringing goods across EC frontiers has as a consequence often been described as a lorry-driver's nightmare. Imports of goods have also been known to be hindered by restricting often undermanned points of entry. The end result is that transport costs are increased and trade is reduced. The Cecchini Report estimates the total cost of customs formalities to be at least 12.5 billion ECUs (over 3 per cent of transborder sales). Moreover, the burden of frontier formalities is borne by small and medium-sized companies. The Commission claims that, among the larger EC countries, Italy imposes the greatest additional cost through these practices, followed by France and the United Kingdom, and Belgium the least. The average total cost of formalities was claimed to be 153 ECUs, or 1.5 per cent of the average consignment's value.

State subsidies   All EC countries give subsidies of various kinds to their industries. Their exact dimensions are difficult to estimate but they are unquestionably of great significance, probably varying between something like 5 and 10 per cent of domestic income in EC countries. These subsidies, although sometimes perfectly logical from a national viewpoint, protect industries and distort trade patterns by effectively reducing costs of production. A particular problem is regional aid, which is allowed by the competition clauses of the Treaty of Rome.

Differing trade and aid policies towards third countries   An example of this is tied aid. It is often the practice for governments in the European Community and elsewhere in the world to grant foreign aid on the condition that it is then spent in the donor country. This clearly has a distorting effect on trade. In addition, despite the CET, EC countries have frequently concluded bilateral deals with countries outside the Community. For example, Britain, Italy and France have restricted the quantity of Japanese car imports, and the Multi-Fibre Agreement sets national quotas for textile imports. Article 115 of the Treaty of Rome allows national governments to exclude non-EC goods coming via a partner, and quota differences therefore lead to price differences which distort trade and lead to resource misallocation.

Different currencies   The existence of different currencies within the Community reduces trade. At the most basic level, it increases the cost of trading by forcing importers to pay the price of changing currency on the foreign exchange markets. More importantly, currency fluctuations increase the risks involved in trade and thus render it a less attractive proposition. Furthermore, a multitude of different currencies reduces the transparency of price differences between different countries, thus reducing the possibility of rational consumer choice. Finally, where the exchange rate is affected by factors other than the competitiveness of traded goods, it can distort prices and thus trade. Arguably, this was the case in the United Kingdom in the 1980s when North Sea oil and the high interest rate policy of the government resulted in an exchange rate for sterling that was higher than the underlying competitiveness of UK manufacturing would have warranted, and thus contributed to de-industrialization. Of course, the increased currency stability brought about by the European Monetary System has reduced the impact on intra-community trade from this source.

National quotas This is perhaps the most obvious of NTBs. There are estimated to be around 1000 of these in existence in the Community.

4.3 LABOUR AND CAPITAL MOBILITY ASPECTS OF THE COMMON MARKET

We now turn our attention to the other aspect of the common market, i.e. the factor mobility aspect of economic integration in the European Community. The Treaty of Rome provides for the free movement of labour and capital within the Community. However, as in the case of the free movement of goods and services, the actual situation differs substantially from the theory.

Looking firstly at capital, it is important to distinguish at the outset between capital movements in their strictest sense, i.e. the transfer of assets between EC countries, and trade in financial services and the right of establishment of business in another member country. The latter two are discussed elsewhere in this chapter, and are usually classified as 'payments', though they are naturally closely related to, and in many ways can be regarded as being part of, capital movements. In general, capital is, hardly surprisingly, substantially more mobile than labour, benefiting from, among other things, fuller information, especially in the wake of the recent improvements in communications which have led to the development of a 'global financial market'. Even here, however, important restrictions have operated.

Foremost among these are the exchange controls that several countries have operated at various times. These exchange controls were allowed to develop because of the fundamental limitations of the free movement of capital clauses of the Treaty of Rome (Articles 67–73), and because of the timid way in which they were interpreted and enforced by the EC authorities and member-states in the years before the Single European Act. The Treaty of Rome in fact lays down no timetable for liberalization in this area, leaving it to the Council to implement free movement by means of Directives adopted by qualified majority voting on Commission proposals. It also contains safeguard clauses, which permit states to impose exchange controls if the free movement of capital disturbs member-states' capital markets or causes balance of payments difficulties. Up to 1986, the Community's policy towards the free movement of capital was governed by two Directives dating back to 1960 and 1962. These divided capital movements into four categories, or lists, each of which was to be afforded different degrees of liberalization. After this, no further progress was made until the start of the '1992' programme, a proposed third directive failing to be adopted after years of fruitless discussion in the 1960s and 1970s. The reluctance of member-states to agree to surrender control over capital movements, even though these have become more and more difficult to operate and less and less effective, is hardly surprising, since these are an important aspect of economic sovereignty, influencing, for example, a country's ability to control its money supply.

The end effect of the above was to permit several member-states, notably Italy and France, to impose strict exchange controls at various times, and wide differences developed between member-states' approaches to capital movements, the Benelux countries, the United Kingdom (from 1979 onwards) and West Germany adopting a broadly liberal approach, in contrast to the protectionist approach adopted by Denmark, Greece, Ireland, France, and Italy (EC Commission, 1988a). The Italian exchange controls have been particularly strict, resulting in many, sometimes hilarious, attempts at evasion by a variety of people ranging from industrialists to film stars. They have arguably, however, permitted the Italian lira to remain within its EMS bands without too many parity changes.

Labour is typically much less mobile than capital. Article 48 of the Treaty of Rome and subsequent directives and regulations provide the basis for the free movement of labour within the European Community, affording EC nationals the legal right to work anywhere in the Community, in theory on an equal footing with nationals of the host countries. Since 1960, the Commission has issued something like 80 directives to promote greater freedom of movement for professionals (EC Commission, 1988b). In practice, however, several factors have acted as impediments to intra-Community labour mobility. These include government restrictions, restrictive practices operated by trade unions and professional organizations, taxation and social security problems, imperfect labour market information, linguistic and cultural differences, skill mismatches, failure to recognize qualifications obtained in partner countries, the very process of integration which may have served to narrow intra-Community earnings differentials, and last but not least the personal costs involved in migration. During the 1980s, unemployment has additionally been high and vacancies have been scarce. In any event labour markets in EC countries have tended to remain balkanized, and what migration there has been has tended to come from areas outside of the Community such as the Mediterranean Basin and North Africa.

4.4   '1992': THE COMPLETION OF THE EC INTERNAL MARKET?

The objective of achieving a free and unified market of 323 million West Europeans by 1992 was agreed at the Milan Summit in June 1985 and was the concept at the heart of the Single European Act of 1986 (see Chapter 2). The next part of this survey will attempt to examine critically the measures that are planned to achieve the objective, progress so far, and the prospects for success.

The major thrust of the programme for '1992' consists of a series of measures and a 'timetable for action' published by the EC Commission in a White Paper in June 1985. This includes over 300 legislative proposals (directives), subsequently reduced to 279, aimed at removing what the Commission sees as being all the technical, physical, and fiscal barriers which prevent the internal market from functioning properly. As a result of the modifications to the Treaty of Rome made by the Single European Act (see Chapter 2), these require a qualified majority in the Council of Ministers in order to be approved (except for directives relating to taxation and professional qualifications, which still require unanimity). The proposals must then be accepted as law by the parliaments of the member-states within two years. All this is supplemented by a series of seemingly *ad hoc* measures aimed at other NTBs and obstacles to factor mobility. The whole is supplemented by the so-called 'social charter' (see Chapter 8), though the UK government has argued that this is not part of the '1992' programme and cannot thus benefit from the preferential voting arrangements in the Council of Ministers that are afforded to measures designed to complete the internal market (see Chapter 2).

The '1992' programme can thus be summarized as follows:

The removal of physical barriers to trade and factor mobility   The Commission has the following objectives in this respect:

1. To simplify administrative checks and move them away from borders. This will have the additional effect of rendering national quota restrictions inoperable.

2. To eliminate all internal frontiers and controls by 1992, for people and capital as well as for goods and services. An interesting by-product of this is likely to be a reduction in the accuracy of statistics on trade flows, the balance of payments of nation-states and national income.
3. To phase out Monetary Compensation Amounts (see Chapter 7) and introduce mutually recognized health certificates for agricultural trade.
4. To develop a common transport policy. This would end transport 'quotas', introduce agreed safety standards to eliminate frontier checks, and allow hauliers to operate freely throughout the Community.

The most important step that has so far been taken in this area has been the introduction of the Single Administrative Document in 1988. This has replaced the 70 separate import forms that were previously in use in the Community. Another has been the introduction of the European passport, which is of considerable symbolic, if not practical, significance. The Trevi Group of Ministers of the Interior and Justice have discussed the harmonization of immigration laws, visa controls, border controls, and asylum policies. They have thus far concentrated on intra-Community movements, but are now seeking agreement on a common policy towards people from outside the Community.

The elimination of technical barriers to trade and factor mobility   Essentially, the strategy here is, wherever possible, to move towards *harmonization*, i.e. introduce common standards and practices that are acceptable throughout the Community. Where this is not possible, then the principle of *mutual recognition* is adopted, i.e. countries must agree to accept technical regulations and standards that are recognized in other member-states, even if they do not meet its own domestic standards. Thus, for example, a drug that has been tested and passed as safe in France can be sold in the United Kingdom without further testing being necessary. The principle of mutual recognition goes well beyond the elimination of national preference, and may in some instances actually result in foreign goods and services being treated more favourably than domestic ones. Specifically, the Commission has the following aims:

1. To adopt Community-wide standards for health and safety, for food, pharmaceuticals and electrical goods, for example.
2. To create a common legal framework for cross-border activities by enterprises to encourage joint projects (the European economic interest grouping), and reform intellectual and industrial property law by creating a Community framework for patents, trademarks, and copyright.
3. To create a common market for services by adopting common rules and making supervision the task of the government of the country where the service company is based. Specifically, the following are envisaged:
   (a) the deregulation of insurance, banking, and other financial services;
   (b) the creation of an integrated European securities market, with liberalized and linked stock exchanges;
   (c) the deregulation of all modes of transport, notably air travel;
   (d) the development of common standards for 'new technologies' to facilitate the growth of this sector on a Community level; and
   (e) the creation of a 'Europe-wide audiovisual area' with common standards of transmission and reception of television and radio programmes, including satellite broadcasts (the 'MAC packet family' of standards).
4. To remove exchange controls.

5. To establish the equivalence of qualifications, i.e. a situation whereby member-states recognize diplomas, degrees, and other qualifications awarded in other Community
   countries, thus promoting the free movement of labour among professionals.

There has been considerable progress in this area so far. Issues such as common price label
rules, levels of pesticide residues in food, the principle of free trade in insurance, and some
relaxation of air transport restrictions have been agreed. Exchange controls have either been
removed or are about to be removed. The ERASMUS programme has been launched to promote student and staff exchanges in higher education. Discussions have begun on a system
of European credit transfer (ECTS) which would permit students to obtain a qualification
by parts of the same course in different Community countries, thus opening up the possibility of
the 'European graduate'. Some proposals in this field are, nevertheless, still at the embryonic
stage.

The reduction of fiscal barriers to trade   The Commission originally decided that, in line
with experience in the United States, a variation of about 5–6 per cent in VAT rates is the
most that is consistent with the customs union. It has therefore proposed that there should
only be two bands of VAT in the Community—a standard rate of between 14 and 20 per cent,
and a lower rate of between 4 and 9 per cent for food, books, medicine, children's clothes, etc.
Even more radically, it has proposed that rates of excise duty be exactly the same throughout
the Community. The original proposed unified rates were 0.17 ECU/litre for beer, 0.17 ECU/
litre for wine, 3.81 ECU/bottle for spirits, 0.43 ECU/litre for petrol, 0.18 ECU/litre for Derv,
and 0.39 ECU + 52–54 per cent for cigarettes (Smith, 1988). Not surprisingly, this has been
one of the most controversial aspects of '1992', particularly in the United Kingdom, and progress has so far been tortuous. So tortuous, in fact that the Commission has recently been
forced to alter some of the more controversial aspects of VAT standardization, and to abandon, for the time being at least, its plans for excise duties.

Opening up public procurement   Rules aimed at open competition in public works and supply
contracts have existed since 1971 and 1978 respectively, and have been singularly ineffective.
The Commission has introduced new proposals that tighten the rules and include powers to
hold up suspect contracts, declare them void, and compensate losers. It is hard to imagine
the UK, French, or Italian governments buying Audi cars for their ministers, for example,
but there is considerable evidence to suggest that public bodies are gradually coming to
terms with the expected new regime.

A firmer application of competition policy   The Community operates a competition policy
which focuses on the trade effects of dominant firms, mergers, and restrictive practices, to the
extent that these affect trade. It also deals with the abuse of subsidies by the governments of
member-states. This has recently been used more vigorously, for example in the case of the
merger between British Airways and British Caledonian, with BA giving up several routes;
and in investigating the role of Hoechst in an alleged secret cartel which was illegally fixing
the price of the plastic polypropylene. The Irish commissioner for competition, Mr Peter
Sutherland, was active in promoting a Community-wide system of merger control, advocating
that the Community take powers to vet all mergers involving more than 1 billion ECUs, and
his successor, Sir Leon Brittan, has also striven to enforce competition legislation vigorously,
for example in the case of the so-called 'sweeteners' paid by the UK government to British
Aerospace in the course of the purchase of the Rover Group. However, despite the progress

on mergers, the Community has probably not got the resources to police effectively the anti-competitive behaviour of firms and governments throughout the Community. Additionally, there is the paradox that the Community also seeks to encourage cross-frontier mergers in order to facilitate the free movement of capital and enable economies of scale to be enjoyed.

The 'social charter'   The role of the 'social charter' in the '1992' programme is discussed in Chapter 8.

4.5   1992: PROSPECTS

Will the Commission's actions and proposals succeed in actually completing the internal market union in the specified time? Clearly progress so far has been impressive, if occasionally tortuous. The Commission has, on the whole, adopted a pragmatic approach, pressing forward wherever possible and modifying its proposals where it meets strong resistance from member-states. There are a number of obstacles to success, some technical, the majority involving political will. The most important of these are the following:

Not all NTBs and obstacles to factor mobility are covered by the programme   There are no credible plans to deal with divergences in external trade policy, for example. Yet these are plentiful in number, important in their effect, and will have to be tackled sooner or later (Yannopoulos, 1989). The danger here is that the abolition of internal barriers might be accompanied by greater barriers to imports from outside, creating a 'fortress Europe'. Additionally, there is the danger of a form of 'pan-European racism' developing around the issue of the free movement of labour, with people free to move inside the Community, but tight controls on people coming from outside.

Most crucially, the European Commission's attitude towards subsidies remains unclear. As we have seen, it has recently attempted to be more vigilant in its enforcement of competition policy. However, the vast structure of subsidies that exists in all EC countries remains largely unchallenged. The issue of state subsidies might become even more significant after 1992, since it will be tempting for governments to use subsidies to replace forms of protection that have been removed. The possibility of a subsidy war would then loom large. Another complication is that there is a credible case to be made for more temporary subsidies to ease the post-1992 transition process.

A central difficulty here is deciding what constitutes an NTB and what constitutes legitimate national preferences and differences, and therefore what degree of harmonization is really necessary to complete the customs union. Indirect taxation is an obvious area of contention here (see Smith, 1988; Guieu and Bonnet, 1987). To take a practical example, how do we regard the British zero-rating of children's shoes for VAT purposes?

Delays in implementing the programme   Change in the European Community is notoriously slow, mainly because of the cumbersome decision-making processes (see Chapter 2). It takes on average three years for a proposal to become law, often much longer in the case of controversial matters. Furthermore, countries tend to be lax in implementing Community law, and complaints to the Commission of infringements are on the increase. Even when the European Court of Justice finds against a country, member-states in one-third of cases have ignored the rulings. The Single European Act has improved the situation for many proposals relevant to 1992 by removing the need for ministerial unanimity in this area. Nevertheless, progress has still on occasions left much to be desired. By the beginning of 1988, for example, the Commission had come up with about two-thirds of the necessary drafts, but the Council of Ministers had agreed only 70 of them—90 less than scheduled. Furthermore, the most thorny issues, VAT and frontier controls, are yet to come. Nevertheless, it is clear that crucial decisions are being made, regardless of the pace.

The political will to complete the programme may be missing   Essentially, progress in the Community on most issues depends on countries' willingness to surrender national sovereignty for what is perceived of as the common good. The power to control one's own affairs at a national level is often an illusion in an increasingly interdependent world. Nevertheless, most countries' political will to make 1992 work will be determined by, among other things, the following:

1. The view that is taken of the process and objectives of West European integration, and therefore the importance a country gives to EC affairs. For example, the UK Thatcher administration tended to be nationalistic in its approach to the Community and took a minimalist view of European integration, emphasizing its economic rather than political dimensions. This, paradoxically, should have made it keen on the completion of the customs union. By contrast, Italy, for example, can be regarded as a maximalist, favouring some kind of political federalism in the Community, and therefore tends to take a supranational approach to Community matters.
2. The strength of pressure groups and vested interests on a European level. The opening up of the internal market will precipitate structural change which will involve winners and losers within individual countries. For example, Lloyds Bank (1989) estimates that in the United Kingdom the pharmaceuticals, food and drink, precision and medical equipment, insurance and airlines sectors are likely gainers, but that other sections of industry will be threatened and face takeover from abroad.
3. National electoral considerations.
4. The costs involved. Completion of the customs union may offer significant advantages to at least some EC countries. The UK service sector will possibly have much to gain, as will sections of French, German, and Italian manufacturing. However, there are also significant dangers and disadvantages involved for most countries. The losses involve the surrender of sovereignty, as well as more tangible factors. For example, 'southern' member-states face a serious threat to their industrial sectors from the 'north'. The German and French insurance, banking, and finance industries will be exposed to strong competition from the United Kingdom. The United Kingdom may well have to impose VAT on sensitive items such as food and children's clothes, while new VAT and excise duty rates might deprive Ireland and Denmark of substantial tax revenue. The signs so far are mixed, but on the whole promising. The French and Italians, and to a lesser extent the West Germans, seem to be on the whole busily preparing for 1992 and welcoming the prospect with open arms as a kind of panacea for Europe's economic problems, despite the costs. The British position is, as ever, a little less clear. They were one of the instigators of '1992', and clearly welcome some aspects of it such as, surprisingly enough, the freeing of trade in financial services. They have also been active in areas such as airline deregulation. However, the position on other issues is rather more ambiguous. The main problems have concerned the harmonization of VAT rates and coverage, and border checks on the movement of people, i.e. the areas that involve the greatest surrender of national sovereignty. There has been the much publicized disagreement between Mrs Thatcher and Lord Cockfield, the former commissioner for the internal market, on this issue. Additionally, the United Kingdom has

dragged its heels on a number of other issues. Despite this, the British are on the whole cooperating, and it is clear that public opinion, especially among the young, is moving in favour of the internal market and European integration in general.

Alternative means of protection There is a clear possibility that these may be sought by countries if the existing ones are removed. The obvious risk is that subsidies might be increased to compensate, with a subsidy war ensuing.

4.6 CONCLUSIONS

What, then, can we conclude from the above? Thus far at least the 'Europe 1992' slogan has started a bandwagon rolling that has to an impressive extent succeeded in turning rhetoric into reality. It is probably fair to say that most EC countries are taking the completion of the internal market more seriously than any Community development for a very long time. Even the United Kingdom, which has been traditionally suspicious of European integration and the loss of national sovereignty that goes with it, is moving forward on most fronts, with the predictable exceptions of taxation, some border controls and the social charter. The desire to promote liberalism is clearly proving an irresistible attraction for the UK government. There is widespread awareness throughout the Community of the implications of 1992, and preparations are advanced in most countries. This would imply that the political will to complete the market is fundamentally present, despite all the difficulties. Thus by the end of 1992 we may not have a complete internal market, but the momentum that has been created will probably ensure that significant and irreversible steps are taken in this direction. One imponderable is, of course, the impact that recent events in Eastern Europe and the imminent reunification of Germany might have on this as well as other aspects of European integration.

REFERENCES/FURTHER READING

Aitken, N. (1973), 'The effects of the EEC and EFTA on European trade: a temporal cross section analysis', *American Economic Review*, **63**, December, 881–892.

Balassa, B. (1975), 'Trade creation and trade diversion in the European Common Market: an appraisal of the evidence', in B. Balassa (Ed.), *European Economic Integration*, North Holland, Amsterdam, 79–118.

Cecchini, P. (1988), '1992: the benefits of a single market', *Report on the Cost of the Non-Europe Steering Committee*, Wildwood House, Aldershot.

European Commission (1985), 'Completing the internal market', White Paper from the Commission to the European Council.

European Commission (1987), 'Europe without frontiers—completing the internal market', European Documentation 4, Luxembourg.

European Commission (1988a), *The Single Financial Market*, Luxembourg.

European Commission (1988b), *A Guide to Working in a Europe without Frontiers*, Luxembourg.

Fleming, M. and Swann, D. (1989), 'Competition policy—the pace quickens and 1992 approaches', *Royal Bank of Scotland Review*, no. 162, June.

Guieu, P. and Bonnet, C. (1987), 'Completion of the internal market and indirect taxation', *Journal of Common Market Studies*, **XXV**, March, 209–222.

Kreinin, M.E. (1972), 'The effects of the EEC on imports of manufactures', *Economic Journal*, **82**, September, 897–920.

Kreinin, M.E. (1981), *Effect of EC Enlargement on Trade in Manufactures*, Kyklos.

Kreinin, M.E. (1989), 'EC—1992, world trade and the trading system', paper presented at the Fulbright International Colloquium '1992, Europe and America', Reading, December.

Lloyds Bank (1989), '1992 winners and losers', *Lloyds Bank Economic Bulletin*, January.

Marques-Mendes, A.J. (1986), 'The contribution of the European Community to economic growth', *Journal of Common Market Studies*, **XXIV**, June, 261–277.

Mayes, D. (1978), 'The effects of economic integration on trade', *Journal of Common Market Studies*, **XVII**, September, 1–25.

Mayes, D. (1983), Memorandum in *House of Lords Select Committee on the European Communities*, HMSO, London.

Pelkmans, J. and Robson, P. (1987), 'The aspirations of the white paper', *Journal of Common Market Studies*, **XXV**, March, 181–192.

Smith, S. (1988), 'Excise duties and the internal market', *Journal of Common Market Studies*, **XXVII**, December, 147–160.

Straubhaar, T. (1988), 'Internal labour migration within a common market: some aspects of EC experience', *Journal of Common Market Studies*, **XXVII** September, 45–62.

Truman, E.M. (1969), 'The European Community: trade creation and trade diversion', *Yale Economic Essays*, **9**, Spring, 201–257.

Truman, E.M. (1975), 'The effects of European economic integration on the production and trade of manufactured products', in B. Balassa (Ed.), *European Economic Integration*, North Holland, Amsterdam, 3–40.

Ugeux, G. (1989), 'Europe sans frontiers: the integration of financial markets', *Royal Bank of Scotland Review*, no. 162, June.

Williamson, J. and Bottrill, A. (1971), 'The impact of customs unions on trade in manufactures', *Oxford Economic Papers*, **23**, 323–351.

Yannopoulos, G. (1989), 'Trade policy issues of the completion of the internal market of the EC', paper presented at the Fulbright International Colloquium '1992, Europe and America', Reading, December.

MONETARY INTEGRATION IN THE EUROPEAN COMMUNITY

5.1 INTRODUCTION

The issue of monetary integration in the European Community came to the forefront of public debate in the United Kingdom in the late 1980s, mainly as a result of the controversy that developed over Mrs Thatcher's refusal to take Britain into the Exchange Rate Mechanism (ERM) of the European Monetary System (EMS) until October 1990, and because of her reaction to the proposals for further monetary integration that were put forward by the Delors Committee. The debate that has ensued has revealed deep political divisions, especially within the Conservative Party, not only about the conduct of economic policy, but also over the whole approach to the process of European integration, which has of course taken on a new dynamic following the Single European Act (see Chapter 2) and the moves towards the by now ubiquitous '1992' (see Chapter 4).

But exactly what do economists mean by monetary integration? What are its possible advantages and disadvantages? What is the precise nature of the EMS? What are implications of membership for Britain? What are the likely future developments in this area? These are the topics that this chapter will examine.

5.2 THE THEORY OF MONETARY INTEGRATION

5.2.1 Nature and definitions

Monetary integration between countries can take a variety of forms. The limiting case of monetary integration, and the model against which current developments such as the EMS should be examined, is a complete monetary union. The popular conception of this is of a situation in which a number of countries decide to do away with their own separate national currencies and replace these by a single currency that is accepted and used as money throughout the whole area. The individual countries then become regions within the monetary union. Thus in the European Community, there would be no lire, francs, pesetas, Deutschmarks, guilders, or drachmas, but we would all do our shopping, pay our debts, and keep our savings in European Currency Units (ECUs), Jean Monnets, europas, gullits, or whatever nomenclature happened to be chosen for the new currency.

It is important to note right at the outset that at least from an economic point of view a single common currency is not strictly speaking an essential prerequisite for a complete monetary

union. For there to be a *de facto* monetary union it would be sufficient for the countries concerned to operate a system of irrevocably fixed exchange rates. The different currencies
would need to be fully convertible, i.e. exchangeable in any quantities and at any time for
each other at the fixed exchange rate. This would have to occur within the context of a completed common market, i.e. a situation in which goods, services, capital, and labour are freely
and fully mobile between the countries involved (which is of course what the Community is
hoping to achieve by the end of 1992—see Chapters 3 and 4). The economic effects of all this
would in many ways be the same as those of having a single currency throughout the area.

The precise importance of having a single currency as well fixed exchange rates and full
convertibility is the subject of some debate (see, for example, Gros, 1989). However, if the single
currency can be regarded as merely the 'icing on the cake', one should nevertheless not
underestimate its importance. The nature of the union would be distinctly changed by a single
currency. It would act as an important symbol of the monetary union. It would also offer significant savings on the transaction costs of changing currencies. It would make some of the benefits
of the union (see below) easier to achieve by increasing the transparency of prices, and by
facilitating the establishment of a 'European monetary identity'. Furthermore, it might help
to provide the political discipline required to make the monetary union stick over time.
While different currencies exist, there would always be the temptation for countries to alter
exchange rates in times of economic difficulty, and thus one could never have total confi-
dence that a system based solely on fixed exchange rates would be completely irrevocable.

A further possibility is to keep national currencies, fix exchange rates irrevocably, guarantee full convertibility, and at the same time establish a parallel currency at the union level.
This is to an extent what the Community is attempting with the ECU (see below) in the EMS,
and it is only of relevance in the context of an incomplete monetary union, or in a phase of
transition towards monetary union. In a complete monetary union in which there is either a
single currency or countries behave as if there were one, a parallel currency would serve no
purpose. In an incomplete union, the hope is that the parallel currency would gradually
become accepted and used, and would eventually eliminate the need for different currencies.
Daniel Gros (1989) has identified four factors that will influence the success of the parallel
currency strategy in an incomplete monetary union: the degree of exchange rate variability;
the expected changes in the exchange rate of the parallel currency against national
currencies; the bid-ask spread in the exchange markets; and the legal tender status of the
parallel currency.

Whether based on a single currency or on irrevocably fixed exchange rates, a central point
about a complete monetary union is that it requires significant amounts of convergence of
economic objectives and outcomes, which in turn necessitate a high degree of cooperation
and joint economic policy-making at the supranational level. The corollary of this is that
individual states have to surrender a considerable amount of national economic sovereignty,
or their freedom to control their own economic destiny and policies in isolation from others.
A crucial point here is whether most countries do in fact have any real economic sovereignty
left to exercise, given the growing interdependence that characterizes contemporary Europe,
and indeed the world (see below).

At the most basic level, a monetary union would necessitate a common policy towards
other currencies outside the union, which would require agreement on whether to fix or float
the joint currency or currencies, as well as probably a pooling of reserves (or at least a firm
commitment to make reserves available to partners), and common exchange controls.

Most centrally, the countries concerned would have to aim to have the same, or at least
very similar, rates of inflation. The rate of inflation in a country affects its international

competitiveness. Broadly, if a country's prices are increasing more rapidly than in other countries, exports become relatively more expensive and imports relatively cheaper. All other things (and in particular price elasticities of demand at home and abroad) being equal, the country would tend to export less and import more, thus putting downward pressure on its exchange rate, which in a free market is determined by the demand for the currency (inflows of foreign currencies in payment for exports, and capital movements into the country) and the supply of the currency (outflows of the home currency to pay for imports, and capital movements out of the country). There would also be pressure on the country's balance of payments. Without the monetary union the country's government would have the option, if it were operating a system of fixing or managing its exchange rate, of devaluing the currency, thus cutting the price of its exports in other currencies and increasing the domestic price of its imports. With floating exchange rates, the market might do the job for them. Either way international competitiveness would probably be restored, albeit with significant lags, without too much effect on key variables such as the level of employment and the rate of growth. With a monetary union, however, the option of altering the exchange rate does not exist. Hence the need for member countries to harmonize rates of inflation. The alternative would be an untenable situation in which higher inflation countries suffer balance of payments deficits and/or relative economic decline and outflows of labour and capital. With a single currency, equalizing inflation rates would necessitate a common monetary policy for the whole of the union, with central determination (assuming that this is possible) of the union money supply and of a union interest rate. With different currencies, monetary policy would have to be, as a minimum requirement, strictly controlled and coordinated.

Apart from the centralization of monetary policy, monetary union requires the joint determination or coordination of other macro- and micro-economic policies which directly or indirectly affect the rate of inflation. For example, fiscal policies (taxation and government spending) and structural policies might have to be centrally controlled. Total standardization would not necessarily be needed, however, and national and regional governments could retain a degree of control over these policies. The extent to which local control of economic policy is compatible with monetary union is the subject of a long-standing and continuing debate. One conclusion that emerges from the above is that a monetary union will result in less sovereignty losses and will therefore stand a better chance of succeeding the closer the economic performance and objectives of the participating countries.

Before leaving the issue of the coordination and centralization of economic objectives and policies, it is important to discuss briefly how these objectives and policies might be determined. In essence there are two possibilities. We might refer to the first as averaging, where countries with different preferences or traditions (for example, the United Kingdom before 1979, which traditionally regarded the level of employment as the main policy objective of economic policy, and the Federal Republic of Germany, which in the post-war period has always placed the control of inflation first) agree to compromise on some mutually acceptable position. Alternatively, one might have a leadership outcome, in which one powerful nation effectively imposes its own preferences and models on everybody else. The latter is arguably the current position within the EMS in which West Germany and the Deutschmark have assumed the dominant role, so much so that the EMS is sometimes referred to as the 'Deutschmark zone'.

All this centralization and coordination of economic policy would require appropriate structures and institutions. For example, a common central bank would probably have to be set up to control monetary policy, and there might have to be something like a common ministry of economic affairs to run other aspects of joint economic policy-making. In a situation of policy leadership within a monetary union, however, the need for specific institutions and structures is greatly diminished. This has led monetary union to be widely regarded as being equivalent to, or at least the precursor of, some form of economic union.

It is often argued that another essential prerequisite of a monetary union is the establishment of some form of redistribution mechanism, by which the countries and regions that suffer the costs involved in membership of the union (see below) can be compensated by those who gain. This may not just be a question of equity, but also one of political reality, since it may be necessary to redistribute resources in order to induce countries to consider it in their interests to join or to remain in a monetary union. This redistribution would probably take two forms: a transfer of resources between countries, and a regional policy.

As mentioned above, full monetary union can be regarded as the limiting case of monetary integration. The United States is the classic example of a monetary union, and most sovereign European countries are full monetary unions. As we shall see, supranational arrangements under the auspices of the Community have been rather more limited in their scope, even though the 'hidden agenda' behind them has for many been monetary union.

5.2.2   Costs and benefits of monetary integration

Most of the costs associated with monetary integration are in one way or another associated with loss of economic sovereignty. This takes two main forms. First, monetary union implies loss of control at a national level over the objectives of economic policy. The analysis of this was pioneered in the early 1970s by two economists, Fleming (1971) and Corden (1972). Countries, as we have seen, would have to set common targets for inflation. If the targets were set by some form of averaging, then all countries would be forced to accept a higher or a lower rate of inflation than their populations and governments would ideally have chosen (we assume that governments reflect the will of the people via the electoral system). If we accept the 'Phillips curve' trade-off between inflation and unemployment, then a country may be partially compensated for a higher rate of inflation than desired by a lower rate of unemployment, or would have to pay the cost of lower inflation by having to accept a higher rate of unemployment than it wants. In either case the 'averaged' union position is a second-best solution and results in a loss of collective welfare at a national level. If policy targets are set by leadership, then of course the leader suffers no losses of this type. The losses then fall exclusively on the other, weaker members of the union. If one favours the 'natural rate of unemployment' hypothesis and accepts the 'expectations augmented Phillips curve', in which the long-run Phillips relationship is taken to be a vertical straight line with the traditional trade-off between inflation and unemployment holding only in the short run, then the outcome is substantially different. In this case monetary union and common rates of inflation can be had without any serious long-term effect on the level of employment.

Secondly, membership of a monetary union deprives a country of control over important tools of economic management. Most obviously, national governments can no longer use the exchange rate to control their economies. As we have seen, altering the exchange rate is a relatively costless method of correcting for differences in international competitiveness. Without this option, the 'burden of adjustment' tends to fall on more painfull areas such as the level of employment, the level of investment, personal disposable income, and the rate of growth, as governments of weaker economies try to control inflation and balance of payments problems by deflationary monetary and fiscal policies. This is of course assuming that a national government would choose to change its exchange rate in preference to deflation, which has not been the case in the United Kingdom recently.

Furthermore, participating in a monetary union would result in partial or even total loss of control at the national level over the operation of monetary policy, since this would have to be determined centrally, or at least harmonized, in order to achieve the economic convergence required to make the union work. In addition, control over important aspects of fiscal policy would have to be surrendered, and it may also be necessary to forfeit the ability of a nation to carry out some aspects of its own micro-economic and structural policies, particularly in order to achieve the completed common market that is an essential prerequisite for a monetary union. It should be noted that the loss of control over key objectives and tools of economic management at the national level is likely to have a regional dimension, exacerbating existing differences between the rich and poor parts of countries. Hence the need for an effective regional policy in a monetary union.

In addition to the above sovereignty considerations, monetary union may result in costs associated with issues of distribution (see the MacDougall Report, EC Commission, 1977, and the Thompson Report, EC Commission, 1973). Regional differences are likely to be worsened, but there is also the likelihood of an inequitable distribution of the gains between countries. Particular countries may even be net losers from the process, hence the need for a redistribution system through a union budget. In principle this should not pose a major problem, since the gainers could compensate the losers and still end up better off themselves. In practice this type of cost is likely to be an important one, since in the real world gainers are notoriously reluctant to compensate losers.

Before leaving the costs of monetary union, two points referred to previously need to be emphasized. First, the size of the costs of a monetary union will be greater the more different participating countries are in their structures and preferences.

Secondly, the costs are only real ones to the extent that the countries concerned do in practice have the ability to control their own economies. Economies are much more open than they were, there is much more international trade and mobility of labour and capital. The international economic environment has an ever-growing impact on the domestic economic scene, and it is in consequence increasingly difficult to pursue economic policies in isolation from the rest of the world. It has always been the case that small countries such as the Netherlands and Luxembourg have been heavily dependent on external events, and have thus been forced to seek alliance and cooperation in order to influence their own economies. Recent evidence, notably the experiences of the Mitterrand administration in France in 1981–3 and of the British Labour government of the late 1970s, suggests that medium-sized European countries may now be in a similar position (see Sachs and Wyplosz, 1986). It is probable that we have reached an historical phase where nation-states, or at least small ones such as those that exist in Europe, are becoming obsolescent as sovereign economic entities. If the only states that can influence important aspects of their own economic performance are large ones such as the United States, then this is a powerful argument in favour of monetary integration, and indeed of other forms of integration at the European level. Nevertheless, old habits and pretensions die hard, and some national governments remain reluctant to surrender economic (and political) sovereignty, and this has been and continues to be a major obstacle to monetary integration.

It must be assumed that for most participating countries the perceived benefits of a monetary union outweigh its perceived costs, otherwise the union would presumably not take place. The exact nature and extent of the benefits of monetary integration depend on the model that is chosen, i.e. a single currency or fixed exchange rates. They can be broadly characterized as follows:

1. Increased welfare resulting from increased trade. This is the customs union aspect of the issue. Fixed exchange rates or a single currency reduce the risks involved in international trade, increase the transparency of prices and (in the case of a single currency) reduce transaction costs. The removal of this important non-tariff barrier to trade is likely to increase its volume, and thus increase welfare through trade creation and scale economies (see Chapter 3).

2. Better allocation of resources as a result of more mobility of labour and capital. This is the Common Market aspect of monetary integration (see Chapter 3). This too can be shown to increase welfare, though it can also result in some costs. Indeed, many economists consider monetary union as an essential prerequisite for the successful completion of the '1992' programme. Padoa-Schioppa (1988), for example, has referred to the 'inconsistent quartet' of free trade, factor mobility, fixed exchange rates, and monetary sovereignty at the national level, arguing that the latter must be sacrificed if the first three are to be achieved.

3. A stronger external position for the union. Members of a monetary union may be less susceptible to changes and shocks elsewhere in the international economy. Furthermore, and especially with a single currency, they may collectively have greater weight in the world economic and political scene. In the European context, this has been referred to as the creation of a 'European monetary identity'. A European currency would probably become a major reserve currency to rival the dollar and the yen, and as a result European countries might be able to enjoy the advantages of *seigniorage*, i.e. the ability to finance balance of trade deficits by having other countries hold the Euro-currency as part of their reserves.

4. A monetary union may result in savings in foreign currency reserves, as a result of pooling arrangements.

5. Centralization of coordination may render economic policy-making more efficient and and effective. If it is true that countries can no longer control their economies separately, then they have no option but to try to do it collectively. This is the inevitability argument for monetary integration. Additionally, some countries may find it beneficial to subject themselves to the discipline imposed by having economic policy determined by a powerful low inflation country such as (West) Germany. This has led to the assertion that monetary union can in some circumstances reduce inflation. The effect of monetary union on the efficiency of macro-economic management would probably become greater as the size and importance of the union budget grows. This could then be used jointly to control more aspects of fiscal policy.

6. Monetary integration is an essential prerequisite of and may act as an engine for political integration. Whether this is a benefit will of course depend on one's views about the desirability of political integration at, for example, the European level. It is also to some extent a 'chicken and egg' argument, since monetary integration is probably not possible without the political will to achieve it.

5.3   MONETARY INTEGRATION IN PRACTICE: THE EUROPEAN MONETARY SYSTEM

5.3.1   Precedents: EMU

Since its creation, the European Community has attempted on two occasions to move towards monetary integration. Before the EMS came European Monetary Union (EMU).

This was set in motion at the Hague Summit in 1969, which took place amid the economic uncertainty that followed in the wake of the political events of May 1968. The debate at the time was concentrated mainly on two issues: whether West Europe was an optimum currency area, i.e. an area in which fixed exchange rates were possible and desirable (see Mundell, 1963); and what was the best strategy for achieving monetary union in the Community. On the latter point there were two distinct schools of thought, sometimes referred to as the 'economists' and the 'monetarists' (the latter having nothing to do with Milton Friedman). The former (mainly the Germans and Dutch, whose views were expressed through the Schiller Plan) favoured a 'gradualist' approach of working towards harmonization and convergence to prepare the ground for fixed exchange rates and a single currency. The latter (the EC Commission backed by the French and Belgians through the Barre Plan) believed in 'shock theory', favouring the introduction of fixed exchange rates as a *fait accompli*, and forcing economies to converge in an ex-post fashion.

The outcome of the debate was the 1970 Werner Plan, the bulk of which was adopted by the Council in March 1971 and put into effect from March 1972. This was broadly a compromise between the two views and created the 'snake in the tunnel' system. Efforts would be made to harmonize economic policies, and the currencies of the ten participants (six full members, plus the United Kingdom, Ireland, and Denmark who were about to join) would be fixed against each other within a band of 2.25 per cent. This was the snake. The tunnel consisted of the bands (4.5 per cent maximum) within which the snake would be allowed to move against the dollar, in line with the Smithsonian Agreements of December 1971. The overall objective was full monetary union by 1980. The scheme rapidly fell apart, however, as the international monetary system fell into disarray after the oil crisis, and the EC states showed that they lacked the political will to subordinate their own national interests to Community ones. As soon as there was any pressure on a country's currency, therefore, it was promptly devalued regardless of the snake. Sterling 'floated away' in June 1972, Italy in February 1973, France in January 1974 and then again in March 1976, and EMU withered away.

5.3.2 The EMS: Structure

The idea of monetary integration was resurrected by Roy Jenkins in 1977, and championed by Helmut Schmidt at the Copenhagen and Bremen Councils in 1978, following widespread dissatisfaction with the often wildly floating exchange rates that existed at the time, as well as a desire to recapture the lost impetus towards European integration. The result was the EMS, which came into being in 1979. In essence the EMS has two main features.

The European Currency Unit (ECU)   This is the Community's alternative money. It has three principal functions:

1. It is the centre of the ERM of the EMS (see below)—the unit currency against which the values of national currencies are expressed; the currency that is used for the credit and intervention mechanism of the ERM.
2. It is the official parallel currency of the Community—the currency used as a means of settlement between different countries, who are also required to accept it as part of their foreign exchange reserves: the currency in which the EC budget is expressed.
3. Increasingly, it has also developed as a private parallel currency. The Community makes its bond issues in ECUs, and so to an increasing extent do national governments and private sector companies. Perhaps most significant from the perception of the general public

is its increased, though still limited, use for ordinary banking purposes. One can have bank accounts in ECUs, ECU credit cards, and ECU travellers cheques. Furthermore, many international credit deals are now conducted in ECUs. It is attractive to business and individuals, since as a composite currency it carries less risk than individual national currencies (see CBI, 1987).

How, then, is the ECU arrived at? As has been mentioned, it is a composite currency, a 'weighted basket' of all the currencies of the EC countries involved. The importance of each national currency is determined by its size, the relative size of the country's GNP, and the relative share it commands of the Community's total trade. The current weights in the basket are shown in Table 5.1.

Table 5.1   Weights of currencies (per cent) in the ECU basket*

Deutschmark (FRG)	34.93
Franc (French)	18.97
Pound sterling (UK)	11.87
Guilder (Dutch)	11.04
Lira (Italian)	9.44
Franc (Belgian and Luxembourg)	9.07
Krone (Danish)	2.79
Drachma (Greek)	0.76
Punt (Irish)	1.13
	100%

*Following the latest realignment of 12 January 1987.
Source: EC Commission, Background Report, 9 March 1989.

It should be noted from Table 5.1 that the Deutschmark is by far the largest influence on the ECU, the 'anchor currency' of the EMS, reflecting West Germany's position as the most powerful economy in the Community. Also, the United Kingdom has always formed part of the ECU basket, and therefore of the EMS, even though it did not participate in the ERM until October 1990. Spain became part of the EMS in response to stage one of the Delors Plan (see below).

The Exchange Rate Mechanism (ERM)   Each currency in the EMS has a value against the ECU, as well as a cross-rate against all of the other EMS currencies. The latter are known as the bilateral central rates. The countries that participate in the ERM commit themselves to fix their exchange rates against each other within a band of 4.5 per cent by not allowing the value of their currencies to rise or fall by more than 2.25 per cent around the central rate. Italy is permitted a margin of 6 per cent either way. (It should be noted in passing that the margins of fluctuation that are allowed against the ECU—as opposed to bilateral fluctuations between national currencies—in this system are in practice less than ±2.25 per cent, since when the value of a currency rises against the ECU it follows that the value of others must simultaneously have fallen. The more important the currency in the ECU basket, the smaller are its effective margins of fluctuation against the ECU before the limits allowed against other currencies are reached.)

This is the 'snake'. There is no tunnel this time, as the ERM currencies jointly float against the dollar and other world currencies. The ERM is not a system of irrevocably fixed exchange rates, since the rates can be changed, or realigned. This flexibility has undoubtedly contributed substantially to its survival. However, the agreed exchange rates are only altered (in theory at least, as Italy demonstrated by unilaterally devaluing the lira in July 1985) by collective decision. The current ERM parity grid, or set of cross-values, in force since 12 January 1987 when the last realignment took place, is shown in Table 5.2.

Table 5.2 Central rates and intervention limits of EMS currencies (parity grid)

		Amsterdam in HFL	Brussels in BFR/LFR	Frankfurt in DM	Copenhagen in DKR	Dublin in IRL	Paris in FF	Rome in LIT
100 HFL	+2.25%		1 872.15	90.770	346.24	33.8868	304.44	67 912.0
	central rate	100	1 830.54	88.752 6	338.537	33.129 3	297.661	63 963.1
	−2.25%		1 789.85	86.780	331.02	32.393 9	291.04	60 241.0
100 BFR/ LFR	+2.25	5.587 0		4.959	18.914 3	1.851 0	16.631 0	3 710.2
	central rate	5.462 86	100	4.848 37	18.493 8	1.809 81	16.260 8	3 494.21
	−2.25%	5.341 5		4.740	18.083 1	1.769 5	15.899 0	3 290.9
100 DM	+2.25%	115.235	2 109.50		390.16	38.182 5	343.05	76 540.0
	central rate	112.673	2 062.55	100	381.443	37.328 1	335.386	72 069.9
	−2.25%	110.167 5	2 016.55		373.00	36.496 4	327.92	67 865.0
100 DKR	+2.25%	30.21	553.0	26.810		10.008 7	89.925	20 062.0
	central rate	29.538 9	540.723	26.216 2	100	9.786 04	87.925 7	18 894.0
	−2.25%	28.882 5	528.70	25.630		9.568 30	85.97	17 794.0
1 IRL	+2.25%	3.087 0	56.511 5	2.740	10.451 1		9.189 0	2 050.03
	central rate	3.018 48	55.254 5	2.678 94	10.218 6	1	8.984 80	1 930.71
	−2.25%	2.951 0	54.025	2.619	9.991 3		8.785 0	1 818.34
100 FF	+2.25%	34.36	628.97	30.495	116.32	11.383 0		22 817.0
	central rate	33.595 3	614.977	29.816 4	113.732	11.129 9	100	21 488.6
	−2.25%	32.847 5	601.295	29.150	111.20	10.882 5		20 238.0
1000 LIT	central rate	1.563 40	28.618 7	1.387 54	5.292 68	0.517 943	4.653 62	1000
	−6.00%	1.472 5	26.953	1.306 5	4.985	0.487 799	4.383 0	
1 ECU	central rate	2.319 43	42.458 2	2.058 53	7.852 12	0.768 411	6.904 03	1 483.58

Abbreviations: HFL, Dutch guidlers; BFR/LFR, Belgium/Luxembourg franc; DM, Deutschmark; DKR, Danish krone; IRL, Irish pound; FF, French franc; LIT, Italian lira.
Source: EC Commission, Background Report, 9 March 1989.

The notional central rates in ECUs for sterling and the drachma have been 0.731 695 and 150.792 respectively. British entry into the ERM was effected on the basis of a bilateral central rate against the Deutschmark of £1 = 2.95 DM, with fluctuations of ±6 per cent permitted.

The biggest problem confronting any system of fixed exchange rates is how to make it stick, and how to keep the currencies within the agreed bands of fluctuation. Ultimately, success depends on the participants having the political will to make the system work. If this exists, creating the nuts and bolts required to keep the system in place is an eminently solvable problem. Nevertheless, there do have to be mechanisms and structures, and in the case of the ERM these consist of the following:

Central bank intervention in the foreign exchange markets   When a currency reaches the upper or lower limit of its permitted range of values against another ERM currency, the central banks of the two countries are required to manipulate the market in order to prevent further divergence from taking place. If, for example, the lira had reached its minimum value *vis-à-vis* the French franc, then the Bank of France would have to buy the Italian currency and the Bank of Italy would have to sell francs, in order to bolster the value of the lira against the franc and maintain the two currencies within their bilateral limits. Any borrowing that is required between the banks to pay for these operations is undertaken and repaid in ECUs. It should be noted that this sort of intervention is the accepted means of influencing the value of currencies, carried out almost routinely by the central banks of countries throughout the world. If it is to be used successfully to maintain a complex fixed exchange rate system such as the EMS, then enormous amounts of money have to be made available for the central banks to call on, not only to finance interventions directly, but also to deter speculators. The ERM members thus have available to them a limited reserve pooling system.

A (limited) reserve pooling system   Short-term financing is carried out between the central banks, and its effectiveness has been considerably enhanced by the Basle/Nyborg Agreement of September 1987 which extended access to short-term finance (mainly Deutschmarks) for ERM central banks who need it. Previously, access had been solely for compulsory operations at the margins of the ERM limits. This new facility has since been used extensively, particularly after the stock market crash of October 1987. Medium-term financial assistance can be provided through the Council of Ministers. In addition, there is a more formal system of pooling which is carried out under the auspices of the European Monetary Cooperation Fund (EMCF). EMS members, including the United Kingdom, have deposited 20 per cent of their gold and foreign exchange reserves with the EMCF, and in return have received the equivalent in ECUs—a notable achievement for supranationalism at the expense of national economic sovereignty. It is planned to replace the EMCF with a new institution, the European Monetary Fund (EMF), with functions more directly appropriate to the imperatives of the EMS. Up to now there has been, however, little sign of this new institution actually materializing. In any case, there is a limit to the extent to which the parities of the ERM can be kept in place by intervention in the markets ('bucking the markets', in Mrs Thatcher's parlance). In the long run pressure on exchange rates can only be eliminated by removing divergence in the economic policies and performance of the participants.

A divergence indicator   In principle, this is an innovatory system whereby as soon as a currency has reached three-quarters of the permitted fluctuation either side of its ECU central rate, the equivalent of an alarm bell is triggered. Following this it is 'presumed' (but not mandatory) that the relevant central bank will take appropriate steps, both in the foreign exchange markets and in terms of its internal macro-economic policy, to remedy the position. In practice the divergence indicator has not played an important role in the operation of the ERM.

Some measures to promote economic policy convergence   These have been predominantly informal and non-compulsory, as is the case with the divergence indicator. However, some policy convergence has in fact occurred. It is also interesting to note that the Single European Act added Article 102A to the Treaty of Rome, urging convergence in economic and monetary policies within the framework of the EMS. Policy convergence, as we have seen, involves costs, and so the ERM also includes a redistribution mechanism.

A (very limited) redistribution mechanism This redistribution mechanism is carried out through the European Investment Bank and the New Community Instrument. This takes the form of subsidized loans for ERM members.

5.3.3 The EMS: evaluation

In evaluating the success of any policy, it is crucial to be clear about its objectives. It is manifest that the EMS in its present form was not intended as a monetary union, though for some that may have been the hidden agenda behind it. It would therefore be unfair to judge the EMS against this paradigm. If one accepts the EMS as having the more limited aims of exchange rate stability and economic convergence, then it can be considered a clear success, not least if one takes into account the immense scepticism that greeted its launch, and of the many economic and political shocks it has survived. The fact that it has arguably also promoted the cause of monetary union is a bonus. The extent of the success of the EMS can be readily seen by considering a number of factors.

Exchange rate stability The EMS has undoubtedly contributed towards greater exchange rate stability (see the statistical findings reported in Artis and Taylor, 1988, and in MacDonald and Zis, 1989). Between 1979 and the present day there have been just eleven realignments, only four of which have occurred since March 1983. There have been no changes at all since January 1987. This stability contrasts with the experience of non-ERM currencies, both inside and outside the European Community, which have been distinctly more volatile. Moreover, what realignments there have been have generally been carried out at the right time and to an appropriate dimension. In other words, the 'collective' decision-making has operated efficiently. Details of the realignments are shown in Table 5.3. Figure 5.1 shows how (with the exception of sterling) ERM currencies have fluctuated less than

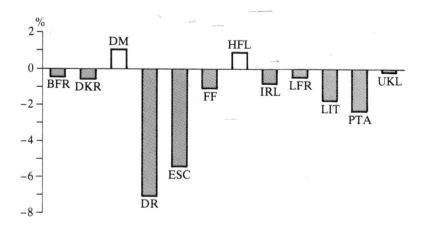

Figure 5.1 Average annual variation in the rates of national currencies against the ECU 1979–88 (per cent). (*Source*: EC Commission, *Target 1992*, no. 4, April 1989.)

Table 5.3   EMS realignments

Sept. 1981	DM +2%, DKR −3%
Nov. 1979	DKR −5%
Mar. 1981	LIT −6%
Oct. 1981	DM/HFL +5.5%, FF/LIT −3%
Feb. 1982	BFR/LFR −8.5%, DKR −3%
June 1982	DM/HFL +4.25%, FF −5.75%, LIT −2.75%
Mar. 1983	DM +5.5%, HFL +3.35%, DKR +2.5%, BFR/LFR +1.5%, LIT −2.5%, IRL −3.5%
July 1985	LIT −6%, others +2%
Apr. 1986	DM/HFL +3%, BFR/LFR/DKR +1%, FF −3%
Aug. 1986	IRL −8%
Jan. 1987	DM/HFL +3%, BFR/LFR +2%

Abbreviations: as Table 5.2.
Source: adapted from Eurostat, *ECU–EMS Information*, no. 3 (1989).

Table 5.4   The value of the ECU relative to the yen and dollar

	The value of 1 ECU in the years		
	1979	*1985*	*1988*
Dollar	1.37	0.76	1.18
Yen	300.47	180.56	151.46

Source: EC Commission, *Target 1992*, no. 4 (April 1989).

those still outside it during the 1980s. Table 5.4 then gives an indication of how the value of the ECU has changed against the dollar and the yen over the last ten years.

Control of inflation   Since 1979, and in particular since 1982, rates of inflation in EMS countries have fallen, have increasingly tended to converge, and have become more stable and therefore more predictable. This can be attributed, in part at least, to an appreciable convergence in economic policy, and in particular monetary policy, in EMS countries. The growth of money supply in these countries has declined and become increasingly convergent and predictable since 1979. In addition the interest rate policy of member countries appears to have become increasingly coordinated recently, an example of this being the coordinated interest rate changes made by Germany and France in November 1987. It should also be noted that the Basle/Nyborg Agreement of September 1987 provides for the coordination of interest rate, as well as other policies, in difficult periods in the exchange rate markets. In effect Germany's leadership of the system has to an extent imposed its price objectives and performance on everybody else. Furthermore, by associating themselves with German leadership, some of the weaker EMS countries have enhanced the credibility of their economic policy-making. The benefits that have ensued have outweighed the losses involved in accepting German leadership. For its part, Germany has managed to maintain its relative competitive position by maintaining an inflation rate lower than that of other members, despite the revaluations of the Deutschmark. It must be pointed out, however, that some at least of this convergence would probably have happened even without the EMS, since the 1980s have on the whole been a decade characterized by widespread agreement on policy objectives (low inflation) and tools (tight monetary policy) among the major industrialized countries under leaders of similar political persuasion such as President Reagan, Mrs Thatcher, and Chancellor Köhl. There has therefore been increased coordination of economic policies between these powers. The Louvre Accord of February 1987, which sought to stabilize the exchange rates of major world currencies, is an example of this. Nevertheless, the EMS, with its limited membership of countries with broadly similar economic structures and political goals, has undoubtedly added to this convergence, not least by helping to change perceptions among politicians.

The growing success of the ECU   The ECU has by no means developed yet into a parallel currency, but its use, particularly by the private sector, has increased substantially in recent years. Table 5.5 shows one aspects of this, the growth of issues of ECU bonds.

Table 5.5   Issues of ECU bonds

	(in million ECUs)	
	1984	*1988*
European Community	7 742	32 344
Rest of the world	1 894	15 615
Total	9 363	47 953

Source: EC Commission, *Target 1992*, no. 4 (April 1989).

Against this it could be argued that the EMS has:

1. Been seriously weakened by the absence of important currencies such as sterling (until October 1990), and by the larger bands of fluctuation allowed for the Italian lira.
2. Failed to develop a common approach among its members towards the major external world currencies, especially the US dollar.
3. Failed to move as far as it might have done in the direction of monetary integration by not making a great deal of use of the convergence indicator, and by failing to establish the EMF.
4. Been too heavily reliant on the German leadership, with the result that the other members have suffered disproportionate losses in economic sovereignty.
5. Only succeeded to the extent that it has because of the favourable external circumstances outlined above.
6. Relied excessively on exchange controls to maintain the ERM parities. This has been particularly the case for Italy and France, and would imply that the liberalization of intra-Community capital movements as part of the '1992' programme will pose serious problems for the system.

Many of the above criticisms are, however, probably unreasonable, and a tentative conclusion might be that the EMS on the whole fulfilled most of its initial objectives, and has furthermore laid the basis for further monetary integration in the European Community in the future.

5.3.4 Britain's position

Britain has been a member of the EMS to the extent that sterling has always formed part of the ECU basket, but the UK government up to October 1990 consistently refused to join the ERM, the official position being that it would join 'when the time is right'. It should be noted, however, that for a period in the mid/late 1980s sterling 'shadowed the Deutschmark', i.e. adopted exchange rate targets that informally tied sterling to the German currency and therefore the ERM. This was after the money supply was abandoned as a policy target by the Chancellor of the Exchequer. In addition, Figure 5.1 shows how stable the sterling exchange rate has been *vis-à-vis* the ECU in the 1980s. The following arguments were put forward for not joining the ERM:

1. Sterling is a 'petro-currency', i.e. because of North Sea oil production, its value depends to an extent on the price of oil. This means that when the international oil price increases, the value of sterling goes up, whereas the value of other ERM currencies tends to fall. Therefore it would have been inappropriate to tie sterling to the ERM currencies. In the late 1980s the validity of this argument was substantially reduced with the decline in the United Kingdom's oil production.
2. Sterling's position as an international currency further complicates the issue. Foreigners hold large amounts of internationally mobile funds in the City of London. These funds are sensitive to interest rate and exchange rate changes, and are therefore a potentially destabilizing force within the ERM. On the other hand, it could be argued that membership of the ERM will help the United Kingdom cope with any flight of capital by collective intervention and reserve pooling.
3. Membership was (in the early 1980s) incompatible with monetarism and the medium-term financial strategy. This implied having high interest rates and a high value for sterling. Membership of the ERM might have constrained the government's ability to pursue such a policy, and in particular might have forced them to adopt a more expansionary monetary policy than desired, in order to stop sterling from rising in value. This is really an application of the loss of sovereignty argument (the Labour government of the late 1970s argued that the weak pound and the United Kingdom's propensity for high inflation would, in the absence of the ability to devalue in the ERM, force deflation and unemployment on the nation). During the mid-1980s it seemed that UK policy was becoming more compatible with ERM membership, but the huge balance of payments deficit of the late 1980s and the exclusive use of high interest rates to attempt to deal with it, seemed to indicate that the United Kingdom had gone back to square one.
4. A recent, and interesting, argument was put forward by Timothy Congdon. This concentrates on the structural difference in the UK economy which results from the high degree of home ownership in this country, and the consequent high level of mortgage borrowing and of the use of housing as a store of personal wealth (both exacerbated by increases in house prices in the mid to late 1980s). This results in more borrowing in the United Kingdom than in other ERM countries at a given interest rate, and a low elasticity of demand for money with respect to the rate of interest, i.e. the government has to increase interest rates by a lot in order to cut borrowing, because much of UK borrowing takes the form of mortgages secured against the equity embedded in one's home. Thus membership of the ERM, if it implied interest rate convergence, might precipitate a credit boom in the United Kingdom. It should be noted, however, that exclusion from the ERM has not exactly acted as a hindrance to credit growth in the United Kingdom in recent years.

In the late 1980s there was widespread agreement in the United Kingdom on the desirability of joining the ERM. Chancellors of the Exchequer have favoured membership, so have the Confederation of British Industry (whose business opinion surveys indicated that most of their members also favoured entry, were keen to enjoy the reduced risk that goes with fixed exchange rates and the increased use of the ECU), the City, most economists, the political parties of the opposition, the TUC, and probably most of the Conservative Party. The United Kingdom did not join during the 1980s because the Prime Minister and some of her close advisers were opposed to membership, probably fearing that monetary integration would lead to political integration, which is not considered desirable. Despite ERM entry there remains a danger, recently publicized by Lord Cockfield (a former British EC commissioner dismissed by the Prime Minister) and Edward Heath, of Britain being 'left behind' other EC members, much as it was in the 1960s. The possibility of a 'two-tier Europe', with the United Kingdom moving towards increased integration at a slower pace than other EC members, has also been raised.

The signs so far are that there has in fact been some change both in the style and in the substance of the way in which monetary integration is regarded by the UK government. At the Madrid Summit in June 1989 the United Kingdom defined the conditions under which 'the time would be right' for Britain to become a full member of the EMS. These consisted of a situation in which the United Kingdom's rate of inflation was reduced to that of other EC members, and in which Italy and France had completed the dismantlement of their exchange controls. Subsequently, the attitude towards membership of the ERM softened somewhat, in response to the perceived need to pre-empt a major bastion of the economic policy of the opposition parties, and to talk up sterling in order to lower the United Kingdom's rate of inflation before the next general election; and also in order to avoid isolation in the European Community and splits in the UK cabinet. This process culminated with full ERM membership in October 1990, albeit with wide fluctuation bands. But severe doubts remain about the true intentions of the UK government, as the incident that led to the resignation of the Trade Secretary Mr Ridley in July 1990 has demonstrated. These doubts have been partly responsible for the sceptical manner in which John Major's proposals for an alternative to the Delors plan for further monetary integration, put before the Dublin Summit in June 1990, have been greeted. This plan is based on creating a new 'hard' ECU—a parallel European currency that could develop into the Community's single currency, not based on the current basket of national currencies. This would stand on its own, not be devalued against other currencies in the ERM, compete with existing national currencies, and be managed by a new EMF. A diversionary tactic to slow down the progress of EMU in the run up to the intergovernmental conferences of 1990/91? Most other EC member-states seem to doubt the UK government's good faith, and regard the proposal as such. The issue of a parallel currency was in fact discussed by the Delors Report (see below), and rejected on the grounds that it would probably be inflationary.

5.3.5 EMS: future prospects

There is a view that the EMS is about to enter a period of crisis. This is based on the following beliefs:

1. The liberalization of capital markets in Europe as part of the '1992' programme may result in serious problems for the EMS, given that exchange controls, especially in Italy and France, have played a major part in keeping the ERM together in recent years.

2. Now that inflation has become (except in the United Kingdom) less of a problem for European countries, the EMS has outlived its usefulness, and members may no longer be prepared to pay the price inherent in accepting German leadership.
3. German reunification and monetary union has radically changed the parameters in the European Community.

These arguments may exaggerate the true situation. Nevertheless, it seems clear that change will be necessary in the foreseeable future if the EMS is to continue to progress along the path of greater monetary integration. Various possibilities have been canvassed for changing the EMS to take it into the 1990s and beyond:

1. One could strengthen the institutions of the EMS. For example, the EMF could at last be established as a formal body for pooling reserves and overseeing the coordination of policy. More radically, one could, as Thygesen (1989) has suggested, create a European monetary authority—the European Reserve Board, modelled on the US Federal Reserve, with policy being made by a European Monetary Policy Committee.
2. One could strengthen the ECU by linking private and official ECUs, which are at present kept quite separate, or by allowing it to compete more fully with national currencies, and eventually displace them. More radically, Padoa-Schioppa (1988) has suggested that an ECU monetary base could be used to regulate monetary aggregates in EC countries.
3. Most radically, one could move towards some approximation of complete monetary union by creating a European central bank and establishing a single currency.

The EC Commission's response to the debate was to set up the Delors Committee, which reported in April 1989 and which was debated by the EC Summit in Madrid in June 1989. The report advocates moving towards a monetary union in Europe run by a European System of Central Banks (ESCB). This is to be achieved in three stages:

1. The first stage (which started in July 1990) consists of strengthening monetary policy coordination and achieving greater economic convergence within the existing institutional framework. All currencies should become full members of the EMS and ERM. Realignment would still be possible.
2. The second stage (undated) would consist of increased collective decision-making, with ultimate control over economic and monetary policy remaining in the hands of national governments. A medium-term framework of common economic objectives would be established, rules for the size of budget deficits and their financing would be set, and the Community would attempt to reach important economic decisions collectively.
3. The third stage (also undated) would see irrevocably fixed exchange rates, preferably a single currency, constraints on national budgets, and the new ESC acquiring and managing the reserves of EC members and managing external exchange rates. The whole would necessitate a change in the Treaty of Rome.

The big problem as ever concerns political will. Nigel Lawson, the former Chancellor of the Exchequer, for example, made it clear that the United Kingdom will attempt to block any move that involved the transfer of sovereignty, stating that the plan would require 'political union, a United States of Europe, which is not on the agenda'. We shall see.

REFERENCES

Artis, M. and Taylor, M. (1988), 'Exchange rates, interest rates, capital controls and the European Monetary System: assessing the track record', in F. Giavazzi, S. Micossi and M. Miller (Eds), *The European Monetary System*, Cambridge University Press, Cambridge.

CBI (1987), 'Survey of UK monetary policy's impact on business', London.

Cobham, D. (1989), 'Strategies for monetary integration revisited', *Journal of Common Market Studies*, **XXVII**, March, 203–218.

Corden, W. M. (1972), 'Monetary Integration', *Princeton Essays in International Finance*, no. 73, Princeton, NJ.

EC Commission (1973), 'The report on the regional problems in the enlarged community' (Thompson Report).

EC Commission (1977), 'Report of the study group on the role of public finance in European integration' (MacDougall Report).

EC Commission (1989), 'Report on economic and monetary union in the European Community' (Delors Report).

Eurostat, *ECU-EMS Information*, various issues.

Fleming, M. (1971), 'On exchange rate unification', *Economic Journal*, **81**, 467–488.

Gros, D. (1989), 'Paradigms for the monetary union of Europe', *Journal of Common Market Studies*, **XXVII**, March 219–230.

House of Lords (1988), 'Twenty-first report of the Select Committee on the European Communities'.

Jenkins, R. (1978), 'European monetary union', *Lloyds Bank Review*, no. 127, January, 1–14.

MacDonald, F. and Zis, G. (1989) 'The European Monetary System: towards 1992 and beyond', *Journal of Common Market Studies*, **XXVII**, March, 183–201.

Mundell, R. A. (1961), 'A theory of optimum currency areas', *American Economic Review*, **51**, 657–665.

Padoa-Schioppa, T. (1988), 'The European Monetary System: a long term view', in Giavazzi *et al.* (Eds), *The European Monetary System*, op. cit.

Sachs, J. and Wyplosz, C. (1986), 'The economic consequences of President Mitterrand', *Economic Policy*, **2**.

Thygesen, N. (1989) 'Decentralisation and accountability within the Central Bank: any lessons from the US experience for the potential organization of a European Central Bank', in P. de Grauwe and T. Peeters (Eds) *The ECU and European Monetary Integration*, Macmillan, London.

Ungerer, H. (1989), 'The European Monetary System and the International Monetary System', *Journal of Common Market Studies*, **XXVII**, March, 231–248.

SIX

THE BUDGET OF THE EUROPEAN COMMUNITY

6.1 INTRODUCTION

In recent years, budgetary conflicts and crises have been a recurrent theme of EC affairs. The long-running dispute over the 'British problem' has since 1984 been replaced by bitter disagreements between member-states over the insatiable appetite of the Common Agricultural Policy and the related problem of diminishing resources. EC budgetary matters have also been at the centre of public clashes between the European Parliament and the Council of Ministers, which have, on some occasions, left the Community without a budget at the beginning of the financial year. The first section of this chapter outlines the economic mechanisms of the budget and highlights the limitations, imbalances and inequities surrounding both the raising and spending of the budget. The latter sections focus upon politics of budgetary policy-making and budgetary reform.

Fiscal policy, i.e. how public authorities raise money and then proceed to spend it, is clearly an issue of major significance both in itself and in terms of the issues it raises for governments, be they local, national, or supranational. In particular, fiscal policy is usually thought to have a key role to play in three areas. First, it can be used to promote the efficiency of the economic system, since governments can use fiscal policy to improve resource allocation and ensure that the 'right' goods are produced in the appropriate quantities. It is generally (but not universally) accepted that the free operation of markets tends to produce outcomes that are less than optimal, since decisions are taken on the basis of the private costs and benefits to producers, rather than with regard to social costs and benefits, i.e. what is desirable or otherwise from the point of view of the community as a whole. 'Undesirable' activities can be curtailed by taxation, while 'desirable' ones can be promoted by subsidies, or by the provision of 'public goods'. A central problem here is, of course, to decide what is desirable and what should or should not constitute a public good. The consensus on these points has changed considerably in Western Europe, and in particular in the United Kingdom, during the post-war period. Secondly, fiscal policy can be used to promote equity by altering the personal or geographical distribution of income, if it is felt that the distribution that results from the operation of the market system is unacceptable. Thirdly, fiscal policy has a role to play in macro-economic management, i.e. the regulation of the economy to promote the classic objectives of economic policy; price stability, full employment, external equilibrium, and economic growth. Just how great this role should be is itself a matter of debate. In the heyday of the Keynsian consensus on economic policy, fiscal policy was considered to be the main instrument of economic management. More recently, with the vogue for 'monetarism' and 'supply-side economics' it has been fashionable to regard it as very much secondary in importance to monetary and structural policies.

In the context of the European Community, fiscal matters are of relevance in two spheres. First, there is the issue of fiscal harmonization. The existence of different fiscal regimes in member-states can impede the free movement of goods, services, labour, and capital. They thus need to some extent to be harmonized in order to allow the EC internal market to function properly. This is discussed in Chapter 4. In this chapter we will concentrate on the other aspect of fiscal policy: the EC budget.

The study of the EC budget is of significance for a number of reasons. First, and most obviously, Community expenditure has an important direct impact on certain areas, notably, as we shall see, agriculture. Secondly, the size, financing, and expenditures of the EC budget, as well as the process by which these are determined by member-states, yield interesting insights into a number of important political aspects of West European integration; for example the nature of the decision-making process in the Community, and the balance between national sovereignty and supranationalism that is considered appropriate by member-states, i.e. the extent to which they are willing to surrender control of key economic and political functions to the Community level. In this sense the budget can be seen as a barometer of the state of European integration. Thirdly, as the process of political and economic integration in Europe continues, one would clearly expect this development to be reflected in an increased role for the EC budget, as more economic functions of government would probably have to be transferred from the national level to the Community level. Indeed an expanded role for the Community budget may in fact be an essential prerequisite for further integration, since it may be necessary to have an effective system of inter-state and inter-regional transfers to compensate the losers from the integration process, in order to secure the political will to move forward.

6.2 THE BUDGET AT PRESENT: SIZE AND LIMITATIONS

Any such expanded role for the Community budget, however, is very much a matter of conjecture. As it is currently structured and operated, the EC budget has a very limited role to play. It fulfils virtually none of the functions of fiscal policy outlined above. Its size both in absolute terms and relative to both total public spending and the national income of the Community is relatively insignificant, as can be seen from Table 6.1 and Figure 6.1.

Despite a steady increase in size throughout the 1980s, and significant expansions in 1983 and 1988, the budget still only accounts for just over 1 per cent of Community GDP and just over 3.5 per cent of total Community central government spending, arguably a very small amount for an organization that has the aspirations of the European Community, and certainly not enough for it to be of any real macro-economic significance in the Community. The size of the budget can be seen in some perspective when one considers that the 1989 total spending of 44.8 million ECUs would be roughly equivalent to the expenditure of a largish ministry in one of the member-states. Nor, at a time when the very notion of public expenditure is frowned upon by economic and political orthodoxy in many Community countries, is there much prospect of significant increase in the foreseeable future. In fact one of the objectives of the wide-ranging reforms agreed in 1988, under pressure from (in particular) the UK government, was to introduce a system of limiting or 'capping' EC expenditure. Thus an overall ceiling for the budget of 1.2 per cent of total Community GNP was agreed, to be introduced in steps as follows:

1988   1.15 per cent
1989   1.17 per cent
1990   1.18 per cent
1991   1.19 per cent
1992   1.20 per cent

Furthermore, the Treaty of Rome obliges the Community to balance revenues and expenditures, thus excluding *a priori* any possibility of using the budget as a means of economic management. It would be illegal to, for example, run a budget deficit at the Community level in order to increase the volume of economic activity in the way member-states have frequently done. As such, the Community budget is a very different and much more modest version of the budgets of the various member-states, and it should be, at least in its present form, regarded as merely a means of operating the existing common policies of the Community. However, it should be noted that both Euratom and the European Coal and Steel Community do have the power to borrow under the Euratom Treaty and the Treaty of Paris respectively, as does the Commission, to a very limited extent and outside of the budget, under the Ortoli Facility introduced in 1978.

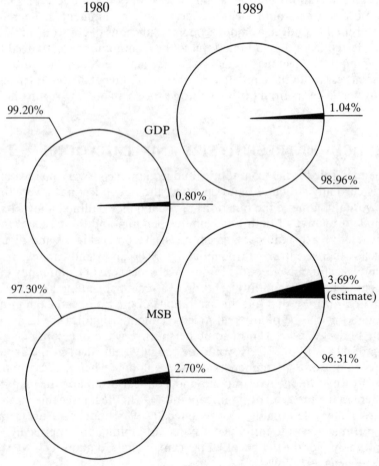

Figure 6.1   General budget in relation to total of member-states' budgets (MSB) and community GDP. (*Source:* as Table 6.1.)

Table 6.1 Growth of Community expenditure in relation to total of member-states' budgets and Community GDP

Appropriations for payments

Year	Expenditure (million ECU)	Growth in money terms (%)	Growth in real terms (%)*	(ECU)	Growth in real terms with constant population (%)†	% of MSB‡	%of GDP
				Per capita expenditure			
1989	44 840.60	+ 2.33	− 2.29 §	138.29	+ 2.77 §	3.69 ¶	1.04 §
1988	43 820.40	+21.16	+17.04	135.41	+16.59	3.56	1.09
1987	36 168.40	+ 2.83	− 1.07	111.99	− 2.23	3.14	0.98
1986	35 174.10	+23.71	+18.11	109.13	+16.86	3.08	0.99
1985	28 433.20	+ 4.35	− 1.65	88.43	− 2.86	2.70	0.92
1984	27 248.60	+ 8.73	+ 2.23	84.95	+ 1.06	2.90	0.98
1983	25 061.10	+13.99	+ 5.34	78.29	+ 4.31	2.70	0.96
1982	21 984.40	+19.26	+ 8.96	68.80	+ 7.33	2.50	0.86
1981	18 434.00	+13.91	+ 2.91	57.83	+ 1.41	2.40	0.81
1980	16 182.50	+12.01	− 0.99	50.97	− 2.84	2.70	0.80

* Deflated by means of GDP (market prices) deflator.
† Deflated by means of GDP (market prices) deflator and rate of growth of Community population.
‡ MSB: member-states' budgets (central government).
§ Forecast.
¶ Estimate. Calculated by reference to member-states' public spending.
Source: EC: The Community Budget, 'The Facts in Figures' (1989).

6.3 FINANCING THE COMMUNITY

How, then, is revenue for the Community budget raised? In essence budgetary funds emanate from three sources. First, the duties that member-countries collect on imports into the Community are paid to the EC. These consist principally of general customs duties (the Common External Tariff—see Chapter 3), to which are added agricultural tariffs in the form of the Variable Levy (see Chapter 7) and levies on sugar imports. Secondly, a proportion of VAT receipts levied by member-states are paid to the Community. Initially 1 per cent of the VAT base (i.e. 1 per cent of the total value added of sales, and not 1 per cent of VAT revenues) was paid to the Community, but this 'VAT ceiling' was raised to 1.4 per cent in January 1986, following agreement at the Fontainebleau European Council in June 1984 (see Chapter 2). Since the 1988 reforms the VAT base has been 'capped' at 55 per cent of GNP at market prices, i.e. a member-state's payments are limited to 1.4 percentage points of the VAT raised from this proportion of GNP. The objective of this is to reduce the burden of finance that is borne by the United Kingdom, Ireland, and Portugal, and thus render the financing mechanism somewhat more progressive. It should also be noted that since the 1984 Fontainebleau Agreement, VAT rebates have been the mechanism by which compensation has been paid to the United Kingdom for its disproportionate net contribution to the budget. These first two sources of income are generally referred to as the Community's 'own resources'. The concept of giving the Community its own separate funds dates back to the Hague Summit in December 1969, though it was not put into practice until 1980, when the harmonization of VAT was finally completed. Before then the Community had been financed by direct contributions from the member-states.

Thirdly, since June 1988, the Community has had a further source of revenue, the so-called 'fourth resource'. As with the VAT 'capping', one of the principles underlying this is to introduce a contribution system based to a greater extent on ability to pay. Thus the difference between the first two sources of revenue and what is required to meet Community expenditure from own resources is raised from member-states in proportion to their national income. The relative importance of these sources of revenue, and their development over time, can be seen from Tables 6.2 and 6.3, and Figure 6.2.

From Tables 6.2 and 6.3 and Figure 6.2 it will be noticed that the contribution of customs duties of various kinds to the financing of Community expenditure has declined steadily over time, and that the gap thereby created has been filled by increased VAT-based receipts and (latterly) by the GNP-based resource, which, however desirable it may be, accounts for only around 10 per cent of total Community finance and is not forecast to grow in importance in the immediate future.

6.4 COMMUNITY EXPENDITURE

We now need to consider how the EC budget is in fact spent. The first thing to note here is

Table 6.2 Structure of revenue (1980–88)

Per cent of total revenue

Revenue	Year								
	1988	1987	1986	1985	1984	1983	1982	1981	1980
Customs duties	24.72	24.97	24.28	29.59	30.56	28.22	31.81	34.65	37.13
Agricultural levies	3.60	4.55	3.49	3.99	4.84	5.44	7.10	6.86	9.65
Sugar levies	3.32	4.11	3.30	3.76	4.52	3.83	3.29	2.62	2.94
Collection costs*	−3.17	–	–	–	–	–	–	–	–
VAT	57.18	65.57	66.01	54.19	55.16	55.31	56.00	49.80	44.61
VAT balances and adjustments to financial contributions	0.92	−1.00	1.12	0.40	−0.43	5.25	–	2.95	1.64
Financial contributions	0.51§	0.59	0.62	0.93	0.85	0.88	0.92	0.90	0.10
GNP-based resource† ‡	10.62	–	–	–	–	–	–	–	–
Miscellaneous and surpluses available	2.30	1.21	1.02	1.26	2.22	1.07	1.24	2.22	4.02
Intergovernmental advances	–	–	0.16	5.88	2.28	–	−0.36	–	–
Total	100.00	100.00	100.00	100.00	100.00	100.00	100.00	100.00	100.00

*From 1988 onwards collection costs constitute negative expenditure. Prior to this they appeared on the expenditure side of the budget.

†Spain and Italy did not pay their shares until 1989.

‡Financed in 1988 in the form of national contributions under an intergovernmental agreement.

§Paid only by Portugal until 1 January 1989.

Source: see Table 6.1.

Table 6.3   Structure of revenue (1989–90)

Per cent of total revenue

	*1989**	*1990*
Customs duties	22.20	24.20
Agricultural levies	2.85	2.22
Sugar levies	2.64	2.66
Traditional own resources (subtotal)	27.69	29.08
VAT	58.47	60.28
GNP-based resource	8.71	8.33
Member-states' contribution (subtotal)	94.87	97.69
Balance from previous year	4.51	1.66
VAT balances and adjustments to financial contribution	p.m.	p.m.
Miscellaneous	0.62	0.65
Total	100.00	100.00
Total in ECUs	44 840 565 470	46 808 721 772

*Including supplementary and amending budget no. 1/89.
Source: see Table 6.1 (adapted).

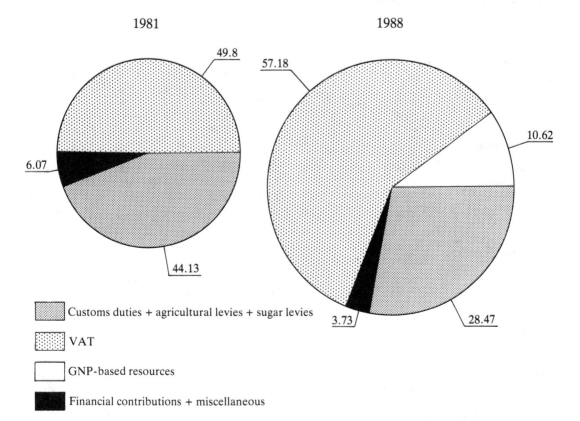

1981

1988

49.8

57.18

6.07

10.62

44.13

28.47

3.73

Customs duties + agricultural levies + sugar levies

VAT

GNP-based resources

Financial contributions + miscellaneous

Figure 6.2   Structure of revenue (1980–88) (per cent of total revenue). (*Source:* as Table 6.1.)

that the 1988 reforms introduced a new classification of budget expenditures to cover the period 1988–92. Expenditure is now divided into six items as follows:

Item 1   EAGGF Guarantee
Item 2   The Structural Funds and Pedip
Item 3   Policies and multi-annual allocations (IMPs and research)
Item 4   Other policies
Item 5   Repayments and administration
Item 6   Monetary reserve

The policy significance of this is that expenditure on each item is 'capped' to the extent that it has to be contained within an agreed rate of increase. Political priorities are reflected in different rates of increase allowed for each item. Thus between 1988 and 1992 items 2 and 3 are allowed to expand more rapidly than the others, thus increasing the relative importance of regional, social, and other expenditures relative to spending on agricultural support.

Nevertheless, it will come as no surprise that Community expenditure has been and continues to be dominated by agriculture, and in particular the cost of the price support mechanism of the Common Agricultural Policy (see Chapter 7). This is evident when one considers Tables 6.4 and 6.5 and Figure 6.3.

Table 6.4   Structure of expenditure by main areas (1980–88)

Appropriations for payments (million ECU)

	1988	1987	1986	1985	1984	1983	1982	1981	1980
EAGGF Guarantee	27 500.0	22 960.8	22 112.0	19 955.0	18 333.0	15 811.0	13 671.3	11 580.0	11 485.5
Agricultural structures	1 222.0	943.2	802.2	687.7	675.1	653.4	773.6	531.8	328.7
Fisheries	281.0	197.3	189.6	111.7	112.4	84.4	87.6	53.5	64.1
Regional policy	3 201.4	2 738.2	2 577.7	1 697.8	1 488.6	2 383.0	2 948.0	1 948.0	722.7
Social policy	2 845.3	2 737.2	2 654.3	1 626.2	1 429.4	1 495.1	1 022.2	732.8	768.8
Research, energy	1 153.6	957.6	758.8	706.8	719.3	1 386.5	435.7	313.9	379.5
Development cooperation	870.5	1 108.9	1 171.5	1 043.7	897.2	992.2	816.8	795.7	641.6
Administration	1 967.2	1 740.0	1 603.2	1 332.6	1 236.6	1 161.6	1 103.3	1 035.4	938.8
Miscellaneous	4 779.4	2 785.0	3 304.8	1 271.8	2 357.2	1 093.8	1 125.9	1 443.1	852.8
Total	43 820.4	36 168.4	35 174.1	28 433.2	27 248.6	25 061.1	21 984.4	18 434.0	16 182.5

Appropriations for payments (%)

	1988	1987	1986	1985	1984	1983	1982	1981	1980
EAGGF Guarantee	62.76	63.48	62.86	70.18	67.28	63.09	62.19	62.82	70.97
Agricultural structures	2.79	2.61	2.28	2.42	2.48	2.61	3.52	2.88	2.03
Fisheries	0.64	0.55	0.54	0.39	0.41	0.34	0.40	0.29	0.40
Regional policy	7.31	7.57	7.33	5.97	5.46	9.51	13.41	10.57	4.47
Social policy	6.49	7.57	7.55	5.72	5.25	5.97	4.65	3.98	4.75
Research, energy	2.63	2.65	2.16	2.49	2.64	5.53	1.98	1.70	2.35
Development cooperation	1.99	3.07	3.33	3.67	3.29	3.96	3.72	4.32	3.96
Administration	4.49	4.81	4.56	4.69	4.54	4.64	5.02	5.62	5.80
Miscellaneous	10.91	7.70	9.40	4.47	8.65	4.36	5.12	7.83	5.27
Total	100.00	100.00	100.00	100.00	100.00	100.00	100.00	100.00	100.00

Source: see Table 6.1.

Table 6.5 Expenditure in the 1989 and 1990 budgets

Appropriations for payments (ECU)

	1989*	*1990* *Preliminary draft*	*Difference* *(%)*
Administration			
Expenditure concerning personnel	1 002 447 000	1 070 524 000	+ 6.8
Buildings, equipment and miscellaneous expenditure	275 713 000	306 948 000	+11.3
Expenditure resulting from special functions	139 225 186	170 021 000	+22.1
Other expenditure	p.m.	p.m.	
Administration—Total	**1 417 385 186**	**1 547 493 000**	**+ 9.2**
Operations			
Agricultural market guarantee	26 741 000 000	26 788 000 000	+ 0.2
Guidance (agricultural structures)	1 552 350 000	2 033 200 000	+31.0
Fisheries	389 240 000	383 700 000	− 1.4
Regional development and transport	4 327 917 300	5 212 450 000	+20.4
Operations in the social sector	3 269 111 400	3 666 905 000	+12.2
Energy, technology, research, nuclear safeguards, information market and innovation	1 463 453 200	1 787 503 000	+22.1
Repayments and aid to member-states	2 912 154 205	2 395 138 772	−17.8
Cooperation with developing countries	1 031 629 500	1 141 232 000	+10.6
Other expenditure	1 000 000 000	1 000 000 000	—
Operations—Total	**42 686 855 605**	**44 408 128 772**	**+ 4.0**
Commission—Total	**44 104 240 791**	**45 955 621 772**	**+ 4.2**
Other institutions	**736 324 679**	**853 100 000**	**+15.9**
Grand total	**44 840 565 470**	**46 808 721 772**	**+ 4.4**

*Including the supplementary and amending budget no. 1/89 and incorporating the changes made to the nomenclature by the 1990 preliminary draft.
Source: see Table 6.1.

Agriculture, including spending on structures, has consistently accounted for around two-thirds of total Community expenditure. Spending in this area has fallen marginally from its high points in the 1970s and mid-1980s, and is forecast to fall modestly into the future, and to undergo a further shift in emphasis away from price support (EAGGF Guarantee) and in favour of structural expenditure (EAGGF Guidance). In fact, as part of the 1988 reforms it was agreed that agricultural price support spending should in future not increase by more than 74 per cent of the rate of increase in Community GNP. Nevertheless, it is and will in the foreseeable future remain by far the main item of EC expenditure, almost like an ominous shadow over the Community. Despite the reforms, EAGGF Guarantee alone accounts for 60.8 per cent of the total budget in terms of appropriations for commitments. One of the many problems associated with this is that a very limited amount of money is then left over for expenditure in other, and arguably just as (or even more) important areas, from the point of view of both the progress of the Community and the welfare of its inhabitants.

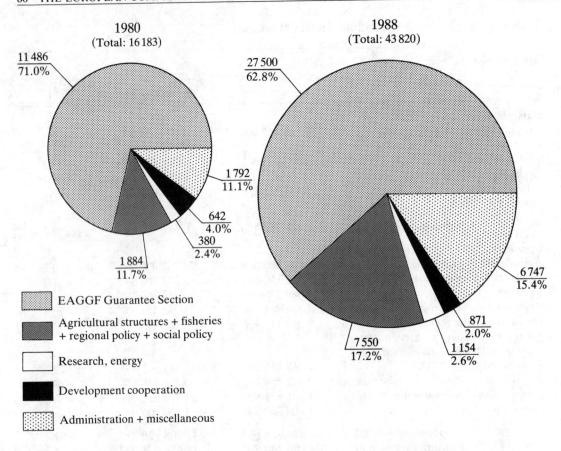

Figure 6.3 Structure of expenditure by main areas. Appropriations for payments (million ECU). (*Source:* as Table 6.1.)

Regional policy, for example, has accounted for only 7–8 per cent of the budget in recent years, though this is forecast to increase to nearly 6000 million ECUs by 1990 and more in the years up to '1992'. Ninety per cent of regional spending is carried out through the European Regional Development Fund (ERDF), while the Mediterranean Programme accounts for just over 5 per cent of spending in this area. Social policy (see Chapter 8), operated predominantly through the European Social Fund (ESF), has similarly been neglected, accounting for again around 7 per cent of the Community budget, though this is also forecast to increase (in terms of commitments, to over 4400 million ECUs by 1990) as the completion of the internal market approaches. Key areas such as education (including the COMETT and ERASMUS programmes) and the environment, which are central to the day-to-day lives of most Europeans, and in which the Community clearly needs to become involved, are relegated to the position of a minor item of social spending, representing just over 3.5 and 1 per cent respectively of total social policy expenditure in 1989. The European Council of February 1988 agreed to double in real terms the spending on the structural funds (EAGGF Guidance, ERDF, and ESF) between 1987 and 1993. Since 1989, moreover, the three structural funds have been set five precise objectives: to promote development in less prosperous regions; to 'convert' areas affected by industrial decline; to combat long-term unemployment; to help young people enter the labour market; and to facilitate agricultural development. Relative spending on each objective is also to be controlled. Objective 1 is to take up 60 per cent of expenditure, objective 2 11 per cent, objectives 3 and 4 14.5 per cent between them, and objective 5 14.5 per cent. All this certainly represents a move in the right direction, but in reality it only scratches at the surface of the issue.

The sums that the Community has spent on research, energy, and development aid have also been paltry, though these areas too are forecast to expand over the next few years as the proportion of the budget spent on agriculture is marginally reduced. In 1990 the Community expects to spend, in terms of commitments, 1723 million ECUs on research and investment, and 63 550 million ECUs on energy. The amount spent directly by the Community on coopera-tion with developing and non-member countries (including food aid) in 1989 amounts to just over 1000 million ECUs (around 2.7 per cent of the budget), though it should be remem-bered that the principal thrust of the Community's operations in the Third World is carried out through the Lomé Conventions with the so-called ACP states (see Appendix B). These Conventions are financed by the European Development Fund which does not form part of the budget.

The European Community is often charged by its critics with being an excessively bureau-cratic organization, which pampers its employees and suffers from inefficiency. While there may be an element of truth in some of these charges, it should also be noted that the admin-istration of the Community takes up less than 5 per cent of the budget (2154 million ECUs in 1989), which is probably not excessive for an organization of such varied interests and aspira-tions. Of this, 65.8 per cent went on the Commission, 18.8 per cent on the European Parlia-ment, 9.2 per cent on the Council, with the Economic and Social Committee, the Court of Justice, and the Court of Auditors accounting for the rest.

Finally, it should be noted that Community expenditure is often divided into two categories: compulsory expenditure and non-compulsory expenditure. Historically, the dis-tinction between the two has been largely political, and it essentially concerns the division of budgetary powers between the European Parliament and the Council (see Chapter 2). Com-pulsory expenditure can broadly be regarded as expenditure that the Community needs to meet its internal and external obligations, i.e. the Guarantee section of the agricultural budget (EAGGF), repayments, aid to member-states, and external commitments concerning the fisheries policy and cooperation with non-member countries. Non-compulsory expenditure is everything else, including the structural side of the EAGGF, the European Regional Development Fund, the European Social Fund, administration, as well as spending on energy, industry, and research. In policy terms, the growth of non-compulsory expenditure vis-à-vis compulsory expenditure can be regarded as a rough indication of the extent to which the Community is diversifying its activities away from agriculture and into other sectors. This has been constrained by limits that have been imposed on the growth of non-compulsory expenditure, but the relative growth of the two types of spending is shown in Table 6.5.

From Table 6.6 it can be seen that such a diversification has to an extent occurred throughout the 1980s, and is forecast to accelerate over the next few years as effects of the 1988 reforms are felt. However, one should remember that this shift concerns relatively small sums of money and is occurring in the context of continued domination of the budget by agriculture.

Table 6.6   Growth rates (per cent) in money terms for compulsory and non-compulsory expenditure (1980–88/89)

		1980	1981	1982	1983	1984	1985	1986	1987	1988	1989
Compulsory expenditure	AC	8.39	13.77	16.96	9.46	7.66	8.87	18.95	2.12	24.44	−4.11
	AP	9.25	16.62	17.81	9.37	7.81	9.21	19.45	1.07	25.13	−3.69
Non-compulsory expenditure	AC	32.85	15.79	14.60	27.77	17.00	−5.34	14.54	8.90	12.22	19.93
	AP	26.47	19.78	25.44	31.16	11.56	−10.20	39.18	8.30	9.58	20.67
Statistical maximum rate*		13.30	12.20	14.50	11.80	11.60	8.50	7.10	8.10	7.40	5.80
Deflator†		13.00	11.00	10.30	8.60	6.50	6.00	5.60	3.90	3.60	4.23

AC: Appropriations for commitments.
AP: Appropriations for payments.
*Article 203(9) of the EEC Treaty.
†GDP (market prices) deflator.
Source: see Table 6.1.

6.5   EQUITY ISSUES AND THE BRITISH PROBLEM: BUDGETARY CRISIS

A principal feature of the way in which the budget operates is that it tends to pay very little attention to issues of equity. There are various aspects to this. From the point of view of the personal distribution of incomes in the Community, the budgetary mechanisms are probably regressive in nature: the financing of a substantial proportion of the budget by means of a flat rate sales tax is one aspect of this, as is the vast expenditure on the price support side of the CAP. This is clearly an issue that will have to be addressed if and when the Community budget comes to take on greater macro-economic significance.

However, the equity issue that is most frequently highlighted by the media and by national politicians is the way in which the budget redistributes income regressively between the member-states. This is due to the fact that, as Ardy (1988) and others have shown, the budget has raised revenue and then allocated expenditure in a relatively haphazard fashion that has paid little attention to the relative wealth of member-states. This problem is compounded by the fact that the Community in fact has possessed no really accurate means of calculating the national incidence of the budget. In particular, this has led to the existence of the 'British problem', the fact that the United Kingdom has been a substantial net contributor to the EC budget, despite having a per capita national income that is one of the lowest in the Community. Godley (1980) estimated that in 1979 Britain was the major net contributor to the EC budget, to the extent of £1203 million in a year in which UK per capita GDP was the third lowest in the then Community of nine (only Ireland's and Italy's were lower). Ardy (1988) has estimated the net UK contribution in the early 1980s to be 1109 million ECUs at 1982 prices (0.32 per cent of GDP), while the Federal Republic of Germany made a net contribution of 2749 million ECUs and France one of 550 million ECUs at this time. The main net recipients were Italy (984 million ECUs), Greece (795 million ECUs), and Ireland (732 million ECUs). Some further insights into this situation can be obtained from Figure 6.4 and Table 6.7, which show how Community income and expenditure respectively have been broken down between member-states.

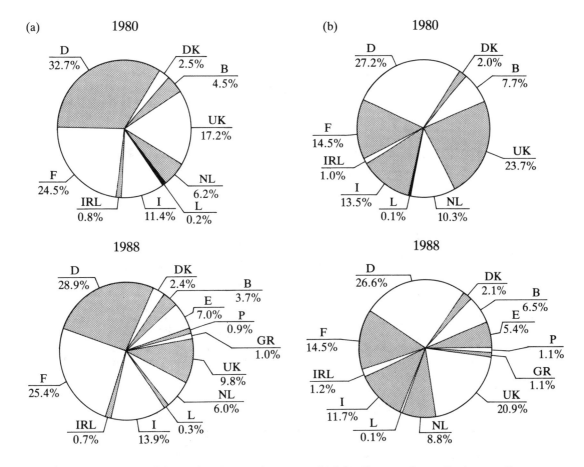

Figure 6.4 Financing of the budget by member-states. (a) Member-states' contributions to Community revenue (VAT + financial contributions and miscellaneous revenue + GNP-based resource in 1988). (b) Member-states' contributions to Community revenue (traditional own resources, after deduction of collection costs in 1988). (*Source:* as Table 6.1.)

From Figure 6.4 it can be seen that the United Kingdom was in 1980 contributing as much to Community revenue as France, which has a roughly similar population and a substantially greater per capita GNP; and considerably more than Italy, which has a broadly similar population and level of per capita GNP. This imbalance is to a large extent attributable to the large and growing extent to which the Community has been financed by VAT receipts. In the course of the 1980s, the situation has largely been remedied, by means of the measures that will be discussed below (the pie charts on the left of Figure 6.4 represent the actual situation, while the ones on the right show what the situation would have been without arrangements to ease the United Kingdom's position). Table 6.7, on the other hand, gives an example of how the United Kingdom receives less than what one might regard as its 'fair share' of Community expenditure.

In fact only 11.13 per cent of total Community spending went to Britain between 1985 and 1988, while France received 19 per cent, Italy 16.5 per cent, and West Germany 14.1 per cent, and the imbalance would have been much greater without the repayments that the United Kingdom has received. The imbalance in UK receipts is almost entirely the result of agricul-

Table 6.7 Categories of Community expenditure (per cent) in each member-state (average 1985–88)

	Belgium	Denmark	FRG	Greece	Spain*	France	Ireland	Italy	Luxembourg	Netherlands	Portugal*	UK
EAGGF Guarantee	42.4	87.3	81.8	69.3	27.8	81.1	67.3	69.5	0.7	90.5	13.9	56.9
EAGGF Guidance	0.9	1.5	2.1	4.7	1.0	3.3	4.2	3.3	0.7	0.6	4.9	2.6
Fisheries	0.0	0.3	0.0	0.0	0.2	0.1	0.2	0.1	0.0	0.1	0.4	0.2
Social Fund	2.8	3.9	2.5	6.2	10.5	5.0	14.5	8.6	0.4	1.6	24.8	13.4
Regional Fund	1.4	1.3	1.6	15.2	14.6	4.2	9.8	10.6	0.5	0.6	31.5	14.2
Transport	0.0	0.0	0.1	0.3	0.1	0.1	0.1	0.1	0.0	0.0	0.3	0.1
Research, energy, and industry	3.8	1.5	3.0	0.3	0.3	1.9	0.6	3.1	0.7	1.9	0.8	4.2
Administrative expenditure	44.1	0.9	1.1	0.3	0.3	0.6	0.5	0.5	95.2	0.6	0.4	0.7
Miscellaneous (including repayments to member-states)	4.6	3.3	7.8	3.6	45.2	3.7	2.8	4.2	1.8	4.1	23.0	7.7
Total	100.0	100.0	100.0	100.0	100.0	100.0	100.0	100.0	100.0	100.0	100.0	100.0

*Average 1986–88.
Source: see Table 6.1

tural expenditure: this, as we have seen, accounts for the bulk of Community spending, and the United Kingdom's agricultural sector, though generally very efficient, is small in comparison with that in other Community countries. Relatively high receipts through the other Community funds cannot hope to compensate for this state of affairs, hence Britain's net contribution.

British politicians, and in particular Mrs Thatcher, have not surprisingly made much of this situation, and have vociferously insisted on compensation and reform. At this stage it must be pointed out, however, that although Britain's position certainly offends against considerations of fairness, the United Kingdom was in fact aware that it would arise before entry into the Community. This was one of the issues in the referendum on British membership of the European Community in 1975. In addition, the sums involved, though of course considerable, in an absolute sense do not really warrant the strong reaction that has been forthcoming from the United Kingdom. One has therefore to consider why the reaction of the UK authorities has been so forceful. It should also be remembered that problems of fairness did not just concern the United Kingdom. From 1981 the Federal Republic of Germany became increasingly concerned by its position as the main contributor to the EC budget, and by the Fontainebleau Agreement it managed to negotiate a one-third reduction in its contribution to financing the compensation given to Britain.

In any event, the British and other equity problems have in practice been tackled in three ways. In the period before the Fontainebleau Agreement, the matter was dealt with on a year-by-year basis through a series of *ad hoc* arrangements negotiated at various European Councils, usually amid considerable acrimony and posturing. For example, the United Kingdom received rebates that reduced its net contribution for 1980 to £370 million, for 1981 to £430 million. This despite the existence from as far back as the Dublin Council of 1975 of complicated correction mechanisms that were never in practice triggered. Secondly, after Fontainebleau, the matter was settled on a more permanent basis. Britain was given a rebate on VAT payments of 1 billion ECUs for 1985, and thereafter would be granted a rebate (paid in practice by reducing the United Kingdom's VAT base) equivalent to two-thirds of the difference between its percentage share of VAT payments and its percentage share of allocated Community spending. This rebate is then made up by the other member-states, according to their percentage shares of VAT payments. As we have mentioned, an exception is made for West Germany, whose additional contribution is reduced by one-third. The complexity of the mechanism reflects the complexity of the political wheeling and dealing that brought it about. Finally, it should be added that the 1988 reforms have contributed to the alleviation of the budget's equity problems, and in particular the British issue, by capping the VAT base, limiting agricultural spending, and introducing the GNP-based 'fourth resource'. The effect of the budget as a whole is now marginally less regressive as a result.

Problems of equity have, however, not been the only ones to have plagued the budget, which, certainly before the 1988 reform, staggered from crisis to crisis, providing a convenient and relatively bloodless battleground for member-states (see below). If, as was suggested above, the budgetary process is to an extent a barometer for the condition of European integration, then the early and mid-1980s were decidedly turbulent. As well as having to contend with the issue of equity, the budget has suffered from inadequate procedures, from disputes between Parliament and Council, and from the fundamental inadequacy of its resources to meet the needs of the Community, especially at a time of expansion and rapidly growing ambition.

6.6   THE BUDGET IN THE FUTURE

To what extent have the reforms of 1984 and 1988 solved these problems? Clearly, they have to a large extent solved the 'British problem', although other, perhaps in the long run more important, equity issues remain. The forward planning introduced in 1988 will also remove much uncertainty from the budgetary process, as well as ensuring that the Community will not become bankrupt. The limited shifts in expenditure away from agriculture and into the structural funds are also to be welcomed, as is the increased targeting of expenditures. The very immediate issues have therefore been dealt with.

However, what the 1988 reforms have also done are to constrain budgetary growth in the years up to 1993. The central problems of the size of the budget and of the distribution of expenditure within it remain, and will be extremely difficult to tackle in the foreseeable future, at least given current national political realities. The fact is that the budget is probably still inadequate to meet the current needs of the Community, particularly since what there is of it is still dominated by agricultural price support spending.

The current situation is arguably such as to give cause for mild concern, but unless the present momentum of the integration progress slows down, in the future the issue may well escalate to the point where the need for an expanded budget becomes irresistible. First of all, the moves that have been initiated towards the completion of the internal market and towards monetary union will create imperatives and throw up problems and issues that the Community will find difficult to tackle with a budget of present proportions. At the most basic level, greater integration will inevitably mean that more functions of government are transferred from the national to the Community level. For example, monetary union would probably necessitate some centralization of monetary policy, and might even lead to centralization of other important areas such as social security (see Chapter 5). Exactly which functions of government are most appropriately carried out at which level of government depends to an extent on the model of integration one chooses to adopt. This sensitive but vital issue is addressed in the literature on fiscal federalism (see Oates, 1972, 1977), and it is clearly an item high on the future agenda of European integration. Broadly speaking, the literature on fiscal federalism tends to suggest that the macro-economic stabilization function of fiscal policy should be carried out at the central level within a federation, while the appropriate level at which to conduct its allocative functions and the provision of public goods depends on the nature of the public goods and on the degree of 'political homogeneity', i.e. the extent of agreement or otherwise at each level in the federation about the nature and quantities of the public goods to be provided. Where appropriate, the centralization of government functions can benefit all by reducing costs through economies of scale. Nevertheless, to the extent that more governmental functions will in fact be carried out at the Community level, there will be a need for more expenditure by the Community and thus a larger budget and greater fiscal integration.

Furthermore, it is generally accepted that any benefits resulting from greater integration will probably not be equitably distributed. This will raise issues both of equity and political expediency, since some compensation will have to be made available to the losers from the integration process in order to secure their cooperation and agreement to proposed changes. This will increase the need for an effective system of inter-country and inter-regional compensation, and thus strengthen the case for an enlarged budget. At the very least, more structural funds will be required to manage the effects of the increased rate of structural change that further integration will entail.

As matters stand, the limited size of the budget probably represents a major potential impediment to further European integration through the European Community, and at some stage this particular nettle will have to be grasped. Tackling this problem would not seem to be so difficult, provided of course that the political will is there to do so. At present, political realities would seem to preclude any substantial growth in the budget, but political realities have a habit of changing rapidly.

From time to time the possibility and consequences of an enlarged budget have been discussed and investigated by the Community. The most significant study that has thus far been carried out in this area was published in 1977, and is usually referred to as the MacDougall Report (EC Commission, 1977). This consists of the deliberations of a group of experts who were invited by the Commission to examine the role of public finance in European integration. The MacDougall Report notes how in most federations, such as the United States, central expenditure tends to amount to something like 20–25 per cent of GNP and plays a significant redistributive role in favour of less well off regions, whereas in the European Community it is only, as we have seen, around 1 per cent of Community GNP and it furthermore has very little effect on the distribution of income between member-states. It briefly looks at the likely impact of increasing Community expenditure to full-blown federal proportions, and to intermediate levels compatible with monetary and economic union, such as 5–7 and 7.5–10 per cent (including defence). These, together with a progressive tax base, are considered to be sufficient to achieve the degree of redistribution (an equalization of around 40 per cent of regional income differentials) found in most federations, as well as significant stabilization effects. The main concern of the report was, however, to consider the impact of the more modest, but politically more feasible, 2–2.5 per cent level of expenditure at Community level, to be achieved by transferring foreign aid, some unemployment benefits, and some vocational training to the Community, and by setting up a system of grants for weaker countries. The extra spending would be financed by increasing VAT on a progressive base. These changes would result in an equalization of 10 per cent of per capita income differentials in the Community and would contribute to stabilizing short-term fluctuations to an extent. They were considered to be probably just about sufficient to render a monetary union possible. The findings of the MacDougall Report are now obsolete, especially following the southern enlargement of the Community. Nevertheless, they give food for thought, and there will probably have to be another similar exercise if moves towards monetary union continue at the present pace.

6.7 EC BUDGETARY POLITICS

As outlined in Chapter 2, the European Parliament has since 1975 enjoyed joint budgetary powers with the Council of Ministers. In contrast to other areas of Community policy-making where the Commission–Council axis is crucial, the budgetary process has been dominated by regular clashes and conflict between the European Parliament and the Council of Ministers. Disagreement between the two budgetary authorities has centred on the overall size of the budget, the classification of expenditure between the compulsory and non-compulsory categories, and the amount of money allocated to non-compulsory expenditure. These disputes reflect the deep-seated tensions between the Parliament over the direction and scope of Community policy, and the Parliament's determination to use its budgetary powers as part of its long-running campaign for more formal powers. As indicated below, though the 1988 budgetary reforms represent a small victory for the Parliament in its battles with the Council, they have not eliminated all grounds for disagreement.

6.8   THE BUDGETARY PROCEDURE

Whereas EC policy-making is normally a lengthy and laborious process, the budgetary time-table must be adhered to if the budget is to be adopted on time. The budgetary procedure is as follows:

6.8.1   Commission's draft budget (January–February)

Prior to the 1988 budgetary reforms, the EC budget was an annual budget which ran from January to December. (See below for the modifications introduced by the 1988 reforms.) The Commission's Directorate-General for Budgets begins preparing the draft budget in January–February of the year preceding its coming into effect. As part of this process the Budget Directorate-General seeks expenditure estimates from other Directorate-Generals and takes into account Community trade, economic growth, and inflation rate forecasts. In accordance with Article 203 of the EEC Treaty, the Commission must send its preliminary draft budget to the Council of Ministers by 1 September. In practice, however, the Commission works to a (pragmatic) deadline of 15 June. A copy of the preliminary draft budget is also sent to the Parliament.

6.8.2   First Council reading of the draft budget (June–September)

Upon arrival at the Council of Ministers, the draft preliminary budget is scrutinized first by the Budget Committee (comprising senior officials from the member-states) and then by the COREPER in an attempt to resolve as many difficulties as possible before the meeting of the Council of Ministers to discuss the budget in July. At the July Council meeting, the finance ministers discuss and adopt the draft budget, acting on the basis of a qualified majority vote (for details of voting procedures in the Council of Ministers see p. 14). The use of majority voting is significant, as it means that it is possible for a coalition of member-states to form a blocking minority (23 out of 76 votes). The finance ministers' meeting is thus typically characterized by extensive behind-the-scenes negotiations between Commission and Council officials aimed at preventing the formation of such alliances. Once adopted, the Council's draft budget is then referred to the Parliament at the beginning of September.

6.8.3   First parliamentary reading of the draft budget (September–December)

The draft budget, as revised by the Council, must be laid before Parliament no later than 5 October, but in practice usually arrives in early September. MEPs then have 45 days in which to consider and vote on it. Detailed scrutiny of the draft budget is carried out by the Parliament's Budget Committee with other specialist Committees (e.g. Social Affairs, External Relations) commenting on specific items. The budget is then debated and voted on at a plenary session which is normally held in early October. At this stage, the options open to the Parliament are as follows:

1. It may adopt the draft budget, in which case the budget is said to be finally adopted. This has happened only once in the case of the supplementary budget in 1987 when the Parliament refused to be associated with the procedure.
2. It may propose *modifications* to compulsory expenditure, acting by a majority of the votes cast.

3. It may propose *amendments* to non-compulsory expenditure acting on the basis of a majority of the membership of the Parliament.

The official deadline for returning the draft budget to the Council is 19 November, while unofficially the deadline is 25 October.

6.8.4 The Council's second reading of the budget (November)

Following a conciliation meeting with a delegation of the Parliament, the Council considers the draft as revised by Parliament. The finance ministers have 15 days in which to act. The voting rules in the Council at this stage are as follows:

1. For *amendments* (to non-compulsory expenditure) the Council may alter each of the amendments adopted by the Parliament by a qualified majority.
2. For *modifications* (to compulsory expenditure):
   (a) If a modification proposed by Parliament does not result in an overall increase in expenditure (i.e. is offset by a reduction elsewhere), the Council may, acting by a qualified majority, reject the modification (the so-called negative majority). If it fails to act, the modification stands as accepted.
   (b) Where a modification proposed by Parliament has the effect of increasing the total amount of expenditure, the Council may, acting by a qualified majority, accept it. If no action is taken, the proposal is rejected.

6.8.5 Parliament's second reading and Adoption of the Budget (December)

At its second reading, Parliament has 15 days in which to act. By now, the Council has already had the last word on compulsory expenditure; attention is thus focused upon non-compulsory expenditure, over which MEPs have the final say. The Parliament, acting by a majority of its members and three-fifths of the votes cast, may amend or reject the changes made to its amendments (to non-compulsory expenditure) by the Council.

Parliament's power to amend—in practice, to increase—non-compulsory expenditure is not, however, unlimited. The upper limit of this increase is determined by the so-called 'maximum rate of increase'. This maximum rate is calculated for each year by the Commission according to a complex formula based upon inflation rates during the previous financial year, the average variation in member-states' budgets, and real GNP growth in the Community. Application of this formula has, for example, produced maximum rates of increase of 8.1 per cent in 1987, 7.4 per cent in 1988 and 5.8 per cent in 1989. Once fixed, the maximum rate of increase can be changed only by joint agreement of the Council and Parliament. Article 203 (9) of the EEC Treaty specifies that the Parliament's *margin of manoeuvre* (i.e. the amount by which it may increase non-compulsory expenditure) is *half* of the maximum rate of increase (i.e. 2.9 per cent in 1989). Furthermore, the Parliament's margin of manoeuvre is guaranteed even if the Council were to use up all the maximum rate in establishing its draft budget. In practice, since 1979 the Council has set as a 'rule of conduct' when adopting its draft budget not to allow increases in non-compulsory expenditure to exceed half the maximum rate. The reasons for this strategy are straightforward: if the Council increases non-compulsory expenditure by less than this amount, Parliament can claim all the remaining portion up to the maximum rate of increase. If, on the other hand, the Council adds on more than half, then Parliament is still entitled to its margin of manoeuvre (Shackleton, 1989). As indicated below, application of the maximum rate of increase has been the source of several budgetary disputes between the Council and the Parliament.

Once the budgetary procedure has been completed, Parliament then votes on the budget and the President of the Parliament declares it to be finally adopted. However, the Parliament has the power under Article 203 (8) to reject the budget at this stage (acting by a majority of its members and two-thirds of the votes cast) and to ask the Commission to prepare a new draft budget. In theory, this course of action may only be taken if there are 'very important reasons' for rejection; in practice, rejection is a political action. The Parliament has rejected the budget three times: in December 1979 (for the 1980 budget); in December 1982 (for the 1982 supplementary budget; and in December 1984 (for the 1985 budget).

In the case of rejection, the Commission is called upon to prepare a revised draft budget. In order to save time, however, the Commission generally modifies the existing draft budget rather than begin the entire budget procedure again. This new version of the budget is then presented as soon as possible to the Council and the Parliament in a 'third reading'. If the budget has not been adopted by the beginning of the financial year, the so-called 'provisional twelfths arrangement' comes into effect. This arrangement allows the Community to spend up to one-twelfth of the preceding year's budget each month, thereby allowing the Community to function until a new budget is adopted.

In practice, the budgetary procedure is much less clear-cut than the above outline might suggest. From the outset, for example, the Commission is lobbied by MEPs, member-states, and key interest groups (notably the agricultural lobby) over the content of the preliminary draft budget. Secondly, the Parliament is not always united over the budget; political groups within the Parliament have special interests that they wish to see supported in the budget. Thirdly, it is oversimplistic to view all budgetary disputes in terms of the Parliament versus the Council of Ministers. In reality, the Parliament often has allies within the Council of Ministers. The British government, for example, has been a firm supporter of the Parliament in its bid to reduce agricultural expenditure while the Iberian member-states have backed MEPs' demands for increases in the structural funds. Finally, it should be borne in mind that the budgetary disputes between the Council and the Parliament are to some extent a device used by the Parliament as part of its deliberate strategy of increasing its powers by stretching its existing powers to the full.

6.9   BUDGETARY CONFLICTS

Since 1979, the Parliament has sought to defend and extend its budgetary powers, which are only grudgingly accepted by the Council. During this period the Parliament has consistently sought to increase the overall size of the community's budget and to switch the balance of expenditure away from compulsory expenditure—especially away from the CAP—in favour of non-compulsory expenditure. For their part, member-states have generally speaking been anxious to limit the size of national contributions to the EC budget and to curb the Parliament's enthusiasm for extending the scope of Community policies. These tensions have given rise to a number of budgetary disputes such as the following:

1980 budget   At its first reading of the 1980 budget the Parliament increased the overall funding in the draft budget, but reduced the allocation for the EAGGF Guarantee section. As the Council at its second reading failed to act on this proposal, the Parliament rejected the budget for the first time ever in December 1979. The 1980 budget was finally adopted in July 1980 after the Council had agreed to increase funding, especially for the Regional Fund.

1982 budget   The 1982 budgetary procedure was marked by conflict between the Parliament and the Council over the classification of expenditure between non-compulsory and compulsory categories, which in turn affected the Parliament's scope for raising the level of non-compulsory expenditure. After the Council refused to enter into negotiations on the matter, the Parliament went ahead and adopted the budget. Subsequently, negotiations were held on the question of classification, which resulted in the June 1982 Joint Declaration on budgetary procedure which sought to clarify the position. At this point, the Council withdrew the Court case it had brought against the Parliament on the matter.

1985 budget   In December 1984, Parliament rejected the draft 1985 budget on the grounds that agricultural spending was covered for only ten months and that no provision had been made for the UK budget rebate. In April 1985, the Council gave in and submitted a new draft budget which covered the disputed expenditure.

1986 budget   During its first reading, Parliament ascertained that the draft 1986 budget did not include sufficient funding to cover the costs of the accession of Spain and Portugal, particularly with regard to the structural funds. Nor, in the Parliament's view, were there adequate funds to cover existing commitments ('the burden of the past'). Since the Council ignored the MEPs' opinion, the Parliament at its second reading went ahead and adopted a budget of 33.3 billion ECUs, i.e. 629 million ECUs higher than the Council's second draft. In response, the Council and several member-states brought an action before the European Court of Justice, claiming that the Parliament had exceeded its powers. This claim was upheld by the Court in its judgment of 3 July 1986 which annulled the 1986 budget and ruled that the Council and Parliament must come to an agreement on the adoption of the budget. A new budget was adopted on 10 July 1986 which was 1.86 billion ECUs higher than the budget adopted in December 1986 and thus satisfied most MEPs!

6.10   THE POLITICS OF BUDGETARY REFORM

As indicated in the earlier sections of this chapter, the *1988 Interinstitutional Agreement* has brought about some important changes in the composition of and regulations surrounding the EC budget. Several factors prompted these reforms. First, as highlighted above, the Parliament has since 1979 repeatedly expressed its concern over the diminishing size of the Community's resources and the spiralling costs of the CAP. Secondly, several member-states have, in recent years, also expressed reservations about the cost of the CAP (though member-states with significant agricultural constituencies have been, for obvious reasons, rather more reticent). Thirdly, during the early 1980s, the problem of the UK budgetary contributions (see above) called into question the whole system of how the budget should be financed. Fourthly, the entry of Spain and Portugal into the Community in 1986 placed further demands on the Community's already stretched resources and increased pressures for structural reform of the budget to increase the structural funds. Finally, the agreement to complete the internal market by 1992 convinced the Commission of the need to ensure that the Community had sufficient resources to implement the necessary accompanying policies (e.g. social policy and regional policy).

The above pressures culminated in the 1988 budget reforms agreed at the Brussels Summit in February 1988 and adopted the following June. As explained earlier in this chapter, the member-states agreed at this meeting to introduce a new source of revenue based on GNP, to bring agricultural spending under control, to double the structural funds, and to establish a five-year perspective for spending. These changes have prompted changes in the budgetary process that seem to have strengthened slightly the position of the Parliament and have, therefore, reduced the tension between the two budgetary authorities. Indeed, the 1989 budget was adopted without disagreement and well ahead of time. The introduction of a five-year frame of reference for expenditure is particularly significant in this respect; the introduction of budgetary discipline has forced the Parliament and the Council to agree expenditure plans, and financial ceilings for all categories of expenditure as well as the maximum rate of increase for the period 1988–92, thereby (in theory at least) removing the basis for annual conflict. The Parliament has also achieved three of its objectives: increased Community resources; a reduction in agricultural spending; and a substantial increase in the structural funds (increased by 22 per cent in 1989). Furthermore, the reforms specify that if, for any reason, compulsory expenditure rises above the planned increase, this will not adversely affect non-compulsory expenditure.

It would, however, be wrong to assume that all grounds for dispute between the two budgetary authorities have disappeared. For example, the Council is now making a distinction between 'privileged' and 'non-privileged' non-compulsory expenditure. According to this formula, the structural funds, research and the Integrated Mediterranean Programmes are regarded as 'privileged' expenditure, whereas policy areas such as environment, energy and transport are designated as 'non-privileged' expenditure. To the irritation of MEPs, the Council is applying a 'maximum rate of increase' to the so-called non-privileged expenditure, while allowing the 'privileged' expenditure to expand at the rates agreed at the Brussels Summit. The Parliament argues that there is no basis in the Treaty for such a practice.

6.11   CONCLUSION

The European Community budget is, in many respects, a barometer of attitudes towards integration. In particular, arguments over the size of the budget, the justice of budgetary contributions and the unfairness of the CAP reveal the extent to which member-governments continue to measure the value of Community membership in terms of national costs and benefits. On the other hand, the 1988 budgetary reforms may prove a significant turning-point in this respect in so far as they reflect a clear acknowledgement on the part of member-states of the need to put an end to the perennial problem of inadequate resources. Analysis of the budget procedure also highlights the way in which the Parliament has used—and sometimes exceeded—its budgetary powers in order to establish its budgetary role. Although it might be argued that the Council remains the more powerful of the two budgetary authorities, it is nevertheless clear that the European Parliament enjoys far more influence over the EC budget than many West European national parliaments exercise over national finances.

REFERENCES/FURTHER READING

Ardy, B. (1988), 'The national incidence of the European Community budget', *Journal of Common Market Studies*, **XXVI**, 401–430.

Denton, G. (1984), 'Re-structuring the EC budget: implications of the Fontainebleau Agreement', *Journal of Common Market Studies*, **XXIII**, 117–140.

EC Commission (1977), 'Report of the study group on the role of public finance in European integration', (MacDougall Report).

EC Commission (1989), 'Community public finance—the European budget after the 1988 reform'.

Godley, W. (1980), 'The UK and the Community budget', in Wallace, W. (Ed.), *Britain in Europe*, Heinemann, London, 72–90.

Nicoll, W. (1986), 'From rejection to repudiation: EC budgetary affairs in 1985', *Journal of Common Market Studies*, **XXV**, 31–50.

Nicoll, W. (1988), 'The long march of the EC's 1988 budget', *Journal of Common Market Studies*, **XXVII**, 161–170.

Nugent, N. (1989), *The Government and Politics of the European Community*, Macmillan, London.

Oates, W. (1972), *Fiscal Federalism*, Harcourt, Brace, Jovanovitch, New York.

Oates, W. (1977), 'Fiscal federalism in theory and practice: applications to the EC', in EC Commission (1977).

Padoa-Schioppa, T. (1984), 'Money, economic policy and Europe', EC Commission, European Perspectives, Luxembourg.

Shackleton, M. (1989), 'The budget of the European Community', in Lodge, J. (Ed.), *The European Community and the Challenge of the Future*, Frances Pinter, London.

Wallace, H. (1980), *Budgetary Politics: The Finances of the European Communities*, George Allen & Unwin, London.

SEVEN

THE COMMON AGRICULTURAL POLICY

7.1 INTRODUCTION

The European Community's Common Agricultural Policy is perhaps the aspect of European integration that has most impressed itself on public consciousness, certainly in the United Kingdom. This is not surprising: expenditure on agriculture accounts each year for something in the region of 70 per cent of all Community expenditure; food is a fundamental item of concern for most people; and 'butter mountains', 'wine lakes', and 'lamb wars' make irresistible copy for the media.

But what is the true nature of the CAP? Is it really all bad as the British perception would imply? If so, what can be done to change it? Why has change proved so elusive? These are the themes of this chapter.

7.2 THE NATURE AND FUNCTIONING OF THE CAP

There are two aspects to the CAP: a price support mechanism, which attempts to create a unified market for agricultural produce throughout the Community; and a structural policy, which attempts to influence such factors as the nature of the workforce, the size of farms, their efficiency, the methods they employ, and the technology they use. Clearly, the structural part of the CAP is potentially of great importance. Thus far it has, however, been comparatively neglected, despite the ambitions of the Mansholt plan in the late 1960s (see Table 7.4). The price support system has been by far the most important and controversial aspect of the CAP and it is on this that we will concentrate.

Essentially, the price support mechanism sets out to guarantee minimum prices for farmers for much of their produce. These prices are normally set higher than supply, demand, and world market prices would dictate, in order to encourage farmers to produce more than they would in a free market. The aims of this are to make the Community self-sufficient (or almost so) in important food items, to provide a reasonable livelihood for people who work on the land, and to promote European integration by achieving a unified market in a key area of economic activity.

Prices for the products covered by the CAP are set each year by the Council of Ministers, following a complex and lengthy series of negotiations between representatives of member-states. It is important to note that prices are not always (or even perhaps usually) set on the basis of economically rational criteria, but are often the result of political negotiation, sometimes involving factors that have very little to do with what consumers want to eat. A target price is fixed for each good covered by the price support mechanism, as is an intervention price (sometimes as much as 30 per cent lower than the target price) below which the market price is not allowed to fall. Broadly, target prices are prices to consumers, while intervention prices are prices for producers. If market forces result in prices falling below the intervention level, Community agencies intervene by purchasing the products in question in the quantities required to push the price back up to the desired level.

This intervention buying occurs when prices have been set too high so that farmers produce more than consumers want to buy. The surpluses that the Community buys up are generally stored, hence the famous or infamous 'wine lakes', 'beef mountains', 'butter mountains,' etc. Whenever possible, the surpluses are exported at the world market price. This is usually below the EC price, and so exporters are compensated by means of Export Restitutions, which are payments equal to the difference between the intervention price and the world market price for the good in question. Sometimes, these disposals touch on political sensitivities, and we see banner headlines of the 'shock horror: cheap EC butter for the Russians!' mould. Occasionally, some of the stored surpluses are distributed to hospitals, old people, the poor, or the starving in the Third World. In some instances, they are changed into other products, e.g. part of the wine lake has been turned into industrial alcohol. All in all, the CAP's surpluses and their disposal has become a major issue in European integration, providing ample and effective propaganda for its detractors.

The integrity of the market and the desired price are protected from competition from outside the Community by a variable levy. This is the Community's Common External Tariff for agricultural products, and, as its name would imply, it is frequently adjusted so as to allow into the Community only sufficient imports to bridge any gap that might exist between internal demand and supply. If the internal price has been set at a level that produces surpluses, then clearly the variable levy would be high enough to exclude all imports. The variable levy is calculated on the basis of the difference between a product's threshold price (the target price less transport and storage costs) and the cheapest consignment entering the Community on any one day.

The essence of the CAP's price support mechnism can be graphically illustrated by means of a simple supply and demand model, which should be accessible to most non-economists. This is shown in Figure 7.1, using the hypothetical example of the market for wheat in the European Community. Here the curve D_{Priv} represents the private demand for wheat by consumers in member countries, i.e. the amounts of wheat that consumers wish to buy at various prices; S_{Eur} represents the EC supply curve for wheat, i.e. the amounts of wheat that EC farmers are willing to produce at different prices; and $0-P_{World}$ is the world market price for wheat, i.e. the lowest price at which wheat is available for import into the Community. $P_{World}-S_w$ is the world supply curve for wheat. For simplicity the 'small country model' is adopted, and $P_{World}-S_w$ is somewhat unrealistically shown as being perfectly elastic, i.e. increased demand by the European Community for imports from the rest of the world does not increase world market price.

With free trade and no CAP the price of wheat in the Community would be $0-P_{World}$, at which consumers would buy $0-Q_5$. $0-Q_1$ of this would be produced by EC farmers, and the rest (Q_1-Q_5) would be imported from the lowest cost producers in the rest of the world. With a totally exclusive variable levy of at least $0-P_{Eq}$ and no CAP price support intervention, the EC price of wheat would be the one that equates internal supply and demand, i.e. $0-P_{Eq}$, at which $0-Q_3$ would be bought and sold. Of course no wheat would be imported.

Assuming, however, that the EC desired price for wheat is set at $0-P_{EC}$ and that the variable levy is completely exclusive, then problems result. At this price producers will put $0-Q_4$

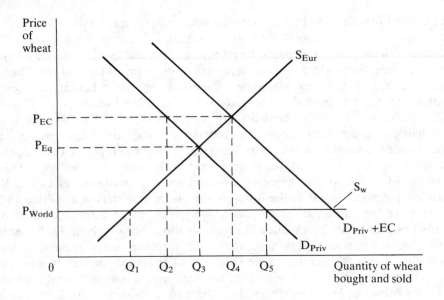

Figure 7.1   The market for wheat in the European Community.

wheat on the market, but consumers only want to buy $0-Q_2$. Therefore a surplus of wheat equivalent to Q_2-Q_4 is generated. Without any action by the EC authorities the market will tend to adjust so that the price of wheat falls towards $0-P_{Eq}$. However, the Community enters the market and buys the surplus Q_2-Q_4, thereby ensuring that the price does not fall below the desired level. This is then disposed of, or goes to form part of the wheat mountain. The curve D_{Priv} + EC thus represents the summation of private demand and intervention buying by the EC.

It is important to note that for most agricultural products the intervention price is not in fact set above the equivalent of $0-P_{Eq}$, surpluses are not generated, and some imports are allowed—not every product has its own lake or mountain! However, CAP prices are very often considerably above the world market price ($0-P_{World}$).

A brief examination of the welfare effects of the CAP provides some important insights into its effects. These are illustrated in Figure 7.2. Here the market for an agricultural product is again modelled in the simplest way possible, with D_{Eur} representing the EC demand curve for the product, S_{Eur} the internal supply curve, and $P_{World}-S_w$ the world supply curve. This time the EC price ($0-P_{EC}$) is assumed to be above the world market price ($0-P_{World}$), but below the self-sufficiency price ($0-P_{Eq}$). At the internal price of $0-P_{Eq}$ consumers buy $0-Q_3$ of the product, of which $0-Q_2$ is produced internally with the remainder (Q_2-Q_3) being imported at the world market price plus a variable levy of $P_{World}-P_{EC}$. With free trade and no CAP the internal price would be $0-P_{World}$, consumption $0-Q_4$, internal production $0-Q_1$, and imports Q_1-Q_4. *Vis-à-vis* such a situation, consumers under the CAP therefore consume less food (an amount equivalent to Q_3-Q_4), and pay more for it (by $P_{World}-P_{EC}$), while EC producers are subsidized to expand their output by Q_1-Q_2. Producers outside of the Community are required to forfeit exports equivalent to Q_1-Q_2 (because of EC import substitution—the production effect) plus Q_3-Q_4 (because of lower demand at the higher price—the consumption effect of the CAP).

In welfare terms, consumers suffer a loss of consumers' surplus under the CAP *vis-à-vis* an

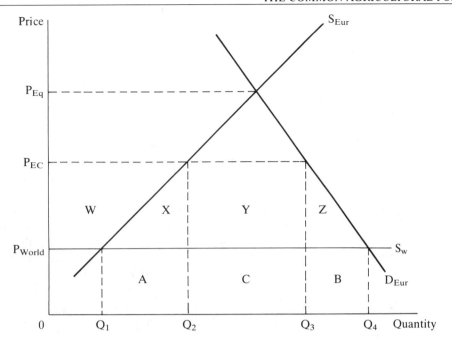

Figure 7.2   The welfare effects of the CAP.

(albeit improbable) free trade scenario equivalent to the area W + X + Y + Z. Of this, W is redistributed to producers in the form of producers' surplus, while Y (the variable levy $P_{World}-P_{EC} \times Q_2-Q_3$ imports) goes into the EC budget in the form of tariff revenues. There is considerable academic debate on whether transfers of this sort are neutral or in fact lead to welfare losses. Nevertheless, what is indisputable is that an amount of welfare equivalent to areas X + Z is not redistributed, but is lost altogether as a result of the CAP, X being efficiency losses from the misallocation of resources in production which results from less efficient producers being permitted to enter the market, and Z being a consumption side loss due to higher price and lower consumer demand. X and Y are sometimes known as the deadweight losses which result from the CAP. Countries outside the Community are allowed exports to the value of area C ($0-P_{World} \times Q_2-Q_3$), but are deprived of sales to the Community equivalent to area A + B. It is important to note that losses of welfare are greater the more the EC price is above world market prices.

7.3   THE BENEFITS OF THE CAP

The much maligned CAP has undoubtedly resulted in some benefits for EC countries since its inception. We will consider the following, which are among the most important:

1. The CAP has ensured that EC countries now enjoy widespread self-sufficiency in agriculture. This has led to:
   (a) Balance of payments advantages. The Community has experienced a major change in its agricultural trading position over the last two or three decades, from being a substantial net importer to now being a large net exporter of many major agricultural products. As will be seen below, this has been achieved at a large internal and external cost.

(b) Abundant food. The CAP has ensured security of supply of agricultural products in the Community. Income permitting, EC consumers have access to plentiful supplies of food and consume a nutritious and varied diet. This is something that we have come to take for granted, but it is none the less an important point in an uncertain world in which there are widespread food shortages, even in developed countries. Again, this has been achieved at a price.

2. The CAP has resulted in higher agricultural incomes than might otherwise have been the case. This has resulted mainly from the artificially high prices that have been guaranteed to farmers for many products. However, as will be considered below, the CAP has proved a somewhat inequitable and inefficient way of achieving this objective, and rural welfare remains an important issue in Europe.

3. The CAP has enabled European agriculture to experience rapid technological change and productivity increases in recent years. Crop and livestock yields have risen rapidly, and the number of people employed on the land has more than halved (from 19 million in 1960 to 7.23 million in 1987 in the Community of ten and from 16.96 million in 1970 to 9.8 million in 1987 in the enlarged Community of twelve). This has happened as a result of high prices, which have led to high profits for the most efficient farmers, which in turn have induced high levels of investment and research and development in the industry. Table 7.1 gives an indication of the increases that there have been in the productivity of EC agriculture in recent years.

However, it should also be noted that this very increase in productivity has contributed to the problem of surpluses by increasing agricultural supply in the Community. The fac-

Table 7.1 Factors in agricultural production and productivity
100 = average 1979–81

	Final production (volume)	Productivity of intermediate consumption inputs	Ratio of farmgate to input prices	Net value-added of the sector (real)	Farm labour	Net value-added per person (real)
1977	90.3	98.6	106.3	103.8	107.1	102.1
1978	95.0	99.0	107.8	104.7	104.6	105.4
1979	98.6	98.2	104.5	104.6	102.3	102.9
1980	100.5	99.7	99.2	96.2	100.5	96.3
1981	100.9	102.2	97.1	99.2	97.3	100.8
1982	105.6	104.8	97.3	109.6	94.1	111.5
1983	105.5	103.5	95.4	106.5	93.9	105.0
1984	108.4	106.2	93.4	108.1	92.2	108.3
1985	107.9	104.3	93.8	102.8	90.5	103.0
1986	110.1	105.5	96.9	105.2	89.3	104.9
1987	108.8	104.2	98.2	98.9	87.0	99.8

Source: EC Commission. 'The agricultural situation in the Community'. 1988 report.

tory farming, chemical-intensive techniques that have tended to accompany productivity increases have additionally contributed to some of the serious ecological problems that are now in the forefront of public consciousness.

4. Finally, the CAP has to a large extent succeeded in achieving the objective of a single and unified market in European agriculture, even if occasional aberrations such as the 'lamb war' between Britain and France do still occur. This has been achieved despite the strains imposed by the southern enlargement of the Community. The economic and political impact of this contribution to integration in Western Europe should certainly not be underestimated. It is probably fair to say that this, along with other advantages of the CAP, tends to be emphasized to a greater extent in EC countries other than the United Kingdom.

7.4 THE DISADVANTAGES OF THE CAP

Despite the above benefits, however, the CAP has been consistently attacked, particularly in the United Kingdom, and interestingly enough from all sides of the political spectrum. This is because the faults of the policy lie both in its equity and its efficiency, and because they tend to be very visible and thus easy to use for propaganda purposes. In assessing the criticisms of the CAP, the reader should bear in mind that most countries and supranational organizations have in the past, do at present, and would in future protect agriculture by some means or other. All subsidy and protectionism involves costs, and so in evaluating the CAP the relevant comparison should probably be not between the CAP and free trade and no subsidies, but rather between the CAP and the system of agricultural support that would be likely to replace it. We can summarize the principal costs of the CAP as follows:

1 The CAP has resulted in high food prices and welfare losses for European consumers. Community prices for most agricultural products are significantly above world market prices as a result of the price support policy, and this has resulted in the kind of welfare losses discussed in the context of Figure 7.2. It is important to emphasize that the essential philosophy of the CAP is to subsidize agriculture by means of the price mechanism, rather than by direct public expenditure. Thus, in contrast to for example the 'deficiency payments' system formerly used by the United Kingdom, the burden of supporting Community agriculture under the CAP falls predominantly on people who buy food, i.e. all consumers, and welfare losses are consequently maximized. The large proportion of the EC budget that is spent on the CAP represents only a small proportion of Community GDP (see Table 7.4) and it is but the tip of a very large iceberg of agricultural subsidy.

Empirical estimates of the internal welfare losses resulting from the CAP vary from 0.32 to over 1 per cent of Community GDP, the higher estimates (e.g. Tyers, 1985; Spencer, 1985; Tyers and Anderson, 1986) being produced by more sophisticated and probably more realistic methods than the lower ones (e.g. Morris, 1980; Buckwell et al., 1982; Tyers and Anderson, 1987), which are based on simpler models. Studies of individual sectors tend to confirm these substantial welfare losses. Harling and Thompson's 1985 study of the poultry estimates the deadweight loss in this sector in the United Kingdom and West Germany between 1975 and 1977 to be around $10.5 million, while Bale and Lutz (1981) estimate losses of $1112.4 million for West Germany, $737.3 million for France, and $112.4 million for the United Kingdom from the price support of beef, sugar, maize, and wheat alone. (For a comprehensive survey of empirical studies on the CAP see Demekas et al., 1988.)

2 The CAP's price support policy has consistently resulted in surpluses in many agricultural products (equivalent to Q_2–Q_4 if we look back to Figure 7.1). Table 7.2 gives an indication

Table 7.2   EC self-sufficiency in selected agricultural products 1980–87 (%)

	1980–81*	1986†	1987†
Cereals (excluding rice)	102.4	112.0	111.5
Rice	77.0	81.1	82.7
Sugar	128.5	129.2	113.7
Fresh fruit (excluding citrus)	87.0	86.0	88.0
Citrus fruit	70.0	74.0	76.0
Wine	106.1	107.4	106.8
Potatoes	101.5	102.4	101.0
Beef/veal	102.2	106.2	107.6
Poultry	107.2	104.1	105.6
Lamb	74.0	78.7	78.9
Pork	100.4	101.8	102.7
Eggs	101.2	102.0	101.4
Fresh milk products	100.4	100.5	100.5

*Ten-member EC.
†Twelve-member EC.
Source: see Table 7.1 (adapted).

of the extent to which Community supply exceeds demand in certain key products. A proportion of the surpluses have ended up as the 'wine lakes', etc. Community 'stocks' of butter, for example, amounted according to the Commission to nearly 1.3 million tonnes at their height in late 1986, though they had been reduced by nearly 50 per cent by the end of 1988 as a result of recent reforms. The skimmed milk powder mountain stood at 846 800 tonnes in 1986 (reduced to 230 000 tonnes in 1988), the beef mountain hovered around 800 000 tonnes in the mid to late 1980s, while the wheat mountain grew to around 12 million tonnes around the same period. CAP surpluses are the consequence of:

(a) Supply-side factors. High prices have directly increased production, while productivity has increased as a result of high levels of investment and research and development in the industry.

(b) Demand-side factors. The income elasticity of demand for food in EC countries is low (estimated at around 0.2), since, as incomes in European countries increase, people tend to spend their extra money on goods and services other than basic foods. Because of this, as well as the fact that the population of EC countries is growing very slowly, demand for basic food products has remained relatively static.

Apart from the dubious morality and waste of having all these mountains and lakes at a time when a large proportion of the world is starving, surpluses provide powerful and very visible ammunition for the opponents of European integration.

3   The CAP has had various redistributive effects, which might be considered on the whole undesirable.

(a) It has redistributed income from the rest of the world to European farmers and governments, through import replacement and the variable levy (see Figure 7.2 above). This will be considered in greater detail below.

(b) It has redistributed income from consumers who pay high prices to farmers who benefit from them (Figure 7.2). This has led the CAP to be characterized by *The Economist* as 'a classic case of the tail wagging the dog'.

(c) It has probably had a regressive effect on the personal distribution of income since it is consumers who pay the bulk of the cost of the CAP, and people on low incomes spend a greater proportion of their incomes on food than people who are better off.

(d) It has redistributed income among EC member-states. In particular, the United Kingdom has suffered from this since the UK agricultural sector is relatively small, albeit very efficient. This has been the cause of all the fuss in recent years over Britain's net contributions to the EC budget and the forcefully pursued negotiations to ensure budget rebates (see Chapter 6). Furthermore, it is important to note that not all agricultural products have been covered by the price support mechanism, and there have been frequent accusations, notably by the Italians and the Greeks, of bias in favour of foodstuffs predominantly produced in Northern Europe. There is also a regional dimension to this latter point. Studies of the extent to which the CAP redistributes income between member-states (e.g. Buckwell *et al.*, 1982; Spencer, 1986) in fact suggest that the United Kingdom, Italy and West Germany are, in order, the main losers from the CAP, while the Netherlands, Ireland, and Denmark are the major net beneficiaries.

More sophisticated studies, using general equilibrium models (Breckling *et al.*, 1987; Stoeckel and Breckling, 1988) generally confirm this ranking, but estimate that France is a net beneficiary of the CAP.

4   The CAP has had adverse effects on non-Community countries.

(a) It has depressed world agricultural trade and has denied farmers in other countries fair access to one of the world's most important markets. There has been a large amount of trade diversion, i.e. cheap and efficiently produced products from the rest of the world being displaced in EC markets by more expensive goods produced by farmers in EC member countries (see Chapters 3 and 4). This has been the result of high internal prices and the variable levy. Returning to Figure 7.2, we can recall that in this example the lost exports amounted to $Q_1-Q_2 + Q_3-Q_4$, with a value equivalent to areas A + B. In the case of a product in surplus (see Figure 7.1) non-Community producers are of course totally excluded from the market.

(b) It has depressed market prices in the rest of the world, to the further detriment of producers elsewhere, by increasing world supply and cutting world demand. Furthermore, the Community's policy of heavily subsidizing the export of surplus produce through export restitutions can be interpreted as dumping, and, as well as being somewhat morally dubious, has the effect of cutting world market prices still further.

Table 7.3 outlines the development of world and EC trade in agricultural and other products over recent years. It can be seen that EC imports of food have fallen, and its exports to the rest of the world have increased in the context of a situation in which world exports of agricultural products have fallen.

Empirical studies (e.g. Koester, 1982; Koester and Valdes, 1984; Anderson and Tyers, 1984; Tyers and Anderson, 1986, 1987; Matthews, 1985) confirm that the CAP considerably depresses world agriculture prices, reducing them *vis-à-vis* complete liberalization by 0.7–13 per cent in the case of wheat, 2.5–14.3 per cent for coarse grains, 4.5–18 per cent for ruminant meat, and 10.5–28.3 per cent for dairy products. The range of findings should warn the reader against taking empirical studies of this sort too literally. The best study in this area, by the

Table 7.3   World exports and EC external trade in all products, agricultural products and other products*

Twelve-member Community	1980	1981	1982	1983	1984	1985	1986	1987
World exports								
All products	1 604.4	1 628.1	1 513.2	1 481.9	1 574.8	1 580.0	1 673.2	1 928.0
of which: agricultural products	243.6	243.1	220.8	217.7	229.6	216.7	230.1	256.9
other products	1 360.8	1 385.0	1 292.4	1 264.2	1 345.2	1 363.3	1 443.1	1 671.1
External EC trade								
Exports:								
all products	305.0	296.9	278.8	269.7	278.5	289.0	336.3	391.7
of which: agricultural products	28.8	30.8	26.4	24.9	26.2	26.1	28.3	32.8
Imports:								
all products	393.9	353.4	327.6	304.8	311.3	310.1	329.1	392.6
of which: agricultural products	62.8	53.6	50.3	48.0	48.6	46.7	51.9	58.7
World exports of agricultural products as percentage of total world exports	15.2	14.9	14.6	14.7	14.6	13.7	13.8	13.3
EC exports of agricultural products as percentage of total EC exports	9.4	10.4	9.5	9.2	94	9.0	8.4	8.4
EC imports of agricultural products as percentage of total EC imports	15.9	15.2	15.4	15.7	15.6	15.1	15.8	15.0
Index changes (1980 = 100)								
World exports:								
all products	100.0	101.5	94.3	92.4	98.2	98.5	104.3	120.2
agricultural products	100.0	99.8	90.6	89.4	94.3	89.0	94.5	105.5
other products	100.0	101.8	95.0	92.9	98.9	100.2	106.0	122.8
External EC trade								
Exports:								
all products	100.0	97.3	91.4	88.4	91.3	94.8	110.3	128.4
agricultural products	100.0	106.9	91.7	86.5	91.0	90.6	98.3	113.9
Imports:								
all products	100.0	89.7	83.2	77.4	79.0	78.7	83.5	99.7
agricultural products	100.0	85.4	80.1	76.4	77.4	74.4	82.6	93.5

*Figures given in milliard USD
Source: see Table 7.1.

OECD (1987), estimates that cutting CAP protection by 10 per cent would increase world prices by a range of 0.55 per cent (sugar) to 2.81 per cent (milk). The same studies also conclude that the CAP significantly cuts world trade and furthermore distorts it, increasing EC exports at the expense of those of other countries. Interestingly, they also support the view that the CAP broadly helps less developed countries (LDCs) at the expense of developed countries (except for Japan), by keeping down the price of temperate zone products (which LDCs import from the developed world). Abolishing the CAP, according to the conventional wisdom, not surprisingly supported by the Commission, would thus harm LDCs by increasing the price of their imports and getting rid of the preferential access to EC markets afforded by the Lomé Conventions. It should be noted, however, that researchers who take a more dynamic view tend to argue that any short-run costs that the LDCs might suffer as a result of the abolition of the CAP are likely to be reversed in the long run, since higher prices for temperate zone products would stimulate this sort of production in LDCs. Using a general equilibrium model which purports to measure indirect effects, Burniaux and Waelbroek (1985) estimate, for example, that abolishing the CAP would increase the real income of LDCs by 2.9 per cent by 1995. Finally, it must be reported that empirical studies tend to show that the CAP has a destabilizing effect on world commodity prices because of its variable tariffs and because it reduces the need to build stocks of food in EC countries.

Sarris and Freebairn (1983), for example, estimate that the CAP has accounted for something like 20 per cent of the variability in the international price of wheat, while others (Anderson and Tyers, 1984) put the figure as high as 50 per cent. The impact on price stability seems to be greatest for dairy produce, accounting for 60 per cent of price variations according to Tyers and Anderson (1986).

All this has been fiercely criticized by third world countries and has generally soured relations between the Community and the rest of the world. Recent examples of this have been the so-called 'pasta wars' with the United States, tension with the United States over grain which has threatened the new round of GATT negotiations, and with Australia and New Zealand over dairy produce. The Australians have estimated the impact of the CAP on the Australian economy to be almost $A1000 million each year.

5 CAP expenditure has dominated the EC budget, as can be seen from Table 7.4. The CAP is financed through the European Agricultural Guidance and Guarantee Fund (EAGGF, or FEOGA to the French). This has accounted in recent years for about two-thirds of total EC expenditure. As a result of this:

(a) Its escalating cost has forced member-countries to increase the size of the budget, and has been largely responsible for the continuing political crises that have occurred over the budget issue in recent years (see Chapter 6).

(b) The cost of the CAP has seriously constrained the ability of the Community to develop effective common policies in other key areas such as industry and regional affairs. As such it has probably hindered the cause of European integration.

(c) A popular tendency to equate the CAP with the whole of the Community has developed, again providing powerful propaganda for the opponents of European integration.

6 The operation of the CAP has become increasingly bureaucratic, complex, and convoluted in recent years. For example, we now have green exchange rates, on which prices and intra-Community trade in food are based. These are fixed annually, and consequently tend to diverge from actual exchange rates, though the EMS of relatively fixed exchange rates has reduced the importance of this. Since changes in green rates result in some countries gaining and others losing, these have come to be part of the EC bargaining round, and we have Monetary Compensation Amounts (MCAs) to compensate losers. Partly because of this complexity there is evidence of a certain amount of corruption and abuse of CAP financial arrangements. This came to light in the course of 1989, again providing ammunition for the CAP's detractors.

7 Despite the large public and private cost of the CAP, the problem of low incomes in the agricultural sector persists. This is because the price mechanism gives support in direct proportion to output, i.e. the more you produce the more subsidy you effectively get. Thus the largest and most efficient 25 per cent of farms are estimated to receive about 75 per cent of

Table 7.4   EC agricultural expenditure (million ECUs)

		1980	1985	1986	1987	1988	1989
EAGGF	Total	11 895	20 464	22 911	23 876	29 998	29 757
	Guarantee	11 315	19 744	22 137	22 968	28 795	28 323
	Guidance	580	720	774	909	1 023	1 434
EC budget		16 290	28 085	35 174	35 783	43 820	45 030
As per cent of budget:							
EAGGF		73.0	72.8	65.1	67.0	68.4	66.0
Guarantee		69.4	70.3	62.9	64.8	65.8	62.9
Guidance		3.5	2.5	2.2	2.5	2.3	3.2
Gross EAGGF Guarantee as per cent of Community GDP		0.56	0.66	0.63	0.63	0.75	0.68

Notes: The Community had nine members to 1980, ten to 1985 and increased to twelve in 1986. 1989 = preliminary draft.
Source: see Table 7.1 (adapted).

budgetary support—in the mid-1980s on average roughly 9700 ECUs per farm per annum—while the rest received an estimated average of only 1100 ECUs each year. Additionally, the large and efficient farms of course receive the lion's share of the indirect subsidy which EC consumers pay via the price system. This system, together with the limited coverage of price support, has led to wide national disparities in farm incomes (see Figure 7.3). There are also significant regional variations within countries in farming incomes.

Furthermore, it should be noted that attempts to cut prices and set quotas for output tend to damage small marginal farmers disproportionately, and this has contributed to the much-publicized discontent with the CAP in some farming communities.

8   The CAP has to an extent proved unresponsive to consumer demand, since it is subsidies, rather than what consumers want, that tend to determine what is produced. Thus, for example, consumer preference would tend to indicate that more organically produced food should be supplied, whereas the price support mechanism encourages the use of fertilizers, pesticides, hormones, and other chemicals to increase crop and livestock yields. Quantity rather than quality is the dominant objective, one that might have been relevant thirty years ago, but is certainly less so now. This has unfortunately had the added effect of contributing to the environmental and ecological problems that Europe, and indeed the world, is experiencing.

9   Finally the CAP probably has serious indirect effects on other sectors of the European economy. If we take what economists refer to as the 'general equilibrium' approach, it can be seen that agricultural support has acted as an implicit tax on other industries such as manufacturing and has probably contributed to de-industrialization. Thus, the employment and balance of payments benefits of the CAP have been achieved at the expense of jobs and trade in other sectors. The Australian Bureau of Agricultural Economics (1985) has estimated that something like 8 per cent of unemployment in EC countries can be attributed to the direct effects of the CAP. This estimate is probably on the high side, given that the

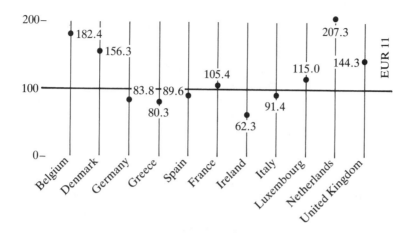

Figure 7.3 Average net value-added per person engaged in agriculture* in the Community and member-states. 100 = average for Community of eleven, 1982–86). (*Source:* as Table 7.1.)

Australians have an axe to grind. Nevertheless, these indirect effects of the CAP are probably significant. Breckling *et al.* (1987) have estimated that manufacturing industries in West Germany, France, Italy and the United Kingdom lose 1.1–2.5 per cent of potential output and 4.4–6.2 per cent of potential exports because of the CAP. The employment loss is put at around 1 per cent. Stoeckel and Breckling (1988) estimate the loss in the same four countries at 1.5 per cent of total income, with a job loss of around 4 million.

7.5 HOW THE CAP MIGHT BE IMPROVED

Suggestions for changes to the CAP have fallen broadly into two categories:

1 On the one hand there are people who consider the CAP to be so fundamentally flawed that only complete and radical change is good enough. This view would imply scrapping the CAP and taking one of the following actions:

(a) Replacing it with a completely different system. Here the old British system of support by 'deficiency payments' has been widely canvassed. With this system of support food would be imported from the rest of the world tariff-free, thus lowering EC internal prices to the level of world market prices (0–P_{World} in Figure 7.1) above. Then the desired level of agricultural support would be achieved by guaranteeing farmers' prices for their output and making up the difference between guaranteed prices and market prices by direct cash transfers from the EC budget. (The subsidy per unit of output would be equivalent to the distance between P_{World} and P_{EC} in the examples depicted in Figures 7.1 and 7.2.) This would have the advantage of providing cheaper food for consumers, of permitting more careful targeting of transfers to farmers, and of shifting the burden of support from consumers to taxpayers. Agriculture would be subsidized with a minimum of welfare losses. It would also eliminate some of the grievances felt since more access to EC markets would be permitted. However, it would also imply a huge increase in Community spending, since the burden of agricultural support would be shifted from consumers to the Community, and as such is probably politically impossible given the loss of national sovereignty involved and the general revulsion that currently exists towards public spending. It could also not be guaranteed to eliminate all the problems of the CAP since the political process might still lead to very high guaranteed prices.

(b) Alternatively, one could 'nationalize the CAP', i.e. replace the common policy with a series of national policies chosen by individual countries. This would leave each member-country free to implement policies suitable to its own requirements and situation. There would still be free intra-Community trade in agriculture. The Community would then be free to pursue other objectives. However, this would in many ways represent a serious retreat from integration and the political implications might be considerable. In addition there is the obvious potential for the outbreak of a 'subsidy war' in Europe, with EC countries competing with each other to support their own food industry at the expense of other countries. A variation on this idea was suggested by Marsh (1977), who advocated national determination of agricultural policy combined with common prices for intra-Community agricultural trade.

2   On the other hand, there have been suggestions for partial reform of the CAP to improve some of its more serious and visible problems. These include the implementation of one or more of the following:

(a) Price freezes or reductions to limit overproduction and reduce welfare costs. These have been consistently recommended by the European Commission and have been to some extent implemented in recent years. However, their scope has been limited by the understandable resistance with which they have been met by farmers, who have to plan output well in advance, and by some national governments. A variant of this has been the suggestion of moving resources from surplus into deficit products by changing relative prices.

(b) Quotas. These are clearly aimed at limiting excess output and have again been implemented to an extent, notably for milk. They are unpopular with some economists since they tend to distort the operation of the market, and thus 'saleable quotas' have been suggested. This would create a market in which the right to produce food would be competed for by farmers, thus further concentrating output in large efficient farms. Quotas have since 1977 been supplemented by 'co-responsibility levies', which are a kind of tax on excess output, to help finance the disposal of surpluses.

(c) Set aside. This is a system that the Community has 'imported' from the United States whereby farmers are paid not to produce anything, to leave their land uncultivated, or to destroy crops and livestock. This apparently absurd measure is of course aimed at reducing surplus output. It is at best a means of tackling the worst symptoms of the CAP's problems, but carries with it substantial scope for abuse and ridicule. A more acceptable variant of this is the encouragement of diversification, i.e. changing land use from farming to alternative activities.

(d) Cash limits on the CAP. This mainly British idea has taken the form of the 'threshold principle' and of 'stabilizers'. These are designed to limit total expenditure on the CAP. In the case of stabilizers the rule is that market support expenditure cannot increase by more than 74 per cent of the increase in gross commodity product.

(e) Direct cash payments to farmers. These are sometimes referred to as income support by French politicians, and they are aimed at tackling the problem of farm incomes and at rendering output restrictions more acceptable to farmers. They have sometimes been supplemented by 'outgoers'—schemes to compensate farmers who have to leave the land as a result of output cuts.

(f) Promoting organic agriculture (i.e. without pesticides, chemical fertilizers, hormones, etc.). This would both help to tackle environmental problems and contribute to reductions in output. It would also considerably improve the wholesomeness of the food we eat. A first step has come in the form of 'extensification', encouraging farmers to adopt less intensive farming methods.

7.6 OBSTACLES TO CHANGE

Despite the deficiencies of the CAP, reform has to be slow and problematic. This is due to a number of factors, of which the following are the most significant:

1 Vested interests. First, several nations as a whole have no interest in reforming the CAP. As we have seen, some EC countries, notably France, but also Ireland, Denmark, and the Netherlands, benefit from the present way in which the CAP is structured and clearly have every incentive to preserve the status quo. Secondly, many farmers, and especially the large and efficient producers, do very well out of the policy. They clearly have no interest in reform. Finally, it must be said that the decision-makers themselves have little incentive to change the policy. Both national agriculture ministers and Community bureaucrats would have their power base reduced by reform, and would have to take considerable criticism in the process. Thus, the political will to effect reform has largely been missing. This is exacerbated by national electoral considerations.

2 National electoral considerations. Farmers are usually well organized and form a powerful pressure group in most EC countries (note, for example, the power of the National Farmers' Union in the United Kingdom). The farming vote is of considerable importance, particularly in countries with proportional representation and a relatively large farming population such as France, Spain, Italy, Ireland, and Greece, where it can make the difference between winning and losing elections. Governments in these countries therefore tend to feel they cannot afford to alienate the farming vote, and are consequently reluctant to support measures that might damage their farming communities. So far this factor has not been of great importance in the United Kingdom where the collapse of the centre parties has left no credible alternative to the Conservative Party in rural areas. Apart from the farming vote, which in any case is shrinking in size, governments are also aware of the importance of pressure groups representing industries that are ancillary to farming, e.g. food processing and packaging.

3 The cumbersome decision-making process in the Community, particularly the veto system in the Agricultural Council of Ministers, which renders change of any kind difficult to achieve (see Chapter 2). This tends to be exacerbated by the short-term nature of much of the agricultural decision-making in the Community. Crisis management and compromise, rather than long-term rational planning, are the order of the day, despite the ambitious-sounding titles of some of the Commission's publications on the CAP (e.g. 'Reflections on the CAP', 'Perspectives for the CAP', 'A future for community agriculture').

4 Fear of breaking up what in many quarters is perceived of as the Community's most concrete achievement in the development of common policies. This, it is argued, might prove a serious blow to the process of European integration, though the opposite might conceivably be true if a more satisfactory alternative were to emerge.

7.7   RECENT REFORMS

Because of the above, very little was effectively done to improve the CAP until 1984, when a reform process was begun. It was the escalating cost of the CAP and the threat of bankruptcy for the Community which concentrated minds, the British making it clear that they would not agree to extra funds for the EC budget unless the problem of the CAP was tackled. Thus the Fontainebleau arrangements of 1984 to extend the budget (see Chapter 6) were accompanied by a serious attempt to tackle at least the most blatant problems of the policy. The principal measures adopted between 1984 and 1988 were the following:

1. The more stringent use of quotas to cut production. The best-known examples are the infamous (according to the farming community) milk quotas, introduced for five years in 1984, with the eventual objective (agreed in December 1986) of cutting output by 9.5 per cent by 1988–89.
2. Substantial real price cuts for most CAP products. For example, the price of beef was effectively reduced by some 13 per cent partly as a result of more rigorous buying-in arrangements, while on average support prices were cut by around 10 per cent between 1985–86 and 1988–89. Details of the most recent price changes are shown in Table 7.5.

Table 7.5   Average change in intervention prices over the previous year

| | 1986–87 | | | 1987–88 | | | 1988–89 | | |
| | Intervention prices | | Inflation 1986‡ | Intervention prices | | Inflation 1987‡ | Intervention prices | | Inflation 1988‡ |
	ECU*	National currency†		ECU*	National currency†		ECU*	National currency†	
Belgium	−0.1	+1.7	3.7	0.0	+1.7	1.8	0.0	+0.4	1.5
Denmark	−0.7	+1.3	4.9	0.0	+2.3	5.0	0.0	+0.7	4.9
Germany	−0.2	−0.2	3.1	0.0	0.0	2.1	0.0	0.0	1.3
Greece	−0.5	+13.5	19.0	−0.4	+13.3	15.7	−0.6	+14.2	14.6
France	−0.3	+2.0	4.7	−0.2	+4.1	2.6	0.0	+1.1	2.8
Ireland	−0.3	+2.5	5.6	0.0	+8.5	2.7	0.0	+0.9	2.6
Italy	−0.6	+4.2	8.0	−0.6	+3.3	5.6	−0.3	+1.9	4.7
Luxembourg	−0.1	+1.7	2.6	0.0	+1.6	0.6	0.0	+0.4	2.2
Netherlands	0.0	0.0	0.7	0.0	−0.5	−1.0	0.0	−0.2	0.8
United Kingdom	−0.5	+1.9	3.5	0.0	+6.3	4.4	0.0	+2.4	4.8
Community of 10	−0.3	+2.2		−0.2	+3.3		−0.1	+1.6	
Spain §	+1.8	+3.3	10.9	+1.8	+7.2	5.7	+1.3	+1.1	5.2
Portugal §	+0.3	+1.7	17.9	+0.5	+6.1	12.1	+0.7	+8.5	8.8
Community of 12	¶	¶		¶	¶		¶	¶	

Note: The figures do not include the effects of co-responsibility levies. For cereals, rice, and oilseeds, the buying-in prices are less than the above intervention prices, and changes in the criteria for buying in are not comparable over time.

* Common prices in ECU (intervention price or equivalent prices) weighted by national agricultural production.

† Common prices in ECU converted into national currency at the green rate including all adjustments of green rates included in the price decisions or adopted since the price decisions of the preceding marketing year.

‡ Rate of inflation for the whole economy (GDP deflator) for the relevant calendar year, latest revisions.

§ Includes alignment of the prices on the common prices following accession agreements.

¶ During the transition period the number of products under common price regimes in Spain and Portugal is very limited, so the calculation of the EUR 12 average is meaningless.

Source: see Table 7.1.

3. More widespread use of co-responsibility levies to limit output. For example, a super-levy of 75–100 per cent was applied to milk. Levies were also extended to cereals.
4. Steps to reduce the size of the various 'mountains' and 'lakes'. For example, a three-year scheme for reducing butter stocks was adopted, which reduced the butter mountain by 1 million tonnes to less than 185 000 tonnes by mid-1988. Stocks of milk powder were also substantially reduced.
5. Structural measures. These had two objectives: first to contribute to the decline in output by measures such as 'extensification', set aside, and changes in land use; secondly, to compensate farmers for lost output by measures such as 'outgoers' schemes.

A further blow for agricultural reform was struck at the Brussels Summit of February 1988. Here, amid scenes of typical brinkmanship, stabilizers were introduced to control agricultural spending further. They now cover about half of all agricultural production, and, crucially, the decision of when the 'maximum guaranteed quantity' has been exceeded can now be taken by the Commission, rather than the Council of Ministers. In addition, the policy of price cutting, set aside, early retirement, extensification, and conversion of production was continued.

So, where do we stand? At long last there has been some serious effort at reform. The mountains and lakes are receding, prices are falling in real terms, EAGGF expenditure seems to be coming under control (see Table 7.4), expenditure on structural policies is taking up a larger (but nowhere near large enough) proportion of the agricultural budget. These developments are to be welcomed, but they must also be put into context. They tackle only the most glaring deficiencies of the CAP, and even then only at the margin. This may be all that is realistically possible in political terms. Nevertheless, the essential nature of the policy remains unchanged, the fundamental problems are still there. It remains to be seen what influence the new round of Uruguay GATT negotiations will have.

REFERENCES

Australian Bureau of Agricultural Economics (1985), 'Agricultural policies in the European Community', *Policy Monograph*, **2**, Canberra.

Anderson, K. and Tyers, R. (1984), 'European community grain and meat policies: effects on international prices', *European Review of Agricultural Economics*, **11**, 367–394.

Bale, M. and Lutz, E. (1981), 'Price distortions in agriculture and their effects', *American Journal of Agricultural Economics*, **63**, no. 1, 8–22.

Breckling, J., Thorpe, S. and Stoeckel, A. (1987), *Effects of EC Agricultural Policies. A General Equilibrium Approach: initial results*, Australian Bureau of Agricultural Economics, Canberra.

Buckwell, A.E., Harvey, D.R., Thompson, K.J. and Parton, K.A. (1982), *The Costs of the Common Agricultural Policy*, Croom Helm, London.

Burniaux, J. and Waelbroek, J. (1985), 'The impact of the CAP on developing countries: a general equilibrium analysis', in C. Stevens and J. Verloren van Themaat (Eds), *Pressure Groups, Policies and Development*, Hodder and Stoughton, London.

Demekas, D.G., Bartholdy, K., Gupta, S., Lipschitz, L. and Mayer, T. (1988), 'The effects of the Common Agricultural Policy of the European Community: a survey of the literature', *Journal of Common Market Studies*, **XXVII**, 113–145.

Fennell, R. (1987), 'Reform of the CAP: shadow or substance?', *Journal of Common Market Studies*, **XXVI**, 61–78.

Harling, K. and Thompson, R. (1985), 'Government intervention in poultry industries: a cross-country comparison', *American Journal of Agricultural Economics*, **67**, no. 3, 243–249.

Koester, U. (1982), *Policy Options for the Grain Economy of the European Community: Implications for Developing Countries*, International Food Policy Research Institute, Research Report **35**, Washington DC. (Cited in Demekas *et al.* (1988).)

Koester, U. and Valdes, A. (1984), 'Reform of the CAP—impact on the third world', *Food Policy*, **1**, no. 20, 94–98.

Marsh, J.S. (1977), 'European Agricultural Policy: a federalist solution', *New Europe*, Winter, 27–40.

Matthews, A. (1985), 'The CAP and developing countries: a review of the evidence', in C. Stevens and J. Verloren van Themaat (eds), *Pressure Groups, Policies and Development*, Hodder and Stoughton, London.

Morris, C.N. (1980), 'The Common Agricultural Policy', *Fiscal Studies*, **1**, no. 2, 15–35.

Organisation for Economic Cooperation and Development (1987). *National Policies and Agricultural Trade*, Paris.

Sarris, A.H. and Freebairn, J. (1983), 'Endogenous price policies and international wheat prices', *American Journal of Agricultural Economics*, **65**, no. 2, 214–224.

Spencer, J. (1985), 'The European Economic Community: general equilibrium computations and the economic implications of membership', in J. Piggott and J. Whalley (eds), *New Developments in Applied General Equilibrium Analysis*, Cambridge University Press, Cambridge.

Spencer, J. (1986), 'Trade liberalization through tariff cuts and the European Economic Community: a general equilibrium evaluation', in T.N. Srinivasan and J. Whalley (eds), *General Equilibrium Trade Policy Modeling*, MIT Press, Cambridge, MA.

Stoeckel, A. and Breckling, J. (1988), 'Some economy-wide effects of agricultural policies in the European Community: a general equilibrium study'. (Cited in Demekas *et al.* (1988).)

Tyers, R. (1985), 'International impacts of protection: model structure and results for EC agricultural policy', *Journal of Policy Modeling*, **7**, no. 2, 219–252.

Tyers, R. and Anderson, K. (1986), 'Distortions in world food markets: a quantitative assessment', *World Bank Development Report Background Paper*, World Bank, Washington DC.

Tyers, R. and Anderson, K. (1987), 'Liberalising OECD agricultural policies in the Uruguay Round: effects on trade and welfare', *Australian National University Working Paper*, **87/10**, Australian National University, Canberra.

EIGHT

EUROPEAN COMMUNITY SOCIAL POLICY

8.1 INTRODUCTION

As part of the '1992' programme leading to the completion of the internal market, the Commission has proposed a series of social measures intended to strengthen the 'social dimension' of the Community. These proposals have been strongly defended by the Commission President, Jacques Delors, as a necessary part of the 1992 project. However, this view was vigorously opposed by the then British Prime Minister, Margaret Thatcher, for whom the so-called 'social dimension' was at best a distraction and at worst a devious means of reintroducing socialism into Britain through the back door. This chapter places the present debate on the social dimension of the single market within the wider context of the origins, aims, and subsequent development of EC social policy since 1957. This analysis addresses key questions such as what is meant by the so-called 'social dimension'? Does the Community have a mandate to impose EC social policy on member-states? How will the European Social Charter affect workers and employers? And why was Mrs Thatcher so opposed to it?

8.2 THE SOCIAL PROVISIONS OF THE TREATIES ESTABLISHING THE COMMUNITIES

EC social policy is primarily concerned with employment matters. In part, this interpretation represents a particular tradition of social policy as something essentially concerned with the totality of relations between employers and workers, the so-called 'social partners' of the Community. But this emphasis is also to a large extent the result of the economic assumptions underlying the setting up of the EC. Although all the EC treaties refer to the need for social as well as economic progress, few clauses deal specifically with social issues. A major reason for this is that at the time the treaties were signed the dominant economic philosophy in Western Europe was one of *laissez-faire*; the unspoken assumption underlying the treaties is that the economic prosperity resulting from the establishment of the common market will lead inevitably to enhanced social benefits. This does not mean that the European Community has never involved itself in other areas of social policy. There are no limits to the areas in which the Community may, if it so wishes, take action, and it has in recent years concerned itself with issues such as sex and race discrimination, poverty, health provision, and family policy. Nevertheless, the formal treaty provisions that constitute the foundations of EC social policy are essentially employment centred (Collins, 1983a). The 1951 Treaty of Paris which established the European Coal and Steel Community (ECSC) states that one of the objectives of the ECSC is 'to promote improved living and working conditions . . . for the workers'. More specifically, provision was made in the Treaty for the following:

- Studies and consultations to facilitate the redeployment of workers made redundant by market development or technical change and to assess the possibilities for improving workers' living standards and working conditions (Articles 46–48).
- Promoting research into occupational safety (Article 55).
- Financing programmes for the creation of new activities and grants for retraining and resettlement of workers (Article 56).
- Guaranteeing adequate wages for workers in the ECSC industries (Article 68).
- Establishing free movement of workers while safeguarding their entitlement to social security benefits (Article 69).

As its name implies, the European Economic Community (EEC) established in 1957 is first and foremost an economic community. However, to ensure that constant improvement in working conditions and employment referred to in the preamble, the Treaty made provision for the following:

- The gradual achievement of the free movement of workers within the Community, accompanied by guaranteed eligibility for social security benefits (Articles 48, 49 and 51).
- Encouraging the exchange of young workers under a joint programme (Article 50).
- Promoting close collaboration between the member-states in social matters in order to facilitate an improvement in living and working conditions and make possible their harmonization while maintaining the improvement. Areas in which the Commission is to promote cooperation between member-states include employment, labour law and working conditions, vocational training, social security, prevention of occupational accidents and diseases, occupational hygiene, the right of association, and collective bargaining between employers and workers (Articles 117 and 118).
- The principle of equal pay for men and women doing the same work (Article 119).
- Setting up a European Social Fund to promote employment opportunities and geographical and occupational mobility for workers within the Community (Articles 123 to 127).
- Establishing general principles for implementing a Community vocational training policy (Article 128).

The 1957 Euratom Treaty, intended to coordinate the promotion of nuclear energy within the Community, refers to the need to protect workers and the general population from contamination hazards associated with nuclear energy production. It provides for the establishment of basic standards for the protection of workers and the general public against the dangers arising from ionizing radiation (Articles 30–39) (European Commission, 1981).

8.3   THE EVOLUTION OF COMMUNITY SOCIAL POLICY

8.3.1   The early years: 1951–72

During the 1950s and 1960s the social provisions of the EC treaties were incorporated into EC law by a series of Council decisions. The principle of freedom of movement—the right of Community citizens to decide where to work in the Community—was gradually extended to the ECSC industries in 1961 and to other sectors in 1968. In theory at least, all wage and salary earners in the Community have, since 1968, enjoyed the right to apply for job vacancies anywhere in the Community irrespective of their nationality, to live in another member-state and be joined there by their families. EC migrants also enjoy the same rights as nationals with regard to working conditions and terms of employment.

The EEC also established a social security system for migrant workers which came into force on 1 January 1959 (workers in the ECSC industries already enjoyed such protection). Three principles underpin this system. First, EC migrant workers are eligible for the same social security benefits as national workers. Secondly, periods of employment and insurance completed in several member-states are aggregated for the calculation of benefits. And thirdly, the beneficiary may, at any time, request the transfer of her or his social security benefits from one member-state to another.

The ECSC High Authority began giving aid to promote the re-employment of redundant workers in the coal and steel industries in March 1954 and the first European Social Fund came into operation in 1960. Its task, according to the EEC Treaty, was 'to improve employment opportunities for workers in the common market and to contribute thereby to raising the standard of living'. As indicated below, the rules governing the operation of the Social Fund have undergone several changes since 1972. However, between 1960 and 1972 the Fund simply considered vocational and retraining projects submitted by the member-governments and funded up to half the cost of these initiatives.

During the period 1958–72 the gross domestic product of the original six member-states nearly doubled in real terms, the increase being more pronounced in the countries that had the lowest levels when the Communities were set up. Clearly, an economic background such as this was conducive to social progress and, as illustrated in Table 8.1, the wages of workers in the member-states increased substantially between 1958 and 1972. However, female employees fared less well than their male counterparts. Under Article 119 pay differentials between men and women doing the same jobs were to have been eradicated by the end of 1961, but this deadline was repeatedly postponed by the Commission throughout the 1960s (Warner, 1984).

The Community took a more active interest during this period in working conditions. The High Authority very quickly drew up a series of safety standards to be introduced in the

Table 8.1 The economic performance of the European Community, 1958–72

	GNP per head*		Percentage increase in real wages 1958–72†
	1958	1972	
Belgium	1154	3351	93%
France	1196	3489	109%
Germany	1096	3840	79%
Italy	612	2008	121%
Luxembourg	1402	3255	75%
Netherlands	845	3193	106%

* US dollar per year at market prices.

† Increase of gross hourly earnings of workers in industry October/October in real terms.

Source: 'The European Community's Social Policy', *European Documentation*, 178/2, p. 5.

ECSC industries and established two Standing Safety and Health Committees (one for coal, the other for steel). Empowered by the Euratom Treaty, the Commission also moved swiftly to establish uniform basic standards with regard to permissible levels of radiation emission, and introduced regular Community monitoring of radioactivity in air, foodstuffs, and water. Outside the ECSC industries the main sectors in which progress was made with regard to working conditions were agriculture and transport. The emphasis, however, was upon voluntary cooperation between the social partners. Joint Committees comprising employers' and workers' representatives were set up to consider working conditions in these industries. These resulted in a series of negotiated voluntary agreements on maximum working hours (agriculture) and Community legislation harmonizing certain social provisions in the transport industry (minimum age for drivers, driving periods, rest periods, etc.) (European Commission, 1983)

By the end of the 1960s, the key social provisions of the treaties had thus been implemented. In practice, however, social policy played only a minor role in overall Community policy-making during the 1960s. The European Social Fund, for instance, operated on a very small scale, Article 119 was still to be implemented, labour mobility was hindered by cultural and social barriers, and no serious attempts were made to initiate collaboration between the member-states in social matters.

8.3.2   Towards a social dimension? The 1974 Social Action Programme

In the early 1970s this minimalist conception of the Community's social role came under attack and a new consensus emerged on the need for a more comprehensive EC social policy. Several factors contributed to this change. First, there was a growing awareness of the unevenness of economic growth within the Community; peripheral areas such as south-west France and the Mezzogiorno in southern Italy were lagging behind the richer core areas. Furthermore, within the labour market, certain groups were relatively disadvantaged. Such groups included the handicapped, women (in theory guaranteed equality of pay with men for equivalent work under Article 119 of the Rome Treaty, but in fact encountering sex discrimination), and certain categories of young and old workers. In addition, migrant workers and their families (including EC migrants whose social rights were supposedly protected by the treaties) suffered problems of social integration and discrimination.

Secondly, there was mounting concern over some of the apparent costs of economic growth, such as the environmental consequences of industrial pollution, low health and safety standards at work, the stultifying nature of many jobs in factories, and the absence of job security and industrial democracy. As profits soared within the Community, these conditions became less acceptable to many people.

There were also important political pressures at work. Key individuals within the Community such as Willy Brandt, the SPD Chancellor of West Germany, and Sicco Mansholt, the Dutch President of the Commission, argued that if the process of economic growth was to continue to be socially and politically acceptable, it would have to be accompanied—and be seen to be accompanied—by an active programme of social reform. Only by giving the Community more of a 'human face' would it be possible to harness the political support of the trade unions to European integration.

More generally, there was a widespread feeling towards the end of the 1960s that the Community was running out of steam. While, in theory at least, the common market had been largely achieved, there was no evidence to suggest that this had created irresistible pressures for further integration. Thus, many felt that a new initiative was needed to accelerate the process of integration and broaden the concept of the European Community from a mere trading bloc to a social community (Shanks, 1977).

Responding to these pressures, the EC heads of government issued a communiqué at the 1972 Paris Summit asserting that they 'attached as much importance to vigorous action in the social field as to the achievement of the economic and monetary union'. The Commission was therefore asked to draw up an action programme by 1 January 1974, 'providing for concrete measures and the necessary resources, particularly in the framework of the Social Fund'. The Commission's proposals for a social action programme were duly adopted in a resolution (non-binding upon member-states in legal terms) by the Council of Ministers on 21 January 1974. Under this resolution the member-states undertook to carry out some forty priority measures during an initial three-year period in pursuance of the Community's three major objectives: attainment of full and better employment; improvement and upward harmonization of living and working conditions; and increased involvement of management and labour in the economic and social decisions of the Community, and of workers in the life of their firms.

Attainment of full and better employment   The adoption of the social action programme in 1974 coincided with the first oil crisis and the onset of worldwide economic recession. Unemployment levels rose dramatically throughout the EC (see Figure 8.1) with certain regions, industries, and categories of workers being particularly hard hit. In consequence, since 1974, reducing unemployment—particularly youth and long-term unemployment— has been the single most important objective of EC social policy. Community action to combat unemployment has focused upon development of the European Social Fund (ESF), promotion of vocational training and the coordination of national employment policies.

The European Social Fund   Following the first reform of the ESF in 1972, the Fund's limited resources were directed towards two priority tasks: the alleviation of labour-market imbalances directly attributable to EC policies, and the reduction of structural unemployment in declining regions (through ESF funding for retraining of redundant workers). Growing concern at record unemployment levels throughout the Community prompted a second major reform of the ESF in 1984 which identified two principal targets for ESF support—young people and disadvantaged regions.

Since 1984, 75 per cent of the Fund's resources has been reserved for the training or employment of people under the age of 25 (who in 1986 accounted for 40 per cent of those registered as unemployed in the Community) are accorded the highest priority by the Fund. Priority is also given to the long-term unemployed, women, handicapped people, migrant workers, and employees who need to learn new technologies. The 1984 reform has also resulted in much greater geographical concentration of the Fund. Seven zones, which together represent nearly one-sixth of the EC working population, are now designated 'absolute priority' for ESF support. These are the whole of Greece, Ireland and Portugal; the Italian Mezzogiorno; the Spanish regions of Castile–Leon, Castile–La Mancha, Estremadura, Andalusia, Murcia, the Canaries, Galicia, and the towns of Ceuta and Melilla; Northern Ireland; and the French overseas departments and Corsica. These areas are guaranteed 44.5 per cent of the Fund's resources. Moreover, whereas the ESF normally covers up to 50 per cent of the eligible costs of any project, this figure may be increased to 55 per cent in the 'absolute priority' zones. The Community also gives priority to other designated 'simple priority' areas, which are characterized by both a significant level of long-term unemployment and a per capita GDP below the EC average.

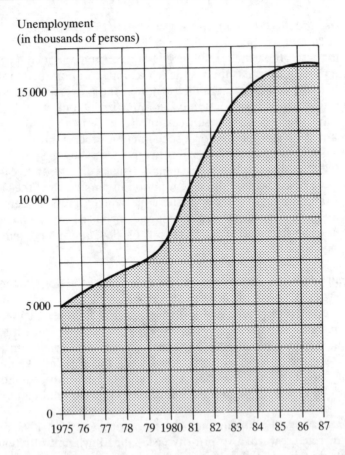

Unemployment
(in thousands of persons)

Figure 8.1   Unemployment in the European Community 1975–87. (*Source:* 'The Social Policy of the European Community: looking ahead to 1992', *European File*, 13/88.)

A major limitation of the ESF is its size, which is strictly limited by the overall size of the EC budget. Though the Fund has been increased over the years (from 30 million ECUs in 1972 to 3150 million ECUs in 1987) it is never able to support all eligible applications for funding. In 1986, for instance, 6449 applications were made relating to 7806 projects, calling for financing in the order of 5200 million ECUs, but due to budgetary constraints only 49 per cent of these bids could be met (European Commission, 1986). To facilitate the selection of projects, the Commission prepares guidelines (which are revised every three years) for the management of the Fund. For the period 1987–89 the guidelines give priority to measures that form part of an integrated programme receiving other forms of EC assistance (e.g. from the Regional Development Fund, the Agricultural Guidance Fund, or the European Investment Bank); operations to promote vocational training and youth employment; projects linked to industrial and sectoral restructuring and the introduction of new technologies; and initiatives to help the socio-vocational integration of certain categories of workers (e.g. language training for migrant workers).

Vocational training   The 1974 Social Action Programme called for the implementation of a common EC vocational training policy. As a first step towards this, a European Centre for the Development of Vocational Training (CEDEFOP) was established in West Berlin in 1977. Run by a tripartite governing council comprising representatives from national governments, the 'social partners' (employers' and workers' representatives), and the Commission, CEDEFOP's main role is to assist the Commission in the preparation of EC training programmes.

Since 1974, the Council of Ministers has adopted in resolution form a series of EC vocational training programmes aimed at young people, handicapped persons, migrants, women, and employees who need to adapt to new technologies (particularly in small and medium-sized firms). It is difficult to quantify the impact of these initiatives, which are typically funded jointly by the ESF and employers, national, and/or local authorities. Certainly, many individuals have benefited from these projects, the existence of which led to increased pressures from employees and trade unions for further training opportunities. But, the impact of the EC action programmes has been limited by inadequate and/or insecure funding and by the fact that they are usually pilot schemes or 'one-off' projects that tend to be small scale and/or short term (European Commission, 1988a).

Coordination of national employment policies   On 27 June 1980 the Council of Ministers adopted a resolution setting out guidelines for a Community-wide labour-market policy. The two objectives of this policy were to reduce the imbalance between the supply and demand for labour and to integrate the EC labour-market. To this end three measures were proposed: greater exchange of information between member-states regarding national employment and unemployment patterns; increased cooperation between national employment agencies and extension of the Community's own placement service, SEDOC (European System for the Diffusion of Registered Employment Offers and Demands); and more concerted, forward-looking analysis of EC labour-market trends by employers and Community ministers. Since 1980, considerable progress has been made with respect to the first of these recommendations; the EC Commission produces vast quantities of statistics on the state of the labour-market throughout the Community. Employment policy, however, remains the responsibility of national governments who have, generally speaking, jealously guarded their autonomy in this key policy area.

Improvement of living and working conditions   In its proposal for a Social Action Programme the European Commission called upon member-states to end 'those patterns of work which tend to dehumanize the worker and change environmental working and living conditions which are no longer acceptable to ideas of social progress'. Under this heading the following initiatives were taken by the Community:

Equal treatment of men and women (Article 119)   The Council of Ministers adopted three equality directives in 1975, 1976 and 1978 to implement Article 119. The first provides for equal pay for men and women doing work 'of equal value'. The 1976 directive guarantees equal treatment of men and women with respect to recruitment and training practices, and the third directive, which came into force in 1984, ensures equality of entitlement to social security benefits (excluding retirement pensions). Two further directives adopted by the Council in 1986 provide for equality of treatment between men and women with regard to private pension schemes and the rights of self-employed persons. These two directives come into force in 1993 and 1989 respectively. Community legislation in this area has been backed by two positive action programmes on behalf of women. The first, which lasted from 1982 to 1985 focused upon the position of women in the workplace (i.e. monitoring implementation of the equality directives). The 1986–90 second medium-term programme for women is aimed at combating discrimination against women outside the workplace in schools, the home, and the media. These policies have been accompanied by the establishment in 1981 of a Women's Employment and Equality Office in the Commission, a permanent Standing Committee on Women's Rights in the European Parliament (established in 1984), and more recently the Commission's 1988 decision to fund an official women's lobby in Brussels. Thus, women's interests have been gradually accommodated into the policy-making framework of the Community (Mazey, 1988; Vallance and Davies, 1986).

Community action against sex discrimination is generally considered to constitute one of the most successful areas of EC social policy. Certainly, implementation of these directives has provided working women with a valuable legal weapon against the most blatant forms of sex discrimination. Likewise, the positive action programmes on behalf of women have also helped to increase public awareness of the problem. However, the roots of sex discrimination lie beyond the workplace and indirect, disguised, discrimination remains widespread.

Health and safety at work   In June 1974 an EC Advisory Committee for Industrial Safety, Hygiene and Health Protection was established whose main task is to monitor national developments and assist the Commission in the preparation of health and safety legislation outside the ECSC controlled sector. Since 1974 several EC directives have been adopted by the Council of Ministers protecting workers against exposure to vinyl chloride (1978), dangerous chemicals and biological agents (1980), metallic lead and its ionic compounds (1982), and asbestos (1983). While this EC legislation has prompted improvements in national safety standards, the effective implementation of these laws remains incomplete. In particular, many workers in the so-called 'second economy' continue to enjoy little protection from harmful substances.

Protection of workers' interests   In 1976 a European Foundation for the Improvement of Living and Working Conditions was established in Dublin. Run jointly by the social partners, member-states, and the Commission, its main function is to prepare EC measures to improve the working and living environment of employees. During the 1970s, the Commission feared that workers' interests would be adversely affected by the growing number of multinational takeovers and mergers taking place within the Community. The following directives were, therefore, adopted to protect employees affected by such developments:

Directive 75/129 (adopted 17 February 1975) obliges an employer contemplating mass dismissals to consult with workers' representatives beforehand.
Directive 77/187 (adopted 14 February 1977) specifies that workers' rights arising from a collective agreement or labour contract must be maintained in the event of a company transfer and that a change of ownership does not constitute grounds for dismissal.
Directive 80/987 (adopted 20 October 1980) obliges member-states to introduce legislation to ensure that workers' outstanding pay claims would be met in the event of their employer going bankrupt (e.g. by forcing employers to insure themselves against such a loss).

The Council also adopted two non-binding recommendations proposing a 40-hour working week and four weeks paid holiday per annum to be introduced throughout the Community by the end of 1978, and more flexible retirement, temporary employment, and part-time working as a means of combating unemployment.

These initiatives have had a limited impact upon the position of EC workers. After its entry into the Community in 1981, for instance, the Greek working week was reduced from 44 to 40 hours by 1 January 1983. But the Commission itself acknowledged in 1988 that implementation of EC legislation in this area is far from satisfactory. In Italy, for example, national legislation on mass dismissals is simply ignored by employers who argue that such matters are for them alone, while in Greece, this directive has yet to be incorporated into national law. Furthermore, the council of Ministers has refused to adopt two additional directives proposed by the Commission in 1982, aimed at protecting the interests of part-time and temporary workers.

Concertation of social security policies Following the adoption of the Social Action Programme, the Commission set up two groups (one comprising senior social security officials from member-states and the other composed of independent experts) to exchange information on national social security systems and discuss common problems (especially budgetary issues) and possible solutions to them. To facilitate this dialogue the Commission introduced the so-called 'social budget'. This is not a budget in any real sense, but a detailed annual statement of social policy expenditure by each member-state with short-term forecasts of planned developments.

The Commission acknowledges, however, that harmonization of social security provision throughout the Community is not, at present, a feasible goal. There are significant differences between member-countries in the levels and scope of coverage which reflect varying degrees of wealth, different priorities, and diverse institutional and funding mechanisms. Nevertheless, the social budget constitutes a valuable source of comparative data for those groups lobbying for increased public expenditure on social policy.

Anti-poverty programme An ambitious innovation in the Social Action Programme was the Commission's proposal for Community measures to help people living in poverty, particularly old people, one-parent families, migrants, and the homeless. An initial five-year programme of pilot schemes and research was adopted in the form of a Council resolution in July 1975. On finding that poverty (defined in relative terms) had actually increased since 1957, the Community adopted a second programme (1984–88) based on further research, medical and food aid (EC butter for the pensioners!).

Promotion of social dialogue A central assumption underlying the Social Action Programme was that active participation and shared responsibility between the two sides of industry were essential preconditions for the attainment of social goals. The Commission attempted to promote such cooperation in two ways: by increasing the role of the social partners in EC policy-making, and by proposing measures to strengthen worker participation within the workplace.

Within the European Community, corporatist interests are represented in the Economic and Social Committee, a consultative body comprising 189 representatives from European employers' organizations, trade unions, and professional associations. The Committee gives its opinion on all EC policies and may also initiate its own reports. In an attempt to strengthen the policy-making input of these interests, nine sectoral committees were established in the 1970s to enable employers' and workers' representatives to discuss problems and EC policies affecting their particular industry. In addition, a Standing Committee on Employment was established in 1974 which brings together employers' and workers' representatives and ministers of employment at least once a year to discuss current trends and

EC labour market proposals. Though the committees provide a useful forum for discussion, their role is limited by their informal status.

Commission efforts during this period to strengthen worker participation within the workplace were unsuccessful. In view of the present debate surrounding the notion of worker participation, it is worth looking in detail at these earlier efforts on the part of the Commission to promote industrial democracy. In 1975, the Commission put forward a draft Directive (the so-called 'Fifth Directive') proposing the introduction of a European company statute. The idea behind this proposal was to facilitate the development of EC multinationals by permitting companies from two or more EC countries jointly to opt out of their respective national legal systems and incorporate themselves as a European company. In practice, it proved impossible to devise a company law statute acceptable to all member-governments. At this time, only West German law required companies above a certain size to reserve one-third of their seats for worker representatives. The West German government feared that unless the European company statute had broadly similar provisions, there could be a mass exodus out of German company law into European company law. From the outset, therefore, the draft statute for a company law was linked to the German model which provided for a two-tier board and worker representation at supervisory board level. The degree of worker participation envisaged in this scheme met with considerable opposition from employers' associations and several member-governments who feared the possible labour-cost increases and political significance of such a development.

Although the proposal for a European company statute languished, the Commission continued to promote the specific issue of worker participation and on 24 October 1980 submitted to the Council the Vredeling Directive (named after the then Commissioner for Labour and Social Affairs). This would have required multinationals and companies with subsidiaries to establish common board structures and procedures for informing and consulting employees on company strategy. Once again, the institutional framework proposed closely mirrored the German model, developed in the context of that country's policy of co-determination.

Several member-states immediately objected that this model was inappropriate to other EC countries which have a totally different system of company law. There was also division within the European trade unions and employers' organizations over the issue of worker participation. While trade unions in West Germany, Denmark, and the Netherlands supported the idea, the major trade unions in France and Italy saw worker participation as a device for incorporating unions into the capitalist system. The British, Irish, and Belgian trade unions had no more than an instrumental interest in participation. The attitude of employers and governments tended to mirror that of the unions. In West Germany, Denmark, and the Netherlands, governments and employers favoured—or acquiesced in—the notion of employee participation. In the United Kingdom, France and Ireland, however, employers' associations were uniformly hostile to the very notion.

The Vredeling Directive was discussed at length in the European Parliament and the Economic and Social Committee before reaching the Council of Ministers in amended (i.e. watered down) form in 1984. Two years later, the Council recommended that the whole issue of worker participation be reconsidered by the Commission as part of its deliberations on the social dimension on the single market.

8.3.3   An evaluation of the 1974 EC Social Action Programme

It is easy to point to the things that the Social Action Programme failed to achieve. Unemployment levels throughout the European Community remained high during this period despite the Community's initiatives. The Commission's objectives of an EC-wide training policy remained unfulfilled and very little progress was made on the coordination of national labour-market policies. Community legislation aimed at improving the living and working conditions of employees was often not enforced and EC attempts to introduce worker participation were effectively resisted by employers and national governments—as well as by some trades unions.

Several factors explain this record. First, the EC treaties—the provisions of which are automatically binding on member-states—gave the Commission few specific powers with respect to social policy. Those sections of the Treaties that deal with social matters are very general in content and with few exceptions (notably Article 119) prescribe no concrete measures. In consequence, the Social Action Programme rested, for the most part, upon secondary legislation (i.e. EC directives and regulations whose adoption required the unanimous support of all member-governments) and positive action programmes that were not legally binding upon member-governments and employers.

Secondly, not all member-governments shared the social protectionist aims of the Commission and its rather *dirigiste* approach towards implementation of the Social Action Programme. In particular, there was a major rift after 1979 between the British Conservative government, whose macro-economic policy was based upon deregulation of the labour-market, and the Commission, which refused to endorse the abolition of workers' legal rights in the name of greater labour flexibility. Moreover, the Commission made little attempt to accommodate national differences in social policy arrangements. Instead, it took as its model in all areas the best practice within the Community (e.g. the German model of worker participation) and tried to impose it on other member-states. Needless to say, this did little to pacify the governments of those member-states such as the United Kingdom, whose existing policies were, by implication, often deemed to be inadequate by the Commission.

Thirdly, the Social Action Programme was launched just as the European economies plunged into a deep and prolonged recession. The sharp rise in unemployment levels throughout the Community after 1974 rapidly reduced the amount of revenue available to national governments for social policy expenditure. Thus, while the Commission was exhorting member-states to commit more resources to the Social Action Programme, most national governments were busily trimming back on social provision. The changed economic background also prompted an important shift in the prevailing political climate within the Community; the social-democratic consensus that had inspired the Social Action Programme had, by the late 1970s, been seriously challenged. The renaissance of economic liberalism and growing opposition to the welfare state within right-wing parties in Western Europe brought with it a questioning of the central assumptions of the Social Action Programme.

What, then, did the Programme achieve? Community laws on equal pay, health and safety at work, and the protection of workers' interests in the event of take-overs and employer insolvency should not—despite their limitations in practice—be totally dismissed. They provide a necessary juridical basis which, as the evolution of the EC equality directives has shown, can be extended and strengthened by subsequent European Court rulings. In addition, the Social Action Programme established an embryonic institutional framework that has played an important role in the preparation of EC social measures to be implemented by 1992 (see below). Also, the 1974 Social Action Programme was the first concerted attempt made at giving the European Community a social dimension. The initiatives undertaken by the Community during this period form the basis for the debate that has now come to the fore in the context of the establishment of the single market. As illustrated below, the Delors package essentially represents a further development of the measures outlined above.

8.4 THE 1980s, EUROPEAN UNION, AND THE SOCIAL DIMENSION OF THE INTERNAL MARKET

The 1980s have witnessed a second relaunching of the European Community, prompted by somewhat improved economic conditions, the entry of Spain and Portugal into the Community, and the appearance on the scene of pro-European figures such as François Mitterrand and Jacques Delors. At the Stuttgart Summit in June 1983, the EC heads of government (including Margaret Thatcher) signed a solemn declaration committing member-states to the creation of a European union. However, as indicated in Chapter 1, the precise meaning of this term remains unclear. Indeed, it is the ambiguity surrounding the concept that lies at the root of the present dispute between so-called maximalists who support further social and political integration, and minimalists (such as Margaret Thatcher) whose understanding of European union amounts to little more than a deregulated market for goods and services. In 1985, the newly appointed Commission President, Jacques Delors (former French socialist Finance Minister) made clear *his* maximalist vision of European union. In his opening address to the European Parliament, Delors stressed that his aim was to establish not simply an economic and financial union, but also a 'social Europe' (*un espace sociale*). To this end the Commission was asked to prepare a programme for the achievement of European Union. This programme, which is now in the process of being implemented, was adopted in two stages:

Completion of the single market by 1992 In order to achieve the common market envisaged in the Treaty of Rome, the Commission proposed some 300 measures to be implemented by 1993 to remove all remaining physical, technical, and fiscal barriers to the free movement of goods, services, and people within the Community. This aspect of the programme was endorsed by EC heads of government at the Milan Summit in June 1985.

The Single European Act To facilitate the achievement of the single market and European union the Commission proposed a number of amendments to the EC treaties in the form of the Single European Act (SEA). The Act was signed by the heads of government in February 1986 and came into force on 1 July 1987 following its ratification by the national parliaments of all the member-states. The SEA commits the member-states not only to the completion of the internal market, but also to monetary and financial integration. Other sections clarify and strengthen EC policies relating to European political cooperation, economic and social cohesion, research and technological development, the environment, and social policy. In order to accelerate the achievement of European union, the SEA also increased the policy-making powers of the European Parliament and removed the need for unanimity within the Council of Ministers from those measures pertaining to the single market.

Three Articles of the SEA—118A, 118B and 130—deal specifically with mainstream EC social policy areas. The first, 118A, commits member-states to the upwards harmonization (i.e. adoption of the highest standards) of health and safety at work regulations. EC legislation in this area may be adopted by means of a qualified majority in the Council of Ministers. Article 118B gives to the Commission responsibility for the promotion of social dialogue between workers and employers, while Article 130 commits member-states to the reduction of regional disparities through more efficient use of the structural funds. Under the same Article a new section entitled 'Research and Technological Development' provides for a series of multi-annual scientific and technological training and research programmes to be funded jointly by the Community and member-governments.

8.4.1   The social dimension of the internal market

On 7 September 1988 the Commission adopted a communication from Vice-President Manuel Marin on the social dimension of the internal market. The document contained a series of detailed programmes of action to be completed by the end of 1992 alongside the completion of the internal market. As outlined below, the measures it proposed are directly related to the internal market, social and economic cohesion, and employment. In several instances, the proposals strengthen and extend existing social action programmes (European Commission, 1988b).

Proposals to promote the free movement of labour
1. A general system for the mutual recognition of academic and professional qualifications between member-states.
2. A Commission investigation into the number of public sector jobs that may be reserved for nationals on grounds of national security (permitted under the Treaty of Rome).
3. The elimination of all forms of discriminatory treatment between EC migrants and nationals with regard to discretionary social security benefits in some member-states.
4. The introduction of a European training certificate, recognized throughout the Community.
5. The introduction of a European citizen's card for the over-sixties, which will entitle holders to concessionary fares on public transport throughout the Community.

Measures to promote social and economic cohesion
1. Reform of the structural funds (agreed by the Council of Ministers in June 1988 and effective from 1 January 1989) to concentrate resources on three priority tasks: assisting less developed and declining regions; combating long-term and youth unemployment; and encouraging the development of rural areas. Member-governments have also agreed to a doubling in size of the structural funds by 1993 (by which date they should total 50 billion ECUs).
2. A second Community Action programme (1988–90) on behalf of handicapped people (adopted in resolution form by the Council of Ministers in May 1987).
3. A third anti-poverty programme (1990–93).

Employment and training initiatives
1. Various action programmes for the long-term unemployed, women (especially migrant women and women setting up their own business), and workers employed in small and medium-sized enterprises (SMEs).
2. Revival of the draft directive (first proposed to the Council of Ministers in 1984) guaranteeing all employees family and parental leave.
3. Promotion of European education and training programmes funded by the Community including:
   COMETT (Community Programme in Education and Training for Technology). Adopted by the Council of Ministers in July 1986 to promote transnational cooperation between industry and universities in the area of training in new technologies by means of student placements in industries in other EC states, transnational training programmes, and the creation of a network of university–industry partnerships.

ERASMUS (European Community Action Scheme for the Mobility of University Students). Adopted by the Council of Ministers in July 1987, ERASMUS aims to increase the geographical mobility of students and academics by means of student and staff exchanges.
YES (Youth for Europe Scheme). Adopted by the Council in 1988, YES promotes youth exchanges among young people not engaged in higher education.
Lingua programme. An EC-funded language training programme for students (but not schoolchildren in the United Kingdom), employees, and vocational and professional trainees.
Youth training. Adopted in December 1987 in the form of a legally binding decision, this legislation entitles all young people to at least 12 months of vocational training after their compulsory school education.

Improvement of living and working conditions
1. An EC action programme on health and safety at work, focusing upon health and hygiene regulations, ergonomics in the workplace, and information and training. Four draft directives have been forwarded to the Council establishing minimum standards for fire prevention, ventilation and lighting, the use of computer visual display units and the handling of heavy goods, and machinery design.
2. EC legislation guaranteeing the rights of part-time and temporary workers.
3. A standard EC work contract.

Promotion of social dialogue
1. Promotion of closer cooperation between management and unions which may result in EC-wide collective agreements. The first such meeting, organized by Jacques Delors, took place at Val Duchesse in January 1985.
2. A European Company Statute guaranteeing worker participation. The proposal adopted by the Commission permits companies to choose between three types of worker participation. One is the West German model (*Mitbestimmung*) of having workers on supervisory boards. Another is the Franco-Belgian model of elected workers' councils (*comités d'entreprises*), and the third is the supposedly British model, which leaves it up to companies to negotiate their own arrangements.
3. The establishment of a European Social Charter guaranteeing employees a plinth of guaranteed social rights. The preliminary outline Social Charter drawn up by the Commission includes provision for a ceiling to working hours, fair and reasonable remuneration, minimum rates of social security, free association in trade unions or professional associations, free collective bargaining, access to training, sexual equality, development of worker participation, protection of children and adolescents, and support for the elderly. At the June 1989 Madrid Summit, the heads of government voted by 11 to 1 (the UK government) to adopt the draft Social Charter prepared by the Commission and to implement the necessary legislation in the near future.

8.4.2   The controversy surrounding the social dimension of '1992'

The Marin proposals have prompted a major row between Britain and the rest of the European Community. While other member-states have voiced opposition to particular aspects of the programme, the UK government is alone in its opposition to the package in principle. Despite signing the Single European Act (which specifically committed the signatories to a strengthening of EC social policy), Mrs Thatcher and her government consistently opposed and obstructed every Commission proposal relating to the social dimension. Thus, in May 1989, the United Kingdom was the only EC state to veto EC proposals to introduce compulsory health warnings on cigarette packets (the legislation was introduced on the basis of a qualified majority) and the EC-wide pensioners' identity card. In the same month, the UK education minister, Kenneth Baker, successfully won his battle to exempt UK schools from the provisions of the Lingua programme. Then, in June 1989, the British government blocked a directive that sought to provide more childcare facilities and parental and family leave. Opposition to the social dimension was a central theme of the Conservatives' 1989 Euro-election campaign and Mrs Thatcher announced her intention of challenging any attempt to introduce the European Social Charter in the European Court of Justice. Underlying this threat is the British government's (controversial) claim that the Charter is *not* related to the single market and therefore cannot be adopted by means of a majority vote in the Council of Ministers.

The British government has invoked both economic and ideological arguments to justify its hostility to the proposed social measures. In accordance with her belief in the free market, Mrs Thatcher repeatedly claimed that economic prosperity and jobs result from deregulation of the labour market and the removal of trade barriers; the imposition of minimum wages, workers' rights and worker participation will—according to this view—serve only to increase employers' costs and render firms uncompetitive.

Government ministers have also claimed that the social dimension is a Trojan horse threatening to reintroduce socialism into Britain. Underlying this assertion is the present government's hostility to corporatist industrial relations. Having worked for the past ten years to curb the rights and powers of British trade unions, Mrs Thatcher had no desire to see these rights restored by the European Community. Hence her warnings about the threat of a supranational, socialist state.

Thirdly, UK government spokespeople have claimed that the Commission is overstepping its powers by unnecessarily interfering in policy areas that are, in fact, the proper domain of national governments. Proponents of this view also assert that the social dimension is undesirable because its implementation would both seriously erode national sovereignty and result in the creation of a massive EC bureaucracy.

The opposing case in defence of the social dimension has been forcefully argued by the Commission. In its view, the completion of the single market must be accompanied by a strengthened social policy for several reasons. First, as highlighted in the Cecchini Report, the predicted economic benefits of the internal market will not be equally distributed throughout the Community (Cecchini, 1988). Backward regions, declining industries, and uncompetitive firms will be adversely affected by the removal of trade barriers. The Commission argues that in the absence of EC social action, the resulting exacerbation of regional disparities would be both economically inefficient and politically unacceptable.

Secondly, the Commission claims that the free movement of labour—an essential feature of an internal market—cannot be achieved without further EC social action. At present, diverse entry requirements for jobs, inadequate training, differences in salary levels and social security provision, linguistic and cultural difficulties all serve to limit the free movement of labour. Elimination of these obstacles can only be achieved by EC action.

Thirdly, the Commission has repeatedly stressed that the European Community will need a skilled workforce, trained in the use of new technologies if it is to compete effectively with the United States and Japan after 1992. In preparation for the completion of the internal market, Community-wide training schemes should therefore be established.

Fourthly, the completion of the internal market will enable companies—including non-

EC ones—to locate in any member-state, thereby gaining free access to the EC market. The Commission fears that in the absence of any EC legislation to protect employees' rights there exists a very real danger of 'social dumping'—i.e. of companies setting up factories in those EC countries with the lowest labour costs (where wages are low and workers' interests poorly protected). Such a policy may seem attractive to some poorer member-governments seeking to attract foreign investment and to reduce imports and unemployment. Finally, the Commission has pointed out that in implementing the social dimension of the internal market, it is simply giving effect to the objectives set out in the EC treaties, the 1983 Solemn Declaration and the Single European Act, all of which commit the signatories (including the UK government) to the promotion of European social as well as economic union (European Commission, 1988c).

8.5 CONCLUSION: TOWARDS A SOCIAL EUROPE?

Within the Community, the UK government is now alone in its total opposition to the social dimension of the internal market. The Commission, the European Parliament, the Economic and Social Committee and the eleven other member-governments have all declared their support for it in principle. Though the British government may succeed in blocking and diluting certain aspects of the social dimension, many social measures relating to the completion of the internal market (e.g. harmonization of health and safety measures) will be adopted by majority vote in the Council of Ministers. Yet, as highlighted above, the social dimensions of the internal market do not constitute a new departure for the Community. The foundations of the social dimension lie ultimately in the EC treaties, and since the early 1970s the scope and importance of EC social policy have been gradually extended by Community legislation and positive action programmes. In many respects, the present social programme marks the culmination of this much longer-term process. Thus, social policy provides a clear illustration of the incremental nature of Community policy-making and European integration. Looking ahead, it should be noted that the Community has recently begun to take an active interest in non-employment related social issues including sexual harassment, cancer, AIDS, consumer rights, and the ageing population.

REFERENCES

Cecchini, P. (1988), *The European Challenge—1992: the Benefits of a Single Market*, Wildwood House, Aldershot.

Collins, D. (1983a), 'Social policy', in J. Lodge (Ed.), *Institutions and Policies of the European Community*, Frances Pinter, London.

Collins, D. (1983b), 'The impact of social policy in the United Kingdom', in A. El-Agraa (Ed.), *Britain within the European Community*, Philip Allan, Oxford.

European Commission (1981), *Thirty Years of Community Law*, European Perspectives, Luxembourg.

European Commission (1983), 'The European Community's social policy', *European Documentation*, 1978/2.

European Commission (1986), 'The European Social Fund', *European File*, 19/86.

European Commission (1988a), *Taking Action about Long-term Unemployment in Europe*, European Foundation for the Improvement of Living and Working Conditions, Ireland.

European Commission (1988b), *Un Espace Social Européen à l'Horizon 1992*, Luxembourg.

European Commission (1988c), 'The social dimension of the internal market', *Social Europe* (Special Edition), Luxembourg.

Lodge, J. (1989), 'Social Europe: fostering a people's Europe', in J. Lodge (Ed.), *The European Community and the Challenge of the Future*, Frances Pinter, London.

Mazey, S. (1988), 'European Community action on behalf of women: the limits of legislation', *Journal of Common Market Studies*, **27**, no. 1, 63–84.

Shanks, M. (1977), *European Social Policy:Today and Tomorrow*, Pergamon Press, Oxford.

Vallance, E. and Davies, E. (1986), *Women of Europe: Women MEPs and Equality Policy*, Cambridge University Press, Cambridge.

Warner, H. (1984), 'EC social policy in practice: community action on behalf of women and its impact in the member states', *Journal of Common Market Studies*, **XXII**, 141–168.

NINE

MULTINATIONAL ENTERPRISES AND COMPETITION POLICIES
NADIA TEMPINI

9.1 INTRODUCTION

Multinational enterprises (MNEs) are once more at the top of the Commission's agenda, for two quite opposite reasons. The question of MNEs and of cross-border mergers, which first erupted towards the end of the 1960s and then subsided again in the wake of the depression of the 1970s, has become topical again in the light of the Community's '1992' programme. The White Paper presented by the Commission to the European Council meeting in Milan on 28 and 29 June 1985 regretted the absence of a Community legal framework capable of encouraging cross-border activities by enterprises and cooperation between enterprises of different member-states. The mobilization of adequate investment resources, particularly in investment-intensive sectors, is more often than not impossible without a pooling of resources between several undertakings. The introduction of a coherent policy on mergers and transnational organizations is therefore rightly felt by the Commission to be of vital importance, if the ability of European business to compete with its American and Japanese counterparts is to be secured (European Commission, 1985a).

At the same time, however, multinationals are seen within the Brussels Commission and by member-governments as a phenomenon that must be tightly monitored and brought within the net of EC controls. Of the 4500 corporations operating worldwide that are loosely classified as multinationals, 2500 have EC-based operations and generate an estimated $750–850 billion. Raytheon, Hertz Rentacar, British-American Tobacco, Massey Ferguson, Black and Decker, Siemens, Warner, Lambert, Litton Industries, Philips, International Telephone and Telegraph, and Citybank-Citycorp have all had their wings clipped at EC level on such matters as plant closures or transfer of production.

This expanding web of constraints targeted on international business, both at the EC level and at the broader international level, is the result of a variety of pressures that started building up twenty years or so ago. Effective control, however, has proved very difficult. But why? This chapter attempts to explain the problems posed by the operation of multinational corporations and the legal and institutional provisions devised by the Community and by other international institutions in order to tackle them.

9.2 MNE: A DEFINITION

It is only in the last two decades that we have seen the emergence of a separate theory of the MNE, the major institution through which international production is organized. The major contribution to this field has been by economists such as Kindleberger, Hymer, Caves, Vernon, Dunning, Casson, and Robson. In spite of the existence now of a substantial body of knowledge on the subject, there is still no generally accepted definition of the MNE. Some economists define a MNE as an enterprise that controls and manages production establishments, i.e. plants, located in at least two countries, home and host (see Caves, 1982). Others prefer a broader definition that includes all 'income generating assets', like for instance sales subsidiaries (Hood and Young, 1979), while others still have preferred stricter definitions, raising the qualifying number of foreign countries to two or even six (Vernon, 1971).

There are also problems in defining 'ownership' and 'control' for purposes of quantification. The usual interpretation of 'direct investment' would require at least 25 per cent of the share of capital of the foreign enterprise to be owned by the parent. Shareholding percentages, however, are a poor measure of control, and it is indeed *control* over a foreign business that is the essential basis of the concept of the multinational. In some cases the MNE is in a unique position to provide and coordinate advanced technology, management skills as well as money capital. Control may therefore be effectively retained by the foreign firm irrespective of the ownership arrangements. In other words, there is no definitive relationship between ownership and control.

Given the lack of general agreement on definitions and the fact that the study of MNEs draws on so many different parts of economic theory, the lack of consensus among economists concerning the theory of the MNEs is hardly surprising. For the purpose of this chapter, however, the essential elements of MNE operations are power of control over decision-making in a foreign enterprise; the collective transfer of resources involving factor inputs such as knowledge and entrepreneurship as well as money capital; and finally, the requirement that the income-generating assets acquired by this process be located in a number of countries. A short, working definition that summarizes these elements is provided by Hood and Young (1979): 'A MNE is a corporation which owns (in whole or in part), controls and manages income-generating assets in more than one country. In so doing it engages in international production, namely across national boundaries financed by foreign direct investment.'

9.3 ECONOMIC CONSEQUENCES OF MNE OPERATIONS: THE THEORY

The current economic theory of the MNE began mainly as an attempt to explain post-war US direct investment in Western Europe. Initially the two main analytical questions posed were: why do the investing firms produce in Europe rather than in the United States?; and, how can they compete with indigenous producers given the additional costs of doing business abroad? The answer to the first question pointed typically to the fact that investments were import-substituting and that local production was made profitable by the avoidance of transport costs and tariffs, as well as providing access, in some cases at least, to cheaper labour. The answer to the second question was provided by the 'technology gap' theory, according to which the cost to US firms of doing business abroad was offset by lower production costs and better quality achieved through superior technology and more professional management (see Casson, 1986).

It was particularly the creation of the two major trading blocs, the EEC and the European Free Trade Association (EFTA) in 1957 and 1959 that triggered the large wave of offensive and defensive investment by American multinationals. The obvious reasons for it were to exploit the economies of scale allowed by the larger markets and to jump tariff barriers raised against exports, in order to maintain rather than increase the old share of the market. In the late 1950s, these large sums of American direct investment were welcomed rather than treated with suspicion, and in fact positively encouraged by the European governments, who competed with each other to attract them, offering foreign investors special advantages, tax concessions, and the like. When throwing their arms open to the MNEs, the various EC governments were probably using a neoclassical framework of analysis, in trying to weigh the advantages of direct investment against its disadvantages.

Within this framework direct investment seemed advantageous to the host countries as it provided new techniques, physical and financial capital, employment opportunities, social overhead capital (such as roads, railways, ports, etc.), and external economies to other industries. According to neoclassical theory, the only disadvantage of direct investment would be its negative effects on the balance of payments, as exchange would have to be provided to transfer the profits abroad. In a regime of fixed exchange rates this would have the effect of depressing domestic investment, via changes of the money supply and upward pressures on the interest rate; while in a regime of flexible exchanges it would probably cause depreciation of the domestic currency. The traditional attitude on this point, however, was to deny the existence of a real 'transfer problem'.

The neoclassical analysis of the operation of the MNE was rejected in the 1960s by Hymer (see Hymer, 1980) who developed a radically different approach, focusing on the monopolistic nature of the 'ownership and location advantage' (such as avoidance of tariffs and transport costs, superior technology, more professional management skills) of the MNEs. Hymer started off by trying to provide an answer to a very simple question: why had US investment in Europe changed from portfolio to direct after World War Two? What was behind the 'control' allowed by the direct investment? The neoclassical explanation of international capital flows based on interest rate differentials could not answer that and was also at odds with the empirical observation that direct capital can flow between countries simultaneously. Why were some European MNEs investing in the United States at the same time that US MNEs were investing in Europe?

Hymer's answer was that direct and portfolio foreign investment were not substitutes for each other. He stressed that the possession of financial capital was not sufficient to explain direct foreign investment. Were capital itself the sole advantage, then portfolio capital alone would flow from low to high interest rate countries. In this case one would have foreign ownership of financial assets, but no control. It is the *control* component that explains the empirical observation that direct capital can flow between countries simultaneously. According to Hymer, therefore, direct investment takes place only when a firm has some major advantage over its competitors at home and abroad and can obtain a peculiar advantage from the international coordination of its economic action. This advantage may be access to capital, which is why capital movements cannot be altogether excluded from the analysis; but it may also be access to a market or monopolistic command over technology, superior efficiency in information gathering, or skill in exploration. Control is therefore retained so as to exploit the full economic rent of the advantage.

Clearly these considerations give a completely new turn to the analysis of the advantages and disadvantages of direct investment. According to Hymer's approach we should be looking at the effects of a process that rests on the economic exploitation of a monopolistic or quasi-monopolistic advantage. The assessment should move along lines quite different from the traditional ones of quantifying the impact of 'neutral', so to speak, capital and trade flows on the balance of payments position of the trading countries. What the analysis should try to identify are then the distortions to production and distribution that always accompany a monopoly situation, only complicated this time by their international setting.

And these are indeed the indications along which research in this field moved in the

1970s. Neoclassical theory maintained that two entities of equal intelligence, maximizing profits in the same economic circumstances, will behave in exactly the same way and that therefore it makes no difference to the conduct of a country's industry that a large part of it is owned by foreigners based in some other country. In the light of what was said by Hymer, this could no longer be true as the total circumstances of an international corporation and a domestic corporation are not the same, even though the two corporations might be identical. The difference lies mainly in the fact that the two firms operate to maximize profits within two different horizons. Crucial differences would therefore emerge in their global strategy, as well as in their use of reserves and depletion funds. MNEs, unlike their national counterparts, are in a position to engage in transfer pricing practices, manipulating costs and internal pricing between different parts of the company. A major effect of transfer pricing practices, apart from their arbitrary redistribution of wealth among nations, is to distort the official figures for trade balance, and, in some cases, the value of currencies.

Much work has since been done to elaborate the themes appearing in Hymer's study. Summing up, the recent literature on the subject seems to point at the ownership advantage (monopolistic or not) and at the internalization and location advantages as the three types of advantage necessary to explain the behaviour of MNEs (see Dunning and Robson, 1987). The final outcome, however, seems to be broadly similar in that MNEs bring about a distortion of the markets in which they operate.

The growth of MNEs as major organizing institutions for the production of goods and services in international trade has also important repercussions on the financial and money markets. Their operations have in fact induced a revolution, as yet poorly studied, in international monetary accounting relations (Davidson, 1982). The growth of MNEs in foreign trade has triggered to a large extent the growth not only of TNBs (transnational banks) (TNBs) (Yannopoulos, 1983), but more importantly of a Eurocurrency system which, under present rules, appears to be outside the control of any national government. The growth of one has helped the growth of the other. Their symbiotic relationship might indeed in the end threaten the ability of national governments to pursue independent public monetary or fiscal policies that are in the best interest of the domestic economy but are perceived by the MNEs to be detrimental to their own interests. MNEs, through their access to borrow in Euromarkets, can free themselves from the confines of restrictive monetary policies in any single nation in which they wish to operate.

9.4   FOREIGN DIRECT INVESTMENT AND WORLD TRADE

Since the end of World War Two, the international sector of the world economy has experienced increasing growth as both world trade and foreign production have expanded more rapidly than world GNP. The United States with its 12.7 per cent, holds the largest share of world trade, followed by Germany (9.6 per cent), Japan (8.3 per cent), and France (5.8 per cent). The market economies of Western Europe together account for 34 per cent of world trade. The foreign trade of the European Community exceeds that of any country, making it the largest trading area in the world, while one half of EC trade is intra-community trade (IMF, 1983).

World trade and foreign production are integrating the world's economies at an increasing rate. The ratio of US exports to GNP nearly doubled during the 1980s. At the same time, the US share of world trade declined by a third. While world trade is becoming more important to the US economy, the share of US trade in total world trade is becoming less important as other nations expand their international sectors. Growth of trade has been experienced in most Western industrialized countries. Like the United States, they too are now experiencing declines in their world trade shares, confirming the growth of trade by the nations of OPEC and the Pacific rim.

Foreign direct investment (FDI) has also grown very rapidly since World War Two. As at the end of 1981, the United States was the world's largest foreign investor, accounting for over 40 per cent of total US FDI. Canada ranks second, as a host country, with 20.7 per cent, while the United Kingdom is the third largest recipient, with 13.2 per cent. There is considerable US investment in Latin America but very little in Japan—only 3 per cent of American firms have far greater amounts invested in developed countries than in developing ones, while industrialized nations invest primarily in each other. The major type of US FDI, approximately 40 per cent, is in manufacturing industries, reflecting the technological advantage of many US firms (Rugman *et al.*, 1987).

What recent statistics also show is that the United States has become the most important and largest host country to FDI. This phenomenon is called 'reversed investment'. Canada (13.6 per cent), the United Kingdom (17.3 per cent) and the Netherlands (22.5 per cent) account for one-half of it. Europe's involvement accounts for 64.3 per cent of FDI in the United States, while Japanese involvement at 7.7 per cent is more than double the percentage of US investment in Japan (US Department of Commerce, 1982). This last decade has confirmed the changes in the pattern of FDI. The former dominance of the United States and the United Kingdom as a result of their technological superiority has declined in relative terms. Indeed, other European and Japanese-based MNEs have been growing more rapidly than US or UK MNEs. Further patterns have emerged in recent years in FDI abroad: an increase in activity by Third World MNEs—firms in developing countries such as Brazil, Hong Kong, Singapore, India, and Mexico have been investing abroad in other third world nations; the oil-exporting developing countries of OPEC have started to make major capital investments in other countries; the emergence of Japanese MNEs (Rugman *et al.*, 1987).

Apart from the sheer size of their operations the other worrying feature of MNEs is their *concentration*. The sources of FDI are concentrated within a very limited number of corporations. There are only about 450 MNEs of significant size in the world and these entirely dominate fifteen or so crucial industries. Take, for example, the largest US, European, Japanese, Canadian, and Third World MNEs: they operate in the same limited but crucial number of sectors of the international economies, sectors that are subject to the economies of large-scale production—petroleum, motor vehicles, aerospace, soaps, and cosmetics, food, tobacco, beverages, rubber, and paper.

Summing up, an examination of world trade and investment reveals that the United States is not only the largest foreign investor, but that it is also the host to more FDI than any other country and holds the largest share of world trade, though this dominant position has been eroded in recent years by the rapid improvement of the position of West Germany and Japan. International trade and investment are now dominated by MNEs. Indeed as the statistics discussed above show, a limited number of MNEs control the majority of foreign investment.

As well as being numerous, powerful, and big, MNEs are also elusive. Until the 1960s, MNEs typically operated relatively autonomous national subsidiaries, each seeing to its national market. The reduction of trade barriers that accompanied the formation of the European Community as well as GATT negotiations, which lowered the Community's common external tariff, the emergence of competition from Japan and other newly industrialized countries exposed European industries to quite new pressures and opened up possibilities for new developments. MNEs operating in Europe responded to the increased pressures in many cases by integrating their operations across borders and specializing their production plants. As a result, each national subsidiary would produce only a small part of a common European product. In industries like electronics, integration often meant locating plants in cheap labour countries in the Far East. This strategy of integration of operations across national borders has added to the problems European governments were experiencing in dealing with MNEs, as they complicated the negotiation of strategies between governments and MNEs.

MNEs, however, vary greatly. It is clear therefore that their behaviour and the nature of the concerns they arouse is modified by a number of factors: their size, their degree of 'multinationality' (as some only operate in one or two countries outside their home base, others in fifty or more); and the nature of their home country. As the statistics discussed show, the United States is still the largest home country, but the phenomenon of multinationals has been spreading and some MNEs are now based in developing countries. Policy considerations and home country perspectives are important factors that can and do modify governmental reactions. The sectors in which MNEs operate also matter: energy companies and those extracting other raw materials are of particular policy importance, just as are those providing high-technology goods; the amount of intra-corporate transfers, as an indication of the scope for possible transfer pricing abuses; and the form of their overseas expansion. Whether they have wholly or majority owned subsidiaries, minority owned associated companies under 'effective' control, or non-equity involvements, are other details of great importance.

9.5   THE NEED TO ESTABLISH COUNTERVAILING POWER

The growing importance of MNEs in the world economy in general and in the European Community in particular became really evident in the 1970s. MNEs, it was then felt, had brought advantages in that the level of economic activity had been undeniably increased, with favourable impact on productivity, growth rates, and overall level of employment, on the dissemination of the new products and processes, and also on managerial know-how. The spread of MNEs, however, had also brought many concerns, mostly related to their concentration of economic power, to the abuse of their dominant market position (entry barriers, price fixing, market sharing), as well as of their international dimension (transfer pricing, tax evasion).

Although the problems raised by MNEs varied from country to country, and from industry to industry, there was none the less one concern about MNEs that was more or less universal: the challenge they pose to national sovereignty and the failure at international level to establish adequate countervailing power. While national governments are clearly not powerless and MNEs not completely free either, their size, the resources at their disposal, their flexibility, and their supranational goals make them less accountable to national policies than purely national firms. Discrepancies in national laws and national circumstances are taken advantage of by MNEs. Their 'global reach' makes for a striking contrast with trade unions, who are still essentially national in scope.

Since MNEs are a world-wide phenomenon, their development stressed the need for a world-wide answer, for cooperation between countries or groups of countries on matters such as tax provisions and anti-trust legislation, as well as the need to establish firm, legally binding guidelines for their activities at the international level (European Community 1981–2). And there was also a common understanding, in principle, within the Commission, at EC level and at the broader international level, on what international agreements on MNEs should aim at achieving. It was necessary to obtain the following:

1. Greater understanding of the way MNEs work and operate world-wide. This could be achieved through more adequate and regular information. Disclosure of MNEs should— as it was in fact stated in the draft document of the UN Code of Conduct for MNEs of December 1978—within reasonable time limits and on a regular basis, but at least annually, provide to the public in the countries in which they operate clear and comprehensible information designed to improve understanding of the structure, activities, and policies of the transnational corporations as a whole. Such information should be disclosed to meet the differing needs of governments, employees, and the public in general.
2. International cooperation and agreements to make information requirements as comparable as possible, in order to facilitate the interpretation of information on a world-wide basis and not give a competitive advantage to companies in countries with slacker requirements. This amounts to the development of international accountancy standards.
3. The development of appropriate reporting standards for various categories of non-financial disclosure. Besides the investment or disinvestment decisions affecting their future, growing public concern in the areas of environment and consumer protection should be responded to in a clear way.
4. The development of an information bank on multinationals, such as the United Nations Centre on Transnationals, should be created.

It was quite clear, in other words, that the policy framework that needed to be constructed could not fall within one neat category of public policy. Within the European Community alone, for instance, it would have had to consist, besides information disclosure, of interrelated decisions and directives in the areas of company law, co-determination, competition policy, and fiscal policy. Progress at international level on these matters has been disappointingly slow. A large number of multinational-related issues stem from clashes of sovereignty, between home and host countries, between countries with a strong system of controls on enterprises and those with more liberal regimes, or which apply lower tax rates, and so on. Countries therefore find that they are competing with each other for new investments from abroad. Agreement at international level on measures to restrain MNEs then becomes very difficult to achieve.

This applies to EC member-countries as well. The interest of the Community countries on this issue are mixed, each member having different concerns as home and host country and as regards the behaviour of Community or non-Community firms within the Community, and of Community firms in third countries.

9.6   INTERNATIONAL INITIATIVES

Since MNEs are a world-wide phenomenon, it is clearly essential to extend international cooperation and exchange of information in this area as well as to establish clear guidelines for their activities at the international level. The following major initiatives in this area have been taken.

9.6.1   The OECD Guidelines

The 'Guidelines for Multinational Enterprises', agreed in Paris in 1976, respond to the concerns about MNEs within a rather cohesive set of industrialized countries. They lay out general guidelines for the international conduct of MNEs and are voluntary in nature.

There is currently much discussion about their effectiveness. It is generally recognized that they are an instrument of potentially great importance in that they lay down certain principles of broad applicability. These principles have already been used to some effect against companies, as in the well-known Badger case, where a combination of the existence of the code as well as of other political pressures forced the parent company in the United States to meet the obligations of a subsidiary that was closed in Belgium, thus finally permitting compensation under Belgian law to staff who were made redundant.

Nevertheless the TUAC (Trades Unions Advisory Council) in particular is not satisfied with the workings of the Guidelines and is still insisting on the need for binding regulations, as well as on the need for national bodies created to review matters stemming from the Guidelines.

The EC Commission itself, in its note to Parliament of 1978, pointed out that 'since they have no legal force the guidelines alone cannot serve to improve the position of, for example, a creditor or a worker who has been made redundant. Furthermore the Badger case demonstrates that the problems of the responsibility owed by the parent companies within a group can be imposed only by adopting binding rules creating legal obligations' (EC Commission, 1985b).

9.6.2   The International Labour Organization

The 'Declaration on Multinational Enterprises and Social Policy', agreed in Geneva in 1977, is a voluntary set of guidelines addressed to governments, labour organizations, and MNEs. Its main interest lies in its tripartite nature, involving representatives of workers, employers, and governments. The Declaration is more detailed and progressive on social policy matters than the OECD Guidelines as it is essentially aimed at improving the social and employment behaviour of MNEs.

9.6.3   The UN Code of Conduct

The 'Code of Conduct for Transnational Corporations' was originally proposed in 1976 and reached its final form in 1983. Preparation of the Code has long been a UN priority.

In sharp contrast to the piecemeal approach adopted by the Community and to the establishment of voluntary guidelines by the OECD countries, the United States led throughout the 1970s a crusade for a comprehensive, legally binding international code of conduct on MNEs. By 1981, however, that had changed in favour of a voluntary code. A prolonged economic slump had altered the climate for the UN Code and its purpose. The proposal for a code stemmed from the pressure to regulate MNEs coming from the developing countries, grouped together in the so-called 'Group of 77', and from the international trade union movement, in particular the European dominated International Confederation of Free Trade Unions (ICFTU, socialist) and the World Confederation of Labour (WCL, Christian) (see Trisciuzzi, 1985).

9.7   EC POLICY ON MULTINATIONAL ENTERPRISES

In addition to these international initiatives, which are of a non-binding nature, it was also clearly essential as well as more immediately practicable to take specific actions at the Community level. Binding regulations at the Community level could be effective in their own right, and also serve as a basis for similar agreements at the international level. Progress at the Community level, however, has been disappointing. The EC attitude and standpoint on the subject has also shifted considerably over the years, together with changing economic circumstances.

In the ten or so years that followed the creation of the six-nation Community, Europe had experienced a decade of unparalleled growth, favoured by stable exchange rates. The initial priority goals embedded in the Treaty of Rome were multinationalization of the six members' economies and unfettered trade in the broader international context. MNEs were seen, at this stage, as the 'natural' product of economic liberalism, and neoclassical analysis encouraged an optimistic assessment of the consequences of their operations. No one thought of restraining or regulating them. In fact European governments competed with each other to attract them.

Economic circumstances changed dramatically in the 1970s. The miraculous growth of the previous decade turned into depression first and then stagnation. The ten years or so of high inflation, rising unemployment, and economic uncertainty that followed the collapse of the Bretton Woods system in 1971 and the oil price shock of 1973 considerably changed the attitudes of the by now ten-nation European Community towards MNEs. Governments started worrying about the size of MNEs and their power on particularly sensitive areas, such as plant closures and job losses. In the second half of the 1970s company regulation legislation aimed at curtailing the activities and autonomy of MNEs began to emerge, as well as some measures of trade protectionism. The change of attitude of the Community and declining liberalism has meant, on the other hand, a substantial shift in business attitudes towards the European Communities. The monitoring of EC political developments (Community proposals, directives, regulations) has since become top priority for US, Japanese, and also European MNEs.

The EC attitude and legislation towards MNEs is not, however, so clear-cut and uncompromising as one might think. It has in fact been fundamentally two-edged—on one hand encouraging multinational activity in transnational European markets, while on the other trying to remedy the disadvantages and concerns caused by this very activity.

Given these conflicting trends, it does not come as a surprise that a global Community policy exclusively addressed to MNEs does not exist. There is indeed no prospect for an EC code of conduct for multinationals in the sense of the OECD Guidelines or the United Nations Code. The EC policy in this respect has been to deal with *specific statutory laws*, but not with general voluntary statements. As Robinson (1985) has pointed out, to the extent that there is a European multinational code, this is the relevant constitutional provisions of the Treaty of Rome. This is not to say that nothing has been done at the EC level to tackle the problems posed by MNEs. There has in fact been plenty of action on the multinational front in Brussels throughout the 1970s and 1980s. This action, however, has taken the form of specific measures for containment of MNEs in particular sectors, rather than the creation of a specific, readily identifiable EC code of conduct. Although, as we shall see, things are beginning to move on this front too in the light of the creation of a single market in 1992.

It was not until November 1973 that the European Commission approved a general policy paper entitled 'Multinational Undertakings and the Community', the first paper on this subject, and submitted a draft resolution to the Council of Ministers, with an accompanying memorandum on what the Community should do in order to resolve the problems raised by the development of MNEs (European Commission, 1973). The paper prepared by Altiero Spinelli pointed out that the existing framework of national regulations was too narrow, and that an effective counterweight needed to be established at the Community as well as at the international level. The Commission called for the Council to adopt the draft resolution in order to provide for a coordinated approach to a number of otherwise scattered proposals. Approving the resolution, the Council of Ministers would have also shown its agreement with the objectives and principles outlined in the communication and its willingness to participate directly in their implementation.

During the period of economic and political uncertainty imposed on the Community and the rest of the world by the oil crisis and what followed, the EC ministers refused to act on the Spinelli resolution and in fact adopted a more flexible approach to competition policy. Almost seven years later, the draft resolution had not been adopted and was withdrawn by the Council. Only a number of piecemeal measures were adopted in the years that followed. That paper, however, remains an important reference point for EC policy on MNEs to the present day. When the Community did start the second part of the early work on implementing MNE legislation, the specific sectors mentioned in the resolution were in fact taken into account. It is therefore useful to look briefly at the analysis developed in that policy paper.

9.8 THE SPINELLI PROPOSAL

The Commission proposal started off by stressing that the measures to be undertaken should not impede the development of a phenomenon 'with recognized economic and social advantages', but that they should merely aim at guarding the Community against its harmful effects with the help of a *suitable legal framework*. This framework furthermore should not contain discriminatory aspects and should apply equally to individuals and to undertakings, whether national, international, Community, or extra-Community.

The Commission was further convinced that the problems raised by the operation of MNEs 'could not be solved by adopting a few spectacular measures or a code of good conduct which by definition would be binding only on undertakings of good will'. Indeed the size of certain problems, in particular relating to security of employment, tax avoidance, or disturbing capital movements, did justify, in the Commission's view, the adoption of *measures of greater constraint*. However, given the MNEs' flexibility and their ability to find effective answers to meet specific isolated measures, the best solution seemed to be to set up a network of coherent measures allowing MNEs sufficient autonomy, essential for the pursuit of their economic and social objectives, but sufficiently finely wrought to prohibit operations considered undesirable by the Community.

Tnis approach led the Commission to list a certain number of measures, the implementation of which, it was felt, should help to solve a large part of the problems raised by MNEs. The measures envisaged covered the following areas:

1. Protection of the general public.
2. Protection of workers' interests.
3. Maintenance of competition.
4. Takeover methods.
5. Equality of conditions of reception.
6. Protection of developing countries.
7. Improvement of information.

The considerations lying behind the choice of these action areas, and the further choice of particularly priority sectors for EC measures, still appears to provide much of the rationale for MNE policy conducted today.

9.8.1   Protection of the general public

The problems encountered in this area concern tax avoidance, security of supply, monetary stability, aid from public authorities, and the protection of shareholders and of third parties.

Tax problems   The area of taxation probably best reveals the inadequacy of nationally devised systems supplemented by bilateral agreements for tackling the phenomenon of the growth of MNEs. The very existence of this disparity has encouraged MNEs to engage in transfer prices and other practices many governments consider improper. Within the harmonization of the EC taxation systems that this situation calls for, special attention should therefore be paid to the problems of transfer prices and licence fees.

Security of supply   Given the concentration of MNEs in the energy sector, it was feared that in the event of a crisis a non-member-state with jurisdiction over a MNE could use this power in a way detrimental to the Community's interests. Measures should therefore be introduced to improve the Community's security of supply.

Monetary problems   One of the principal measures in this area should lead to a better knowledge of the financial flows accompanying companies' transnational operations. Better statistical information should also be collected to assess the impact of MNEs' capital flows on the balance of payments of the Community and of its member-states.

Aid from public authorities   In many cases, international investment plays an important role in the implementation of regional policies developed by public authorities. By being in a position to decide on the location of their establishments, not within the constraints of a national dimension but in terms of all the possibilities provided in the geographical area of the common market, MNEs can place the different members in competition with each other, to gain the greatest advantage for themselves. In order to eliminate the possibility of this happening a better coordination and harmonization of national and particularly *regional* aids needed to be developed.

Protection of shareholders and of third parties   The Commission called for the need of a 'law on groups of companies', which would legally recognize the subordination of the interests of particular companies to the group interests and therefore legalize the application of a uniform management policy for the group in relation to the companies forming part of it. Provisions should also be introduced to protect external shareholders; the parent company should guarantee to cover the failure of a subsidiary company.

9.8.2   Protection of workers

The MNEs' power to affect substantially employment in the countries in which they operate causes much anxiety among workers. A trade union counterweight should be set up for a balanced solution to this problem. This however, was *not* an EC task, although the Community could certainly encourage the growth of European collective agreements. Guarantees as regards security of employment could be achieved by pursuing the introduction of directives on large-scale dismissals; the protection of employers' existing rights in the event of mergers or rationalization; and the harmonization of national laws on mergers between companies (i.e. information of and consultation with employees prior to merger decisions by general assemblies).

The following actions were also deemed necessary:

1. Adopting the European Company Statute which would ensure that employees of branches do actually participate in the supervising of the management of the parent company, and which would also ensure the possibility of concluding collective agreements between employees and administrative organs in the European company.
2. Harmonization of labour law in order to guarantee real participation in the works council of the parent company for employees of companies that are members of a group.
3. The provision of information for, and the participation of employees in cases where either the parent company or any of the member undertakings of the group are situated outside the Community which raise further substantial problems that the Community will have to tackle.

9.8.3 The maintenance of competition

Most MNEs are of considerable size and control substantial sections of markets. They are therefore in a position to restrict competition and to abuse their dominant positions. EC rules on competition need therefore to be enforced by the following means:

1. The adoption of the draft regulation under Articles 87 and 235 establishing the incompatibility of anti-competitive merger operations within the common market and laying down the obligation to give prior notice of merger operations involving groups with a turnover in excess of 1 billion units of account.
2. Active surveillance by the Commission in accordance with Articles 85 and 86 of oligopolistic situations.

9.8.4 Takeover methods

The increasingly frequent purchasing of competitor companies with or without the latters' consent calls for the need to draw up a code of obligations concerning the ways in which such operations are to be carried out (Community rules on public takeover bids; good conduct rules allowing or disallowing takeovers in the light of the Community's economic and social aims).

9.8.5 Equality of conditions of reception

Not all third countries are as liberal in the conditions they grant to foreign companies as member-states of the Community. The restrictions in question apply to the right of establishment and financing opportunities, the right of foreigners to hold capital in or directorships of companies, profit repatriation, application of national unit-trust provisions, etc.

The Community's aim in this field, as in others, should not be to apply restrictive or discriminatory measures but to make liberalization measures more widespread. In order to eliminate discriminatory situations, the following actions would be necessary:

1. Negotiating the harmonization of conditions with the United States and Japan, and tackling the problem, among others, of tax facilities.
2. Pressing for the general adoptions of a comprehensive and comparable set of measures on MNEs by the OECD member-states.

9.8.6   Protection of developing countries

A substantial proportion of investment in developing countries is made by MNEs. Their economic and financial power can, in certain cases, result in substantial imbalances in the economic development of the developing countries, often incompatible with their long-term development aims. The Community should make every effort to ensure that investments by MNEs of Community origin are closely compatible with the economic and social aims of the host countries.

9.8.7   Improvement of information

Many of the problems and anxieties posed by the operation of MNEs could also be reduced by the widespread distribution of an annual report containing straightforward information on large national and international undertakings. This would allow all interested parties to arrive at their own conclusions on the policies carried out by the MNEs. This information should, among other things, include the following:

1. Funds invested, reinvested, and transferred to the country of origin.
2. The origin and composition of the capital.
3. The number of jobs created and abolished.
4. Declared profits and taxes paid, as percentages of the turnover.
5. Expenditure on research and income from licences.
6. The information requirements listed above should be broken down into home and host countries.

9.9   MULTINATIONAL ENTERPRISES AND MERGER CONTROL POLICIES IN THE SINGLE MARKET

The present EC line on MNEs is very close to the one initially spelt out in the 1973 paper and summarized above. A measure of the operational significance of that resolution, never adopted as such by the Council, is that many measures have now been adopted which have changed national legislation in precisely the priority areas outlined in it.

Partially encouraged by the adoption in June 1976 of the OECD Guidelines for Multinational Enterprises, a new wave of rules and decisions affecting MNEs in a wide variety of sectors, such as employment protection, and anti-trust and information disclosure, was indeed started in 1977. Heightened activity during this period, as Robinson (1985) remarks, reflected disparate causes: external political pressures for control of MNEs exerted on the EC, such as the start of UN negotiations for a 'Code of Conduct' in 1977; UNCTAD IV's May 1976 resolution on transfer of technology by MNEs; the arrival of pragmatist Etienne Davignon to head EC industrial policy; the creation of a small MNE policy office at the Community headquarters in Brussels; the increasingly successful drive of European anti-trust officials against MNEs abuses through the creation of precedents based on Article 86 of the Treaty of Rome.

Retaining the priority sectors for actions outlined by Spinelli in 1973, the Community has pushed ahead with policy measures in selective areas. Large-scale dismissals, employee protection in merger cases, mergers, harmonization of company law, corporate disclosure, co-operation to tackle corporate tax evasion, have all been dealt with in one way or another in recent years and proposals in virtually every other area have been actively pursued (a summary of EC legislation on MNEs is given at the end of this chapter).

The last few years, however, have witnessed a clear change of attitudes and some active movement on these matters. The campaign for new powers to regulate mergers and to control the transnational activities of MNEs has found in the creation of the single market a vital source for renewed institutional momentum, and in the former Irish Commissioner for Competition Policy, Peter Sutherland, 'the most vigorous and committed Competition Commissioner Europe has ever had' (Owen and Dynes, 1989, pp. 112–124). Presenting the Commission's 16th annual report on competition policy in July 1987, Sutherland stressed his intention to revive the long-standing 1973 Community draft directive on mergers and takeovers (the 10th Directive on Company Law) and his determination 'to use the full force of Art. 85 and 86 to fill the gap in the present legislation' (Sutherland, 1985). 'My aim', Sutherland had already anticipated at the 8th Annual Competition Law Conference in Brussels in November 1985, 'is not only to administer but to improve competition policy in several respects' (Robinson, 1985). He intended to strengthen:

- the enforcement of anti-trust rules, to deal with, in particular, clear infringements of Articles 85 and 86;
- the effective application of the recent 'block exemption regulations' in order to ensure a maximum of legal certainty;
- the decentralization of enforcement by having EC merger regulation laws applied by national courts;
- the adoption of measures intended to 'fill the gaps' that still existed in the EC policy, particularly in relation to the proposals submitted to the Council concerning pre-merger control;
- clarity and legal security in areas of franchising, know-how, licensing and joint ventures;
- the effective application of competition policy in the public sector, and in particular the full use of Articles 37 and 90.

For a competition policy programme, it was a very substantial one, and one that Sutherland stuck to in his four years of office.

As Sutherland had pointed out in his programme, the provisions of the Treaty of Rome had already given the European Commission considerable powers to monitor certain categories of business activity. All the Commission needed was the political will to use them to the full. Article 85 prohibits as incompatible with the common market any form of price-fixing and market-sharing agreements. The Commission, however, has also the power to give its approval to any restrictive practice when such agreement contributes to improving the production or distribution of goods or to promoting technical or economic progress. Enforcement of Article 86, on the other hand, allows the Commission to investigate any business suspected of abusing its dominant position. However, under Article 86, mergers that would create a dominant position likely to be abused can only be investigated *after* they have taken place. This, in the eyes of Sutherland and the Commission, is the Achille's heel of the Treaty's provisions, as it substantially weakens the powers of competition enforcement of the Commission, now more damaging than ever, given the new wave of transnational mergers and takeovers triggered by the imminence of the 1992 single market (Owen and Dynes, 1989, p. 113).

A short-term solution to remedy this loophole in the existing provisions could be found by 'stretching' Articles 85 and 86 to cover the difficult cases of 'potential competition'. An important step in this direction was taken in November 1987, when the Court of Justice, ruling over a takeover bid by the US company Philip Morris of a large minority stake in the UK-based Rothmans International, stated that 'the Commission had a legal obligation to investigate any merger or acquisition *that could lead to* the creation or consolidation of a market dominance, and thereby violate the Community's competition code' (European Court of Justice, 1987; italics added). This ruling for the first time stretched the applicability of Article 85 from price-fixing or market-sharing arrangements to 'mergers and acquisitions that might restrict competition' *before* they took place. In so doing, the ruling was trying to fill the gaps—to use Sutherland's expression—and make up for the limitations of Article 86.

A new, revised comprehensive draft directive on mergers control policy was then put forward in March 1988. This new draft directive proposed that the Commission should have the power to regulate all mergers where the combined turnover of the companies exceeded £690 million (European Commission, 1988). The United Kingdom and France were the only two member-states who failed to recognize the need for such Community policy and refused to give their 'approval in principle' to the new draft directive. France, however, was eventually won over in June 1988, and the United Kingdom followed suit in January 1989. Although Sutherland had failed to get a merger control directive passed during his term of office, which ended in 1988, he 'had managed to push the issue to the top of the European agenda' (Owen and Dynes, 1989, p. 117).

9.10 A FINAL ASSESSMENT

Why has progress on regulation and control of MNEs proved so difficult? 'Because member-states' views differed' could be a very simple answer. As for many other areas of possible EC intervention, conflicts of views stemmed from a conflict of interests. The fundamental ambivalence that the Community has displayed over the years on MNE-related issues is in fact the result of a number of different economic interests, as well as of diverse national, political, and institutional factors.

The European Community is both home and host country to MNEs. Control measures for MNEs are therefore likely to have a direct impact on a large section of international companies, either at headquarters or at subsidiary level. The figures for MNE activities in the Community discussed above are enough to give an idea of the huge conflict of interests that legislative measures proposed to control their activities are likely to arouse. Member-states have diverging economic interests and different legal traditions; their economies display different degrees of 'openness'; the attitude of some of their governments has also shifted over the years on the MNE issue. The 'issue' itself is extremely complex, as we have seen. It affects politically sensitive areas such as worker participation, employees' information, job protection, and corporate disclosure. MNE issues have also become very politicized and therefore more likely to polarize attitudes. This is partly due to the strong ideological opposition to MNEs of the European trade union movement. The ETUC, the European Trade Union Confederation, has been the strongest non-governmental supporter of EC measures designed to curb international business. Support for them has also come from the ICFTU, the International Confederation of Free Trade Unions.

The creation of an internal market in 1992 should provide the Commission with a real incentive to speed up the process of political as well as economic integration in the Community, through the establishment of a common legal, taxation, and financial system and through the simplification of procedures for the reorganization of the legal structure of companies. We might, therefore, be just about to witness more decisive action also on MNE regulation. Many changes that the single market will bring about, like the harmonization of the taxation system, will in any case deeply affect the way MNEs operate today.

Still, the fundamental ambivalence displayed by the Community on the MNE issue is likely to remain as it rests on conflicts of interest of difficult solution and on a basic contradiction at institutional level, as Robinson (1985) has pointed out. On one hand, the European Community was formed with an idea of building a multinational market for trade and enterprises, pulling down national trade barriers, liberalizing and releasing the 'free forces' of a European market; on the other, it simultaneously saw itself as a pro-active, policy-creating institution aimed at controlling and regulating, through a complicated legal system, those very forces it was fighting hard to release.

Mergers and transnational operations are unproblematic as such, providing that they do not diminish effective competition and hence the freedom of action and choice of suppliers, buyers, and consumers. This aspect, as we have seen, is governed by the rules on competition in the Treaties of Rome and Paris. Article 220 of the EC Treaty even refers to the desirability of encouraging the development of larger companies in Europe as a way of improving competitiveness *vis-à-vis* American and Japanese companies. Pro-competitive transnational mergers integrate the internal market, facilitate risky investment, encourage innovation and transfer of technology, reduce structural overcapacity, and improve the industry's competitiveness. They do appear, therefore, to be the logical economic consequence of the provisions of the Treaty of Rome.

At the same time, however, MNE operations can and do have anti-competitive effects that run counter to the Community's general economic objectives. This is the case when MNEs lead to transfer-pricing practices, raising entry barriers, and in general to excessive concentration of market power. Their power and pervasiveness is then seen as an abuse of their dominant market position and a threat to the national sovereignty of governments.

As a result, the EC policy towards MNEs has been double-sided and fundamentally ambiguous. It has encouraged multinational activity in a transnational European market, and, at the same time, it has tried to minimize the side-effects of this activity by binding legal measures of containment, rather than a single EC code of conduct (Robinson, 1985). It still remains to be seen whether the single market of 1992 will bring about real harmonization of EC company laws and a genuine political will to implement them.

REFERENCES

Casson, M. (1986), 'General theories of the multinational enterprise: the relevance to business history', in P. Hertner and G. Jones (Eds), *Multinationals: Theory and History*, Gower, London.

Caves, R.E. (1982), *Multinational Enterprise and Economic Analysis*, Cambridge University Press, Cambridge.

Davidson, P. (1982), *International Money and the Real World*, Macmillan, London.

Dunning, J.H. and Robson, P. (1987), 'Multinational corporate integration and regional economic integration', *Journal of Common Market Studies*, **XXVI**, no. 2, 103–126.

EC Commission (1973), *Multinational Undertakings and the Community*, S.15/73.

EC Commission (1985a), *Completing the Internal Market*, COM (85) 310 Final.

EC Commission (1985b), SEC (78)2860.

EC Commission (1987), *Sixteenth Annual Report on Competition Policy*.

EC Commission (1988), *Amended Proposal for a Council Regulation on the Control of Concentration between Undertakings*, COM (88) 97.

European Court of Justice (1987), *Proceedings of the Court of Justice of the European Communities*, 24/87, Luxembourg.

Hood, N. and Young, S. (1979), *The Economics of Multinational Enterprise*, Longman, London.

Hymer, S.H. (1980), *The Multinational Corporation*, Cambridge University Press, New York.

International Monetary Fund (1983), *International Financial Statistics*, Washington, DC.

Owen, R. and Dynes, M. (1989), *Britain in a Europe Without Frontiers*, Times Books, London.

Robinson, J. (1985), *Multinationals and Political Control*, Gower, London.

Rugman, A., Lecraw, D. and Booth, L. (1987), *International Business: Firm and Environment*, McGraw-Hill, New York.

Sutherland, P. (1985), 'Towards positive guidelines on joint ventures', paper presented at European Studies Conferences, Brussels, November.

Trisciuzzi, G.S. (1985), 'Multilateral regulation of foreign direct investment', in B.S. Fisher and J. Turner (Eds), *Regulating the Multinational Enterprise*, Gower, London.

US Department of Commerce (1982), *Survey of Current Business*, Bureau of Economic Analysis.

Vernon, R. (1971), *Sovereignty at Bay*, Longman, London.

Yannopoulos, G. (1983), 'Growth of transnational banking' in M. Casson (Ed.), *The Growth of International Business*, George Allen & Unwin, London.

LIST OF RELEVANT EC DIRECTIVES

Company law

1. *First Directive.* Council Directive 68/151/EEC of 14 March 1968 governing the disclosure, validity of obligation entered into by the representative organs, and the nullity of public limited companies and private limited companies. OJ no. L65, 14.2.1968.

2. *Second Directive.* Council Directive 77/91/EEC of 13 December 1976 relating to the formation of public limited liability companies and the maintenance and alteration of their capital. OJ no. L26, 31.1.1977.

3. *Third Directive.* Council Directive 78/855/EEC of 9 October 1978 concerning mergers of public limited liability companies. OJ no. L295, 20.10.1978.

4. *Fourth Directive.* Council Directive 78/660/EEC of 25 July 1978 governing the annual accounts of certain types of companies. OJ no. L222, 14.8.1978.

5. *Fifth Directive.* Amended proposal for a Council Directive concerning the structure of public limited companies and the powers and obligations of their organs. OJ no. C240, 9.9.1983.

6. *Sixth Directive.* Council Directive 82/891/EEC concerning the division of public limited liability companies. OJ no. L378, 17.12.1982.

7. *Seventh Directive.* Council Directive 83/349/EEC on consolidated accounts. OJ no. L193, 13.6.1983.

8. *Eighth Directive.* Proposal for a Council Directive on the professional qualifications of statutory auditors. OJ no. C317, 18.12.1979.

9. *Ninth Directive.* Draft proposal for a Council Directive on links between undertakings and in particular in groups (unpublished).

10. Amended proposal for a regulation on a statute for European Companies, presented by the EC Commission to the Council on 13 May 1975, *Bulletin of the European Companies*, 4/75.

11. Council Directive 80/390/EEC of 17 March 1980 coordinating the requirements for the drawing up, scrutiny, and distribution of the listing particulars to be published for admission of securities to official stock exchange listing.

12. Council Directive 82/121/EEC of 15 February 1982 on information to be published on a regular basis by companies on the official stock exchange listing. OJ no. L48, 28.2.1982.

13. Amended proposal for a Council Regulation on the European cooperation grouping (ECG). OJ no. C103, 28.4.1978.

14. Amended proposal for a Council Regulation on the control of concentrations. 11150/86 of 2 December 1986, COM (86)76.

15. *Tenth Directive.* Amended proposal for a Council Directive concerning cross-border mergers between firms, COM (84) 727. At present cross-border mergers are rendered impossible by the legal obstacle placed in their way by the legislation of almost all member-states. The proposal would allow public limited companies to extend their cooperation as far as merger, with the aim of achieving the size and the economies of scale necessary to take full advantage of the European market, and strengthening their ability to compete with large undertakings from non-member-states.

Labour law

1. Council Directive 75/129/EEC of 17 February 1975 on the approximation of the laws of the member-states relating to collective redundancies. OJ no. L48, 22.2.1975.
2. Council Directive 77/187/EEC of 14 February 1977 on the safeguarding of employees' rights in the event of transfers of undertakings, businesses, or parts of businesses. OJ no. L61, 5.3.1977.
3. Council Directive 80/987/EEC of 20 October 1980 on the approximation of the laws of the member-states relating to the protection of employees in the event of the insolvency of their employer. OJ no. L283, 28.10.1980.
4. Amended proposal for a Council Directive (Vredeling) on procedures for informing and consulting employees. OJ no. C 217, 12.8.1983.

TEN

BRITAIN AND THE EUROPEAN COMMUNITY: THE IMPACT OF MEMBERSHIP
MICHAEL NEWMAN

10.1 INTRODUCTION

> We have not successfully rolled back the frontiers of the state in Britain, only to see them reimposed at a European level, with a European super-state exercising a new dominance from Brussels. (Margaret Thatcher, Bruges, September 1988)

The European Community seeks to harmonize important aspects of the policies of the member-states. Analysis of its impact must therefore deal with some factors—such as the status of European Community law—which would be similar in all states. Yet each state has entered the Community with its own tradition (or traditions), which have continued to affect its 'European' role and its attitudes towards the Community's institutions and policies.

In this discussion of the impact on the United Kingdom, particular attention will be paid to the elements that have occasioned the most debate in that country. This means that emphasis is placed upon key issues in the controversies that have surrounded membership and, in particular, upon the question of 'sovereignty'. However, it will also be suggested that many of the problems that have been identified apply to other states and, in the conclusion, it will be argued that the era of '1992' raises urgent political questions for the Community as a whole.

10.2 CONTINUING CONTROVERSY

The European Community has been a recurrent source of political controversy and conflict in the United Kingdom.

Until very recently it appeared that the Labour Party had the most serious difficulties in formulating its attitudes to the Community. Not only did Labour reject the original terms of entry in 1971, but this led it to conduct a renegotiation, and the suspension of collective Cabinet responsibility in the subsequent campaign for the referendum over membership in 1975. Nor did the positive result of the referendum curtail the controversy. By 1980 the Labour Party had again opted for withdrawal from the Community, if re-elected, and this decision was an important factor in splitting the parliamentary party and leading to the formation of the Social Democratic Party the next year. Although the Labour leadership quietly abandoned the withdrawal commitment after its electoral defeat in May 1983, and made a relatively positive declaration about the Community at its 1988 conference, it would be rash to suggest that the party's attitude is now settled.

While the Labour Party has often been overtly hostile to the Community, Conservative attitudes have become increasingly complex. Under the leadership of Edward Heath in the early 1970s, the party appeared enthusiastic, with the 'anti-marketeers' occupying a marginal position. However, this changed under Margaret Thatcher's leadership. Between 1979 and 1984 her strident demands for 'our money back' epitomized a new tone of populist national-ism in her dealings with the Community, and in 1988–89 the theme of 'national sovereignty' became ever more prominent in government propaganda. Conservatives continued to pro-claim their 'Europeanism', but simultaneously projected an increasingly negative image of the Community.

'Public opinion' is notoriously difficult to assess, but by 1989 polls suggested that the majority was now reconciled to membership. However, there was still little public interest in the Community and the UK turnout for the Euro-elections was lower than in any other EC country in 1979, 1984, and 1989.

Much of this indifference to 'Europe' is rooted in British political culture, arising from Britain's historical experience as an island power with a world-wide empire rather than a specifically European involvement. Such attitudes were reinforced by post-war factors: the humiliation of a declining great power initially rejecting West European integration and subsequently being rebuffed when it sought entry into the Community. This historical back-ground needs to be appreciated for it provides the context in which certain issues are seen as controversial in the United Kingdom (which may be easily accepted elsewhere in Western Europe). The debates have, however, normally concentrated on matters that appear more concrete. In particular, two broad areas have remained at the forefront of concern ever since Britain joined the Community:

1. Economic and financial questions, particularly about the cost of living and employment effects.
2. Constitutional and political questions, particularly about sovereignty and democratic control.

This chapter concentrates particularly on the second area, but because the issues are often closely linked, it begins with a brief discussion of the first.

10.3 THE ECONOMIC IMPACT

10.3.1 The general context

There is little doubt that after the United Kingdom entered the European Community, her economic position deteriorated in various respects. Unemployment rose to an extent that had previously appeared inconceivable in the post-war period, manufacturing industry declined ever more sharply, and the number of families living in poverty increased (accord-ing to most indicators). It is true that, after 1981, the growth rate improved and unemploy-ment declined, but it remains a matter of controversy whether this reflected a long-term improvement or simply a partial compensation for the particularly severe recession experi-enced between 1979 and 1981. But if the United Kingdom underwent an economic crisis dur-ing the decade after she joined the Community, how far, if at all, was this attributable to membership? Or has the Community had any positive role in preventing the development of a still worse situation? Before even attempting to discuss these issues (which were at the heart of the controversy between the Labour and Conservative Parties in the late 1970s and early 1980s), it is necessary to make two preliminary points:

1. The United Kingdom's economic performance prior to 1973 was, in crucial respects, worse than that of the original six members of the European Community. From a position of relative economic strength *vis-à-vis* the majority of devastated West European states in 1945, the United Kingdom subsequently experienced relative economic decline, manifested by comparatively slow growth, a decline in competitiveness, and balance of payments problems. Between 1955 and 1974 the UK share of the exports of the eleven main exporting countries fell from 19.9 to 8.5 per cent (El-Agraa, 1983) and during the 1960s the domestic consequences of this shift became ever more apparent. It was in this context that successive governments and commentators argued that EC membership was the solution to the difficulties—a catalyst that would generate new competitiveness by providing tariff-free access to a large and growing market. Given this long-term background, any argument that the Community has been the *primary* cause of the United Kingdom's economic decline must be oversimplified.

2. Britain joined the Community just at the time that the international economy was entering the worst recession that had taken place since the 1930s. Signs of the downturn had been accumulating since the late 1960s, but the rapid rise in oil prices in late 1973 precipitated a crisis in industrial capitalist economies from which they have not yet recovered. Whereas the EC countries had experienced high growth in the late 1950s and early 1960s and moderate growth thereafter, all of them now suffered from the impact of the international recession. It is certainly true that the general phenomena of de-industrialization and high unemployment were experienced particularly acutely in the United Kingdom. But there are two major reasons for scepticism about the view that EC membership has been the crucial factor in this:

   (a) Since the United Kingdom was already vulnerable as an economy prior to 1973, the sharper competition for markets (both international and domestic) during the recession placed particular strains on her industries. It is therefore highly probable that many of the depressing aspects of the United Kingdom's situation would have occurred whether or not she had joined the Community.

   (b) The sharpest rise in unemployment and de-industrialization occurred after 1979 when Margaret Thatcher's Conservative government assumed power. This administration was committed to the fight against inflation and the freeing of market forces rather than the protection of employment or industrial output. The impact of such policies was greater than that of the EC as a specific factor.

10.3.2   The economic and financial obligations of membership

The most important economic and financial obligations that the United Kingdom accepted when joining the Community were the following:

1. The Common Agricultural Policy (CAP).
2. The budgetary contributions.
3. The elimination of tariffs within the Community and the establishment of a Common External Tariff with all third countries (except those with which special arrangements are made by the Community as a whole).
4. The harmonization of competition policies.

The CAP   Prior to 1973, the United Kingdom operated a 'cheap food' policy: that is, food was bought at the lowest available world price and the exchequer provided a subsidy to UK farmers so as to provide them with a reasonable income. Although the CAP has encouraged UK farming production to increase its degree of self-sufficiency in temperate foods from 60 per cent in 1973 to more than 80 per cent in 1986 (*The Times*, 23 August 1986), from the British point of view it appears to have major defects:

1. The abandonment of a 'cheap food' policy has had a cost-of-living impact on the consumer. Since food costs are a far higher percentage of the expenditure of the poor than of the well-off, any price rise will adversely affect the least wealthy sections of the population. Only approximately 2.5 per cent of the population are employed in agriculture in Britain, so gains in farming incomes would not compensate for the generally negative cost-of-living impact. While this criticism is valid, the specific effect of CAP in the rise of food prices remains controversial. Between 1971 and 1981 food prices certainly increased dramatically—by almost 300 per cent. However, it has been argued that only about 10 per cent of this rise can be attributed directly to the CAP, as the major part of the increase reflected world-wide rises in food prices (European Commission, 1983). On the other hand, this no doubt understates the negative cost-of-living impact of the CAP on the United Kingdom for it is probable that the Community, as a major food producer, has itself contributed to the increase in world food prices. The Labour Party thus still claims that every family in the Community has to spend more than £13.50 per week to finance the CAP (Labour Party, 1989).

2. The CAP system involves a diversion to agriculture of resources that could be devoted to more beneficial uses. The most notorious aspect of this in the United Kingdom is through disproportionate budgetary contributions to the Community (see below) which spends up to 70 per cent of its income on the CAP. The United Kingdom derives far less benefit than other member-states from such expenditure because of the tiny percentage of its population involved in agriculture. Since the CAP is a mandatory expenditure item, the constant increase in the cost of farming support simply decreases the amount available for other funds (regional and social) from which the United Kingdom could derive more benefit. Furthermore, the CAP system encourages overproduction throughout the Community (including the United Kingdom), thereby drawing resources away from other possible economic uses and simultaneously damaging the environment. A recent study thus argued that the cost of agricultural price support in the 'big four' has led to a loss of between 1.1 and 2.5 per cent of potential gross output and of between 4.4 and 6.2 per cent of exports in manufacturing industries (excluding food processing). This has led to a total reduction of employment of about 860 000 jobs, with the United Kingdom and West Germany suffering most severely (Breckling *et al.*, 1987, cited in Demekas *et al.*, 1988).

These are serious concerns, but there are two provisos that are often neglected. First, the inequities between the United Kingdom and other Community countries are not as vast as the British are sometimes led to believe. Most analysts would agree that the CAP should be reformed because it is, in many respects, iniquitous and inefficient. But the specifically British aspect of the injustice is far less important than is normally implied. Thus if the CAP itself is considered (rather than its financing), the United Kingdom just about breaks even (Ardy, 1988). Secondly, even if the United Kingdom did not participate in the CAP, the Exchequer would need to subsidize agriculture in some way, and the costs of so doing were increasing fast during the 1960s. When the Labour Party considered withdrawal from the Community, its research department calculated that there would be a net saving of 1000 million pounds even if the previous support system was fully restored (Labour Party, 1981b). If these figures are accepted (and they are controversial), they suggest that freedom from the CAP would increase the funds available to the UK government by a significant, but undramatic, amount. The UK government was instrumental in negotiating a modest reform of the CAP in 1988 (see Chapter 7) but it seems unlikely that this will have a radical impact on the United Kingdom's position in relation to the policy.

Budgetary contributions From the end of the transition period in 1978 until the Fontainebleau Summit in 1984, the United Kingdom's budgetary contribution was a major issue in domestic and Community politics. Although the problem was anticipated in 1973, British dissatisfaction was hardly surprising since the contributions were not related to per capita income, but flowed automatically from levies and customs duties on imports from third countries, and a proportion of VAT receipts. As the United Kingdom imports relatively greater amounts from third countries than most EC members (as a result of long-term trading patterns), the budgetary contribution was assessed as the second highest (after that of West Germany) of the then nine members, although the UK GDP per capita was the third lowest. The United Kingdom therefore suffered from two disadvantages: a higher contribution than that warranted by her economic performance, and receipts that benefited a very small sector of the population. This problem became particularly acute in 1979 and 1980 when the net contributions mounted very sharply and, until 1984, an annual compromise was needed so that the United kingdom received rebates. This meant that she never actually paid the full amounts that would otherwise have been due. At Fontainebleau a longer-term solution was negotiated which diminished the UK budgetary contribution, although the percentage of VAT receipts transferred to Brussels by all member-states was raised (from 1 to 1.4 per cent).

None of this has fully resolved the problems, however (George, 1987). The Community budget soon entered a new period of crisis with its expenditure surpassing the agreed VAT limit as agricultural expenditure escalated. Nor has the general basis for assessing budgetary contributions been fundamentally changed. The Fontainebleau compromise does not therefore tackle the underlying iniquities in the national incidence of budgetary contributions. Ultimately, these can only be remedied either by relating contributions to an assessment of relative levels of national wealth or by increasing the percentage of Community expenditure on regional and social policies. The latter change (which was envisaged in the Brussels agreement in 1988 and in the various discussions on the Social Charter) would be the more *Communautaire* and should also ensure that the benefits were derived by regions and groups suffering relative deprivation, rather than by national exchequers. But a prerequisite would be a substantial reduction in the proportion of expenditure devoted to the CAP, and there is little sign of this at present, even though the 1988 reform of the budget (see Chapter 6) has to an extent reduced CAP expenditures and improved the United Kingdom's position by introducing the GNP based 'fourth resource'.

The British therefore still have justification for regarding their position as unfair in terms of the relationship between contributions and receipts. However, resentment should be tempered by two important considerations. First, it must, once again, be stressed that the problem is not specifically a British one. A recent study of the budget thus concludes that the distribution of contributions and receipts across the Community as a whole is arbitrary (Ardy, 1988). Secondly, it must be emphasized that the amounts involved in budgetary contributions are still relatively small, for EC contributions have not constituted as much as 1 per cent of government expenditure since 1980. The United Kingdom's economic performance would not be transformed even by their complete curtailment.

The elimination of tariffs   The United Kingdom's trading relationships are of far greater importance than the CAP or the budgetary contribution in the context of her overall economic performance and, since 1973, her trade with the rest of the Community has increased sharply. Whereas in 1972 visible trade with the Community accounted for 31 per cent of the United Kingdom's total world exports, by 1985 the rest of the Community accounted for 46.3 per cent of UK exports, and by 1988 this had risen to 49.8 per cent. The reverse trend was equally marked, with the percentage of the United Kingdom's total imports coming from the Community rising from 31.8 per cent in 1972 to 44.3 per cent by 1985, and by 1988 this had risen to 49.2 per cent (based on Eurostat, 1989). However, while there has been an increase in trade flows in both directions, imports from the Community rose far more quickly (particularly between 1973 and 1979), leading to a serious deficit in the United Kingdom's balance of payments with the rest of the Community.

The crucial question in this context is the extent to which the considerable and increasing deficit in trade with the rest of the Community, with all its implications for the level of employment in the United Kingdom, can be attributed to the removal of tariffs which is implicit in membership of the Community. This is a difficult question to answer, since in order to isolate the EC effect on trade flows one has to create an *anti-monde*, or an estimate of what would have happened in the absence of membership. One factor to consider here is that UK trade with the Community had been growing steadily prior to membership—indeed this was one of the reasons for the applications to join. Thus, whereas imports from the Community were 20.2 per cent of the United Kingdom's total imports and 21.2 per cent of total exports in 1959, by 1970 the respective figures were 27.3 and 30.1 (El-Agraa, 1983). Given the post-war tendency for industrial countries to trade more with one another, and the geographical proximity of the continent, it is highly probable that there would have been an increase in mutual trade whether or not the United Kingdom had joined. There was, in any case, a reduction in tariffs between the Community and EFTA, of which the United Kingdom was a member prior to 1973, and this would also have promoted reciprocal trade. Nor are tariff barriers always of such crucial importance as might be thought: Japan's ability to 'jump over' tariff walls and the growing phenomenon of multinational companies that circumvent such restrictions both demonstrate this. Nevertheless, there can be little doubt that the European Community fosters intra-Community trade and that membership has been an important factor in explaining the increased trade flows in both directions. However, it would be unfair to attribute the United Kingdom's deficit in trade, and in particular manufacturing trade, solely to EC membership. The United Kingdom has long been experiencing a deterioration in her trading position *vis-à-vis* the rest of the world, and in fact the deficit in manufacturing trade with Japan and the United States has deteriorated to a far greater extent. UK exports have consistently failed to maintain their share of world markets, while one of the central features of her economy has been, and, on the evidence of the recent huge balance of payments deficit, continues to be, a high marginal propensity to import. When the disposable income of UK citizens increases, domestic industries cannot meet the ensuing increased demand and imports rise disproportionately. This phenomenon arises from the underlying lack of competitiveness of British industry and has resulted in the process of de-industrialization, or the relative decline in the importance of manufacturing industry in the economy, which the United Kingdom has been undergoing since at least World War Two, and arguably much before. This process of de-industrialization was in the 1980s probably exacerbated by purely domestic factors such as continuing micro-economic deficiencies, and macro-economic factors, including the overvalued exchange rate that resulted from North Sea oil and the policy of high interest rates. Demand management policy might not have helped either, since, for example, the then Chancellor Sir Geoffrey Howe chose to deflate in a recession in 1981, although he would argue that he was merely 'removing the dead wood' of UK industry.

Nevertheless, the best estimates available support the thesis that membership of the Community reduced UK output of manufactures and worsened the trade balance in this area to a significant extent. Winters (1987) suggests that a conservative estimate of the gross loss of output that resulted from accession would be in the order of £3 billion (1.5 per cent of GNP), but that the actual figure might well have been twice as great. Winters, however, also argues that the resulting unemployment and other supply-side losses might well have been outweighed by increases in economic welfare that UK consumers enjoyed as a result of the increased availability of cheaper foreign manufactures.

It might also be argued that membership will have improved the United Kingdom's industrial structure by resulting in increased direct investment from abroad. The attractiveness of the United Kingdom as a location for US and Japanese direct investment will have been improved by the prospect of tariff-free access to other EC markets. There will also have been increased intra-Community investment into the United Kingdom, though much of this may have been in the support networks required to service the increased exports to the United Kingdom. On the other hand, some of this has probably been offset by increased UK investment in other member-countries, particularly after the abolition of exchange controls in 1979 (although the bulk of recent UK foreign direct investment has been directed towards the United States). The extent of these investment effects is of course very difficult to quantify, though evidence produced by Mayes (1985) suggests that changes in investment flows have not been as great as changes in trade flows. Dunning (1989) shows, *inter alia*, that between 1972 and 1985 investment by US companies in the United Kingdom rose marginally more rapidly than in the rest of the European Community, increasing the UK share of the EC capital stake of US companies from 37.6 to 40.7 per cent. This was in a period during which the UK share of EC sales of manufactured goods fell sharply from 31.1 to 29.4 per cent. In addition, it is clear that the United Kingdom has attracted much more Japanese direct investment than any of the other EC states in recent years. By March 1987 the stock of Japanese direct manufacturing investment in the United Kingdom amounted to $488 million out of a total of $2357 million for the twelve members of the Community. The next most favoured location was Spain with $461 million, while the stock in France amounted to $310 million, and in West Germany $277 million. If one considers non-manufacturing direct investment, the United Kingdom's performance is even more striking, with a stock in March 1987 of $3586 million out of a total for the twelve-member Community of $10 375 million. The next highest stocks of non-manufacturing Japanese direct investment are to be found in Luxembourg ($2305 million), the Netherlands ($2133 million), and West Germany ($1025 million) (O'Cleireacain, 1989). It should be noted, however, that foreign direct investment can be a mixed blessing, since it may also result in loss of economic sovereignty and long-run negative balance of payments effects. Further measures to remove non-tariff barriers and create the single market will be likely to reinforce this tendency. If this is so, what significance does it have in relation to the United Kingdom's economic plight?

This question has been discussed in a propagandist manner by both advocates and opponents of membership. The former have sometimes pointed to the amount of UK exports to the rest of the Community to argue that all these exports (and hence the jobs that go with them) would be at risk if the United Kingdom withdrew from the Community. But this is clearly simplistic for it cannot seriously be maintained that the whole EC market would disappear if the United Kingdom was not a part of the Community. Furthermore, the '1992' process might well offer opportunities for the United Kingdom, to the extent that it leads to increased trade in services, in some of which (in particular financial services) the United Kingdom enjoys a clear comparative advantage.

Harmonization of competition policy   A fundamental feature of the Treaty of Rome is that competitive conditions should be equalized throughout the area of the Community. In fact a plethora of barriers to this remain, despite frequent statements of intent by the governments of the member-states. Ultimately, competitive conditions can be equalized only to the extent that the Community becomes a single economy, equivalent to that within existing nation-states: i.e. with a single banking and monetary system, the elimination of national preferences in consumers' purchases and public contracts, real mobility of labour, a common taxation policy, and so on. The Community is nowhere near this stage, but implementation of the commitment to achieve a single market by the end of 1992, and the goal of monetary union, would constitute a very significant move in this direction.

In any case, the harmonization policy is a crucial feature of the Community and the Commission devotes a great deal of time trying to equalize commercial conditions throughout the EC area. Much of the policy is aimed at company level, but a large part is also directed at governments to ensure that they both enforce EC competition laws, and refrain from distorting competition themselves. The ramifications of this can be extremely wide-ranging: for example, during 1989 the Commission argued that UK restrictions on the percentage of shares in defence industries that could be owned by foreigners was discriminatory and, although a compromise was reached, it held that such restrictions would ultimately have to be lifted to ensure compliance with Community laws. A further crucial aspect of EC competition policy is that it precludes governments from granting financial aid or subsidies to industries or regions unless these are specifically authorized by the Commission.

Moreover, opponents of membership, such as the Labour Party in 1981, pointed out that the trade balance appeared far worse from the United Kingdom's point of view if oil was separated from general export sales to the continent and particular attention was given to manufactured goods. Two principal reasons could be given for this. First, oil is not expected to remain as a long-term resource for the UK economy; secondly, it does not provide employment on the scale of manufacturing industry. The Labour Party therefore argued that if the trade balance in manufactured goods alone was considered, the situation appeared far worse from a British perspective. Whereas such goods accounted for an increasing proportion of UK imports from the Community (74 per cent in 1980), they constituted a shrinking proportion of UK exports to the Community (66 per cent in the same year) (Labour Party, 1981b). Moreover, since 1982 the United Kingdom's total trade in manufactured goods has gone into sharp deficit and the greater part of this has been accounted for by imports from the Community. On the other hand, 'anti-marketeers' have often exaggerated in claiming that this deficit was necessarily due to membership or that it could be remedied either by rebuilding export markets with third countries or by domestic protectionism (Benn, 1979).

It is, in fact, extremely difficult to arrive at any definite conclusion about the impact of the Community on trade flows—important though the subject is. Many analysts have argued that relative price levels, the rate of inflation, government monetary and fiscal policies, and the state of non-Community markets have been more important factors than the removal of tariffs in stimulating the increase in British trade with the Community since 1973 (Morgan, 1980; El-Agraa, 1983). Above all, the maintenance of sterling at a high exchange rate, particularly after 1979, increased the price of UK exports and lowered that of imports, thereby creating both balance of trade difficulties and furthering the process of de-industrialization.

Since 1973 and, more particularly since 1979, the UK government has removed a whole range of subsidies to the regions and the nationalized industries (and it has of course privatized many industries). It has also eliminated restrictions on the free movement of capital, and has generally sought to reduce government expenditure. All this has clearly had a marked effect upon the UK economy and much of it is in harmony with the Community's competition policy.

Yet it would be wrong to conclude either that the UK government has followed this line *because* of EC requirements or that more interventionist policies would be incompatible with membership of the Community. Since 1979, the UK government has adopted a strategy in accordance with its *own* philosophy and, in the 1989 Euro-elections, the Conservative Party proclaimed its successes in converting the Community to the free market (e.g. in steel production), and its intentions of leading the way in sweeping aside the remaining restrictions (Conservative Party, 1989). Indeed the clashes between the Community and the Conservative government during 1988–89 stemmed largely from the latter's strident commitment to the *laissez-faire* approach (see below). On the other hand—as will also be discussed below—it is true that the Community's competition policy impeded some of the interventionist measures proposed by the 1974–79 Labour government.

Overall, it has been argued that the discernible impact of the Community upon the United Kingdom is extremely difficult to isolate from other factors. The negative features of the CAP and the budgetary contribution are significant but relatively small in relation to total economic performance. The removal of tariffs has had some impact in promoting intra-Community trade, but other factors also account for this tendency. It is also possible that the United Kingdom's international trading position and ability to attract external investment has been enhanced by its membership of a powerful trading bloc (but credible dissenting arguments can also be put forward). As for harmonization policy, the criteria for assessment are clearly dependent upon general value questions about economic policy: is well-being to be attained primarily through the market, through public intervention and control, or indeed, through an abandonment of the goal of economic growth (Green Party, 1989)? But whatever solutions are advocated, it would seem that membership of the Community has, *thus far*, been less important in explaining UK economic performance than either the international economy as a whole or domestic factors.

Yet this conclusion immediately raises further crucial questions. Given the general process of internationalization of economic forces, and the specific development of the European Community, how much distinction remains between the 'domestic', the 'European', and the 'international'? In particular, as 1992 approaches, with a move towards a single market, probably reinforced by a form of monetary union, how much national economic independence will exist? Such questions demonstrate the intimate relationship between the economic and political spheres, for they lead us to the second main area of UK concern: that of sovereignty.

10.4   CONSTITUTIONAL/POLITICAL ASPECTS

At the time the United Kingdom joined the Community, and during the referendum of 1975, proponents and opponents of membership differed fundamentally over their assessments of the impact on sovereignty. Anti-marketeers claimed that the crucial powers would be lost, while the pro-marketeers maintained that participation in the Community would enable the United Kingdom to regain its power through 'pooling sovereignty'. This debate has constantly recurred, but at least two different, though interrelated, issues have always been involved:

- *National sovereignty and independence* The issue of whether the United Kingdom as a state could continue to make its own policies or whether it would forfeit its national sovereignty to a supranational European Community.
- *Parliamentary sovereignty and power* A range of questions concerning the ways in which EC membership might affect the position of Parliament both as the source of legislation and as an institution that seeks to control executive power.

10.4.1   National sovereignty

Unless 'national sovereignty' is taken as a purely abstract notion, we must deal with the issue in a relative rather than an absolute way. By 1973 the United Kingdom was already a member of international organizations, such as NATO and GATT, which had limited her autonomy, and, because she was a declining power, successive governments had experienced serious constraints on their ability to carry through their strategies at home and abroad. Nevertheless, there were two ways in which membership of the European Community had implications for the issue of national sovereignty. First, in entering the Community, the United Kingdom was accepting the whole basis of the treaties and all subsequent enactments and amendments. This meant that a UK government was supposed to circumscribe its range of legislation so as to conform with Community policies. Secondly, in relation to the development of subsequent initiatives, the United Kingdom would be only one voice within the Community and, to this extent, would also forfeit aspects of sovereignty. These two issues will be considered in turn.

In accepting Community law, the United Kingdom is, at least in theory, renouncing the right of national sovereignty whenever a policy that it devises conflicts with a Community policy. And in the case of conflict, the judgment is ultimately to be made by the European Court of Justice. In fact there are relatively few well-documented instances of such conflicts. The United Kingdom has been taken to the European Court a number of times on equal opportunities' issues, quite recently in 1986 when it was found to be in contravention of Community law in the treatment of women looking after relatives with disabilities. It has also been notoriously slow on such matters and has been criticized in Brussels. Other contraventions have been on tachographs in lorries (1979), and in regard to restrictions on the import of poultry, eggs, and egg products (1982). Furthermore, in July 1989 the European Commission warned the UK government that it would face prosecution unless it came forward within two months with adequate assurances that EC water purity standards would be met after privatization of the water industry. At the time of writing, it was not clear whether such assurances would be forthcoming, although the government has, in the past, complied with the treaty when a contravention has been upheld.

The 1974–79 Labour government was also forced to make concessions on such matters as regional employment premiums, temporary employment subsidies, and government aids to offshore drilling supplies, and other member-states constantly protested about the government's aid to the steel industry. At other times the Community has not intervened even when the United Kingdom has been prima facie in breach of EC policies because it has judged it politically unwise to do so: there was thus no intervention when the Thatcher government granted state aid to Chrysler (UK) and British Leyland. On the other hand, the Commission did intervene in 1988 to reduce the amount of Rover's debts that the government was prepared to underwrite to secure the takeover by British Aerospace. The general position is that there is an obligation for member-states to inform the Commission of any financial aid that they intend to give their industries. The Commission has the right to ask for a change in policy if such aid infringes Community rules against unfair competition and, if unsatisfied, it may refer the matter to the European Court.

National sovereignty is not only involved on these relatively infrequent occasions of overt conflict. For governments, advised extensively by the home civil service as well as permanent officials in Brussels, will normally seek to ensure that their legislation is in conformity with the European treaties. In this way they are, in advance, effectively elevating Community law above potentially deviant policy choices.

We can now consider the second issue: how far is UK national sovereignty affected by the Community decision-making process?

In the early 1970s the opponents of membership tended to take the constitutional aspirations of the Community very seriously. They noted the commitment of the preamble of the Treaty of Rome to work for 'an ever closer union', and the semi-federalist discourse of much 'Euro-speak', and held that, eventually, UK ministers would be forced to accept majority decisions in all spheres of policy. The proponents of entry adopted pragmatic arguments when countering these points, claiming that some 'pooling of sovereignty' was necessary to ensure that common policies were attained, but that the United Kingdom could withstand external pressures more effectively in association with the Community than as an isolated and weakened state. They normally stressed the Luxembourg compromise of January 1966 as a guarantee that the United Kingdom would be able to check any initiatives that appeared to threaten greater supranationalism.

In the years since the referendum both major political parties have continued to stress the importance of the national veto and have been prepared to block Community progress unless their demands have been satisfied. Above all, Margaret Thatcher repeatedly ridiculed all proposals implying institutional supranationalism and maintained intergovernmentalism as the only basis for decisions. In reality, however, the situation is far more complex than the rhetoric implies.

In May 1982 a British attempt to veto an increase in agricultural price rises was superseded by various other member-states, led by the French. Despite the claim by other EC members that this was in line with normal decision-making procedures, it appeared to call into question the status of the Luxembourg compromise and the defence of 'national interests'. Subsequently, the impetus to institutional reform developed, leading eventually to the Single European Act, and an increased use of majority voting (See Chapter 2). Although the UK government claimed at the time that the effects of the change were very limited, this was seriously misleading. The legal adviser to the House of Commons Select Committee on European Legislation has thus recently argued that the social measures to which Mrs Thatcher was so opposed could be imposed by a majority vote of the European Council, in accordance with the terms of the Single European Act (Select Committee on European Legislation, 1989). In such circumstances, it can hardly be maintained that the national veto is a firm guarantee of national sovereignty.

In any case, the stress on the importance of the veto was always exaggerated, for no member of the Community could even attempt to use a veto power on more than a few occasions without Community business grinding to a halt. The United Kingdom has always been involved in the continuous process of bargaining and 'horse-trading' described in Chapter 2. When, for example, the government secured a temporary compromise on its budgetary contributions in 1980, the probable *quid pro quo* was acquiescence in the French demands in the 'lamb war'. Similarly, it is probable that part of the hidden agreement behind the Fontainebleau budgetary settlement was the United Kingdom's acceptance of the increase in the ceiling on VAT contributions the next year.

All of this suggests that membership of the Community has limited UK national sovereignty *to some extent*. But the position is not static, and '1992' can be expected to project new dynamism into the semi-supranational processes.

10.4.2 Parliamentary sovereignty

According to constitutional convention, the British parliament has been the source of all law in the United Kingdom: it was parliament rather than government that legislated. However, the reality of late twentieth-century policy-making bore little relationship to seventeenth-century constitutional theory, as government introduced the overwhelming majority of legislation and relied on its parliamentary majority to ensure that its programme was passed. In these circumstances the party in power needed to work hard to secure support only in the comparatively rare situations when its majority was threatened, and private members' bills stood virtually no chance of reaching the statute book unless supported by the government. This reduction in parliament's primacy as a legislative body was not the only difficulty under which it was labouring, for it was also facing problems in scrutinizing and controlling an increasingly dominant executive. Indeed throughout the 1960s there had been a spate of tracts arguing that parliament should be reformed so that its relative decline *vis-à-vis* the executive could be reversed.

Both the act of accession itself and, more significantly, the legal basis of the Community appeared further to weaken parliament's role. In accepting the EC Act in 1972 parliament accepted all existing Community legislation embodied in the Treaty of Rome and as subsequently interpreted: naturally, the House of Commons debated only a minute proportion of such laws and could not be said seriously to have scrutinized so wide a range of legislation. Perhaps still more fundamentally, the UK parliament accepted a key feature of the Treaty of Rome which asserted its legal supremacy over domestic law (see Chapter 2). Not only did this mean that UK legislation could be declared invalid, but it appeared to affect one more aspect of British constitutional conventions: that 'no parliament could bind its successor'. In theory, each new parliament could undo all previous legislation and begin again. However, the supremacy of Community law apparently invalidated this for, while the United Kingdom remained a member of the Community all parliaments were bound by its law.

A second relevant aspect of parliament's role concerned not so much legislation *per se* as a series of matters concerning the scrutiny and control of the executive. According to convention, ministers are responsible for government policy and accountable to the UK parliament for their actions. Once again, the pre-1967 reality was far less 'pure' than the conventions implied, and there had been growing concern among Members of Parliament and political analysts about crucial aspects of the existing system of accountability. Nevertheless, it seemed that membership of the Community could reinforce some of these problems or generate new ones:

1. The European Commission's position could, in itself, affect the notion of ministerial responsibility, for it could initiate policies that the elected UK government may not have anticipated. Legislation emanating from the Commission would also increase the output

of UK government departments and could therefore be expected to exacerbate the problems of ministerial responsibility and parliamentary control.

2. The issue of external initiation of responsibility, whether by the Commission or the Council of Ministers, raised a still more fundamental problem. In the Community, UK ministers—or prime ministers—could be outvoted by their partners. In these circumstances a minister could claim not to be responsible for policy, but a reluctant acquiescer in a majority decision. If this became a typical occurrence, the issue of governmental accountability would be affected still more markedly than by the difficulties already noted. In what ways would parliament be able to hold a minister responsible if the latter claimed that the policy was outside his or her control?

When such questions were raised by the opponents of membership, the normal governmental response was, on the one hand, to stress the desire of the Community to reach decisions through consensus and, on the other, to suggest that parliament's role could be protected if an adequate scrutiny body was established. We can therefore assess the actual impact of the Community on parliament's position, at least in part, by considering the issues in relation to this body.

Parliamentary scrutiny procedures   'Scrutiny committees' were established in the House of Lords and the House of Commons as soon as the United Kingdom entered the Community, but the first major stage in establishing more extensive arrangements came in May 1974 when a 16 member European Legislation Committee (ELC) was set up in the Commons and a far larger committee (currently of about 80, including co-opted members and subcommittees) was created in the Lords. Although the two committees confer, their functions have differed: while the Lords committee has discussed the merits of EC policies and has made detailed suggestions for changes, the Commons is particularly concerned with alerting parliament to matters emanating from the Community that may have important political or constitutional implications. It is thus seen as an 'early warning' device rather than a body that seeks to examine the merits of proposals. Because of its greater relevance on the issue of parliamentary sovereignty, only the Commons committee will be discussed here.

Over time, and as a result of problems it has identified, the ELC has been able to strengthen itself in some respects: its support staffing has been increased; its terms of reference have been widened so that it can consider EC documents with long-term implications even if they involve no immediate legislation; its status has been heightened by its conversion to the role of a permanent committee; and in 1980 the Commons resolved that ministers should not normally agree to any proposal for European legislation unless it has been recommended by the Committee. Nevertheless, the ELC has serious short-comings as a controlling mechanism:

1. The Committee scrutinizes approximately 700 statutory instruments per year and recommends a relatively small proportion of them for debate in the whole House (e.g. 81 in the 1980–81 session). However, this is minimal in comparison with the output of the Community and with the extent of the United Kingdom's involvement in EC affairs. Nor is the Committee even empowered to scrutinize legal instruments which the Commission can promulgate under its delegated authority, of which there are approximately 5000–6000 per year (Gregory, 1983). Of course, the majority of these matters are highly technical and are often restricted in scope, but it is inevitable that the committee has difficulty in alerting parliament to legislation that may have constitutional or political significance when confronted with this mass of information.

2. The ELC is in a relatively weak position to influence European legislation at an early stage, but amendments are far less likely to be accepted by the time the committee is involved. By the time they reach the ELC most of the bargaining between the 12 member-states has already taken place and the legislation is almost fixed. (The only exceptions to this are in regard to very slow-moving legislation and this is often of the most technical kind.)

3. Because the Commission does not formally notify national parliaments about its legislative proposals, the ELC is largely dependent upon the goodwill of the government in supplying information. The committee has sometimes complained about the government's tardiness in this respect.

4. Despite statements of good intent by successive governments (and the Commons' resolution of 1980), ministers will not be bound by any requirement to secure the blessing of the ELC (or the Commons as a whole) before agreeing to EC policies. Nor will they reveal their bargaining positions for EC negotiations in advance.

In addition, the position of the ELC is clearly dependent upon the general situation of decision-making in the Community and, in particular, on the status of the 'Luxembourg Compromise'. When originally recommending the establishment of a Scrutiny Committee in 1973, the Commons report argued that it would be possible to control EC legislation at least to the same extent as domestic delegated legislation *so long as the practice of unanimity was required*. For in these circumstances MPs would have some chance of lobbying ministers prior to the taking of a decision, and holding them responsible if they failed to impose a veto when this was regarded as necessary. However, the overriding of the attempted British veto in May 1982 seriously worried the ELC, which feared that its existing control functions could be jeopardized if majority decision-making were introduced. Moreover, the ELC immediately saw that the Single European Act—with its increase in majority voting—could compromise the role of the Committee, and hence that of the Commons as a whole. It feared that there would be increased pressure on parliamentary time, that majority voting would reduce the power of any individual member-state to impose any sort of brake on progress, and that parliament might become still more dependent upon the government to provide accurate information, particularly over details of legislation involved in the cooperation procedure (Select Committee on European Legislation, 1986).

Many of the Committee's fears have proved very prescient and there is now a widespread conviction that, in the era of '1992', the existing scrutiny and control mechanisms are inadequate. There have thus been calls for the establishment of a more powerful committee, of which the ELC would become a subgroup, which could report on all the issues involved in such notions as the Delors plan for economic and monetary union. It has also been suggested that the Committee should have access to working drafts of EC proposals *before* directives were formally published. The government is expected to introduce changes in the scrutiny procedure by the end of 1989, but it is unlikely that they will be as extensive as those sought by either the Labour Party or Conservative backbenchers.

The Commons as a whole   In the first five years of membership, debates on EC issues were held late in the day, the government gave little notice of its intentions, and MPs could not even identify the importance of the subject matter. In 1977 the problems were recognized by the government of the day but nothing was done until 1980, when a Standing Committee was established, more time was set aside for EC debates, and the government committed itself to providing fuller explanations of its EC policies. However, in 1989 MPs were still complaining that the government continually staged crucial EC debates late at night. It was reported that the Leader of the Commons accepted this criticism and was considering the introduction of various reforms. In addition to that of a reformed committee structure (mentioned above), there has been talk of the establishment of a regular weekly EC 'Question Time', with the Foreign Office and the Department of Trade and Industry (DTI) putting up ministers to account for their handling of the latest directives; a greater use of morning standing committees; more debates on future contentious issues emanating from Brussels; and the allocation of more parliamentary time for debates on EC proposals which currently get through parliament because the Commission is working during the parliamentary recesses.

It remains to be seen how extensive a series of reforms are initiated by the government, but, in any case, some fundamental problems will remain whatever the changes in the structure of the Committee or the procedures of the Commons:

1. It is extremely difficult for MPs to know whether policies emanate from the Community or not. Since the Community permeates such a wide range of concerns, government policy does not come neatly labelled 'EC', but is absorbed into departmental legislation and general activities. For example, the recent Education Act gave greater status to EC languages within the national curriculum than to other languages. There is nothing in the Act to indicate that this decision is influenced in any way by Community membership, although it is, in fact, compatible with the EC's Lingua programme which no doubt accounts for it. This is one obvious instance of a continual process.
2. Except on emotive issues, EC matters have a low level of salience for most MPs, particularly as the majority are inevitably comparatively ill-informed about the Community. This problem is exacerbated by the highly technical nature of much EC legislation. Yet, while each individual item might appear narrow and technical, the cumulative impact could be significant with regard both to substantive policy and parliamentary control.

Overall, it therefore seems clear that EC membership has increased the problems of scrutiny and has contributed to the weaknesses of parliament as a controlling mechanism. This does not suggest that the Community *created* the major problems, or that the most notorious examples of recent governmental disregard for parliamentary rights have been related to EC membership. But those who predicted that membership would exacerbate some of the problems have been vindicated, even if many statements by critics of the Community were alarmist and sensational. Once again, it is also true that the current moves towards '1992' and monetary union will add to the difficulties (see further below).

Government accountability   The closer the United Kingdom's involvement with the Community becomes, the more the EC dimension permeates the work of government departments. Yet the ways in which it does so are exceedingly difficult to perceive. For example, in 1980 the Ministry of Agriculture and Fisheries sent approximately 2500 civil servants to attend 1200 meetings (Stack, 1983). Similarly, an issue such as farm subsidies will sometimes take several hundred hours of discussions at lower level before being referred to COREPER and finally to the Council of Ministers. The degree of involvement of the DTI in EC affairs is also massive, and UK officials in Brussels (UKREP), representing the Whitehall departments most affected by the Community, participate on average for 100 days per year in COREPER meetings (Stack, 1983). What this means is that there is sometimes a continuous dialogue between the Commission and Whitehall departments, and that the actual location and level of decision-making becomes more obscure. All this naturally exacerbates the problems of control and accountability.

One final aspect is also important. So far control and accountability have been discussed in relation to parliamentary control over government. In fact, however, EC membership involves two other issues of control: political control over the civil service and Cabinet control over ministers.

In general, new UK Cabinet ministers will be little more informed about the complexities of the Community than the average MP; certainly they will be far less knowledgeable than civil servants working in UKREP, the relevant section of the Foreign and Commonwealth Office or the European Secretariat of the Civil Service. This is, of course, a general problem of government, but it has particular significance in relation to EC affairs because of the need to ensure the compatibility between UK policy and Community legislation. If civil servants are more aware of the interpenetration of domestic and EC affairs than new government ministers, they can alert ministers to the need to make domestic policies conform to those of the Community. But they could also gain a means of pressure against the legislative programme of elected governments. In other words, EC membership could reinforce the potential power of civil servants in key areas of policy-making.

The second point is perhaps more speculative. In theory, the Cabinet is the final decision-making body in the UK political system. In practice, many analysts had discerned an increasing trend to prime ministerial government long before 1973. And it is no doubt true that this trend has been reinforced since 1979 by factors that have nothing to do with the Community. However, it is probable that membership has had some impact in reducing the role of the Cabinet as a collective decision-making body. This follows from the Community's own policy-making process: contentious issues are ultimately resolved either in the Council of Ministers or in the European Council. But this means that the minister or prime minister is locked into negotiations with his or her counterparts in 11 other states. The Cabinet can set general parameters for the UK position, but cannot necessarily anticipate all the dynamics of the negotiating process. Nor is it always possible for the minister in question to halt the negotiations in order to refer back to London (and certainly not to refer back to the Cabinet as a whole). At present, political analysts do not have the information that would reveal how often UK ministers have departed from a prior Cabinet position, but there is some evidence that John Silkin, as Secretary of State for Agriculture in the Labour government, did so. Furthermore, such departures seem to be almost inevitable given the Community's decision-making processes. Of course, this phenomenon is not only a feature of the policy process in the Community, but the frequency of meetings of the Council of Ministers and European Council, and the range of policy covered by the Community, would seem to reinforce a trend towards the weakening of the Cabinet. Under Margaret Thatcher's leadership it may also have led to a situation in which the scope for ministerial autonomy was thwarted by her insistence on taking key decisions on the Community herself.

It would therefore seem that involvement in the Community has contributed to a process whereby decision-making becomes ever more complex and opaque. It therefore becomes more difficult to understand at what level policy is determined and whether and where it can be controlled. Once again, it must also be noted that the Single Act, the Single Market, and monetary union would exacerbate all these problems.

10.5   CONCLUSION

It has been argued that, in both the economic and political spheres, the European Community has had significant effects on the United Kingdom, but that their impact has been to reinforce trends that were already present. Yet, as has been noted, the Community has continued to engender a degree of controversy that may often appear disproportionate in relation to its discernible effects. Why is this?

One important reason—touched on in the Introduction—is the existence of a particularly deep-rooted attachment to the nation-state in UK political culture. The belief that British institutions had some specific virtue has been a conventional wisdom of politicians in both major political parties and was reinforced by the tradition of separateness from the European mainland. In these circumstances the claim that a potentially unpopular measure emanated from 'Brussels' could easily be used to stimulate nationalist feelings. Sensitivity about national sovereignty remained just below the surface—a raw nerve that could easily be irritated. Such arguments have been still more potent, however, when harnessed to other forms of ideology, as was the case with the Labour Party in the years 1980–83 and the Conservative government, particularly since 1988. The explanation for this is straightforward. If EC policies are broadly in line with those favoured by domestic political forces, they will not normally be regarded as threatening or even as external. But if a party wants to make fundamental alterations to the status quo that run counter to EC priorities, the argument about sovereignty is likely to be projected to the forefront of debate. We can illustrate this point in relation to both major parties, and their changing stances on the Community.

After losing the 1979 general election the Labour Party moved to the left and argued that the only way to revive the British economy was by the adoption of an 'alternative economic strategy' which would involve import controls, extensive state intervention, and subsidies for declining industries. However, such measures were incompatible with fundamental features of the Treaty of Rome, and the party claimed that, rather than precipitating a major conflict, the United Kingdom should withdraw from the Community (Labour Party, 1981a).

The concern here is not with the merits of Labour's arguments at the time (Newman, 1983). It is rather to illustrate the point that, once the party had adopted a strategy that departed fundamentally from the EC consensus, the impact of the Community appeared far more dramatic—it now seemed to represent a barrier to the goals that were being sought. Hence the vehement reassertion of the importance of national sovereignty. Between 1983 and 1989, however, the Labour Party's position shifted once again for three main reasons. First, the leadership feared that the withdrawal policy had contributed to the electoral disaster. Secondly, it came to see it as an impractical policy in view of the ever-increasing economic integration with the rest of the Community. Thirdly, it became apparent that there was more support for reformist policies in the Community than in 'Thatcherite' Britain. In these circumstances by 1989 the party was saying much less about sovereignty and tried to present an image of 'Europeanism'.

Although Margaret Thatcher had never called for withdrawal from the Community, in 1988–89 she adopted a line on sovereignty that showed some striking similarities to that which the Labour Party had just abandoned. In this case the reason was not so much the fear that the EC consensus represented a barrier to her goals, as that it might undermine the policies that she had implemented in the United Kingdom.

After 1979 the Conservative government had deliberately used a high exchange rate to reduce domestic demand, and subsequently deregulated the economy to a greater extent than had previously been conceivable. The public sector and trade unions were progressively weakened and market conditions were allowed to prevail. In these circumstances Margaret Thatcher saw the European Monetary System—and still more full monetary union—as threatening because a Conservative government could thereby be deprived of an important deflationary instrument. And she viewed the European Social Charter with horror as it could re-establish social rights (and powers), which the Conservative government had sought to eliminate. This was the context for the Conservative Party's strident campaign against the Commission's 'creeping socialism' in the name of 'national sovereignty'.

The European Community has thus become controversial when it has appeared to threaten cherished policy goals of the major political parties. Yet there is good reason to believe that the actual process of interpenetration between the Community and national dimensions is far more complex and significant than is implied by current political rhetoric.

While the specific economic and political effects of the Community on the United Kingdom have thus far been relatively undramatic, and difficult to disentangle from other forces, it is evident that the pace of change within the Community is now increasing. The Single European Act has led to a greater use of majority voting, and a more important role for the European Parliament, and the Single Market will have a major impact in sweeping away non-tariff barriers in the Community. Such changes initiate a dynamic process, with implications on areas such as education, social policy, and civil liberties. If, as is probable, all this is accompanied by a form of monetary union, the political and economic powers of national governments will be affected very dramatically.

In reality, this era is already underway and Margaret Thatcher's government has been an active participant in the process. Although she has denounced supranationalism, the UK government has embraced the notion of free market and the Conservative Party has called for a 'bonfire of controls' (Conservative Party, 1989). But a free market *removes* the controls that governments have traditionally used to regulate domestic demand and maintain a favourable balance of payments position. It represents a further internationalization of the economy rather than national control. It is also evident that the position of the UK government within the Community is far less powerful than it likes to admit. It may proclaim that it maintains national sovereignty, but at the Madrid Summit in June 1989 Margaret Thatcher was forced to accept a compromise on monetary union and it is probable that some form of 'Social Charter' will ultimately be agreed.

International economic and financial forces exercise such powerful constraints that the price of non-cooperation within the Community normally becomes too high for the individual member-state to bear. But if this is the world that now exists, UK political discourse is obsolescent. In other words, if the Community is an entity in which it is becoming increasingly difficult to differentiate between the 'national' and 'European' dimensions, rhetoric about 'sovereignty' is unhelpful. If, as is currently the case, both major political parties now accept membership of the Community, their programmes have to address existing circumstances rather than imply that the United Kingdom is still the independent force that it was a century ago.

In its manifesto for the 1989 Euro-elections, the Green Party made the point that nobody was in control of the political and economic forces that were affecting the lives of the 320 million members of the Community (Green Party, 1989). It is not necessary to be a 'Green' to recognize the force of this argument. For, as this chapter has shown, the UK parliament can not effectively scrutinize or control the government on EC legislation. But nor are Community decisions controlled by the European Parliament.

The power and impact of the Community is therefore increasing, while scrutiny, accountability, and control remain wholly inadequate. The Conservative Party said nothing about this problem in its 1989 Euro-manifesto, while the Labour Party still highlighted the importance of parliamentary control at national level. However, it is difficult to see how improved procedures at Westminster could—in themselves—bring about democratic control of the Community. This has been recognized by the European Parliament, which, in February 1989, called for far greater cooperation between itself and national parliaments, and their scrutinizing committees (European Parliament Research and Documentation, April 1989).

After 1992 it will become increasingly difficult to talk of a specific Community impact on the United Kingdom, as the interpenetration of national and supranational levels can be expected to move on inexorably. The most urgent task is therefore not to bemoan the loss of national sovereignty, but to seek to influence the direction of EC policies and to establish democratic controls—at all levels.

REFERENCES

Ardy, B. (1988), 'The national incidence of the European Community budget', *Journal of Common Market Studies*, October, **XXVI**, 401–430.

Benn, Tony (1979), *Arguments for Socialism*, Cape, London.

Conservative Party (1989), *Leading Europe into the 1990s* (Conservative Party Manifesto).

Demekas, D.G., Bartholdy, K., Gupta, S., Lipschitz, L. and Mayer, T. (1988), 'The effects of the Common Agricultural Policy of the European Community: a survey of the literature,' *Journal of Common Market Studies* **XXVII**, 113–145.

Dunning, J. (1989), 'European integration and transatlantic foreign direct investment: the record assessed', paper presented at the Fulbright International Colloquium, '1992: Europe and America', Reading, UK, December.

El-Agraa, A. (1983), *Britain within the European Community*, Macmillan, London.

George, S. (1987), *The British Government and the European Community since 1984*, University Association for Contemporary European Studies, London.

Green Party (1989) *Don't Let Your World Turn Grey*, (Green Party European Election Manifesto).

Gregory, F.E.C. (1983), *Dilemmas of Government: Britain and the European Community*, Martin Robertson, Oxford.

European Commission (1983), *Britain in the Community, 1973–1983: 10 Years in Europe*.

European Parliament (1989), 'Bodies within National Parliaments Specialising in EC affairs', *European Parliament Research and Documentation Papers*, National Parliament Series No. 3, April.

Eurostat (1989) 'External trade—monthly statistics', Luxembourg.

House of Commons Select Committee on European Legislation (1986), *The Single European Act and Parliamentary Scrutiny*, HMSO, London.

House of Commons Select Committee on European Legislation (1989), *Charter of Fundamental Social Rights*, HMSO, London.

Labour Party (1981a), 'Withdrawal from the EEC', Statement by the National Executive Committee to the 1981 Conference.

Labour Party (1981b), 'Withdrawal from the EEC', Research Papers, Labour Party Research Department, September.

Labour Party (1989), *Meeting the Challenge in Europe* (Labour's Manifesto).

Mayes, D. (1985), 'Factor mobility', in A.M. El-Agraa (Ed.), *The Economics of the European Community*, Philip Allan, Deddington, 124–150.

Morgan, A.D. (1980), 'The balance of payments and British membership of the European Community', in W. Wallace (Ed.), *Britain in Europe*, Heinemann, London, 51–71.

Newman, M. (1983), *Socialism and European Unity: The Dilemma of the Left in Britain and France*, Hurst, London.

O'Cleireacain, S. (1989), 'EC policies towards Japanese trade and investment: implications for US–EC relations', paper presented at the Fulbright International Colloquium, '1992: Europe and America', Reading, UK, December.

Stack, F. (1983), 'The imperatives of participation', in F.E.C. Gregory, *Dilemmas of Government: Britain and the European Community*, Martin Robertson, Oxford, 124–152.

Winters, L. Alan (1987), 'Britain in Europe: a survey of quantitative trade studies', *Journal of Common Market Studies*, **XXV**, no. 4, 315–335.

THE 1989 EURO-ELECTIONS IN PERSPECTIVE

In June 1989 European voters elected the third directly elected European Parliament. As with the previous Euro-elections in 1979 and 1984, the election campaigns in most member-states tended to concentrate upon national rather than Community issues. The results of the elections nevertheless highlighted three trends that appear to be European, rather than national in scope: a surge in support for Green parties throughout the Community; continuing support for extreme right-wing parties in France, Italy, and Germany; and a slight shift in favour of social-democratic parties in several EC countries. The largest political grouping in the newly elected Parliament remains the Socialist group, which has been strengthened by the elections. The Socialists will be able to count upon the support of the European Greens, Communists, and the centrist Christian Democratic group on many issues. The new President of the assembly, the Spanish Socialist, M. Enrique Baron de Crespo, has declared that the Parliament will concentrate its efforts over the next two years on three areas: implementation of the single market; the development of EC social policy (especially the introduction of the Social Charter); and further institutional reform of the Community.

A.1 THE ELECTORAL SYSTEM

The failure of the Council of Ministers to agree on the adoption of a common electoral system for the European elections meant that the 1989 poll—like those of 1979 and 1984—was conducted according to diverse electoral systems and regulations in the member-states. The biggest single difference in this respect is between the United Kingdom (excluding Northern Ireland), which uses the first-past-the-post system (in single-member constituencies), and all other member-states, which apply some method of proportional representation. There are, however, several differences between these countries in the precise form of proportional representation used. Ireland, for instance, is alone in its use of the single transferable vote system, while in West Germany and France, parties must obtain at least 5 per cent of the poll in order to gain any seats in the Parliament. Some countries allow voters to indicate a preference for particular candidate or candidates. Moreover, as indicated in Table A.1, there are also considerable differences between member-states regarding the voting age and the size of constituencies. Regulations concerning the duration and funding of election campaigns, candidate eligibility, and voting rights for foreign residents also vary between states. Finally, there is as yet no agreement among the member-states as to which day of the week the elections should be held; in the United Kingdom, Spain, Ireland, the Netherlands, and Denmark, voters went to the polls on Thursday, 15 June while their counterparts in Belgium,

Table A.1   Electoral systems used for Euro-elections

Country	No. of MEPs	Age of eligibility	Electoral system	No. of constituencies	Average no. of voters per seat
Belgium*	24	21	Proportional representation with preference vote	3	411 500
Denmark	16	18	Proportional representation with preference vote	1 (nation)	320 563
France	81	23	Proportional representation, no preference vote and 5% vote threshold	1	688 321
Germany	81	18	Proportional representation, no preference vote and 5% vote threshold	10 + 1	756 976
Greece*	24	25	Proportional representation, no preference vote	1	416 667
Ireland	15	21	Single transferable vote (proportional)	4	235 934
Italy	81	25	Proportional representation with preference vote	5	708 630
Luxembourg*	6	21	Proportional representation (mixing lists allowed)	1 1	62 000
Netherlands	25	18	Proportional representation with preference vote	1	588 600
Spain	60	18	Proportional representation, no preference vote	1	648 567
Portugal	24	18	Proportional representation, no preference vote	1	427 917
United Kingdom	81	21	Simple majority in single-member constituencies (Northern Ireland proportional)	78 (+ 1 Northern Ireland: 3 seats)	703 914

* Compulsory voting.
Sources: 1989 Elections Handbook (European Parliament Publication, 1989); 'Résultats des Elections Européennes', *Le Monde—Dossiers et Documents*, July 1989.

France, West Germany, Greece, Italy, Luxembourg, and Portugal voted the following Sunday. The absence of a uniform electoral system is regarded as a problem by MEPs and European integrationists who argue that the present arrangement whereby each state determines its own procedures serves to reinforce the view that the European elections amount to no more than a series of national elections.

A.2 THE ELECTION CAMPAIGN

Back in the 1970s, European federalists argued that the introduction of European elections would be decisive in establishing the legitimacy of the Parliament and fostering a sense of European political identity among parties and voters. European elections, they believed, would provide an opportunity for voters to debate issues of European interest and pass judgement upon the performance of the European Parliament. Bearing these aspirations in mind, we should address three questions when looking at the 1989 Euro-campaign: how important were Community-related issues in the campaign; what role did the transnational party groupings play in the organisation of the campaign; and what were the attitudes of national political élites towards the elections?

Clearly, public awareness about the Community and the European Parliament is, generally speaking, greater than it was in 1979 when Euro-candidates had, first of all, to explain to voters what the European Parliament was. Furthermore, recent government publicity campaigns in all member-states on the socio-economic implications of the planned completion of the single market in 1992 ensured that some discussion took place during the campaign in all member-states of related Community issues such as the Social Charter and European monetary integration. Widespread public concern about the state of the environment combined with the concerted efforts of Green parties throughout the Community also meant that at least one European-wide issue—the environment—figured in the campaign in all countries.

Nevertheless, the Euro-election campaign was in most member-states dominated by national rather than Community issues. This was particularly true in Greece and Ireland where the European elections were totally eclipsed by national elections scheduled for the same day. In Greece, the campaign centred upon the personal and financial scandals surrounding the Socialist Prime Minister, Andreas Papandreou, while in Ireland, the European campaign was overshadowed by the unexpected decision of the Fianna Fail Prime Minister, Charles Haughey, to call a general election in an (unsuccessful) attempt to increase his party's majority in the national parliament. Elsewhere, the campaign tended to focus upon the performance of the national government. In West Germany, debate centred upon the waning fortunes of the Christian Democratic Chancellor, Helmut Köhl, and his failure to stem the growing support for the extreme right-wing Republican Party, while in Spain, the domestic economic policies of Felipe Gonzáles's ruling Socialist Party came under attack. In Italy, where the European elections coincided with the collapse of the 48th post-war government and where there is an all-party consensus in favour of European integration, political debate centred upon the likely composition of the next coalition government. Meanwhile, in the United Kingdom, the key issue during the election campaign was the public rift between Mrs Thatcher and other leading Conservatives (notably the former Prime Minister, Edward Heath) over Britain's commitment to the European Community. Though in one sense, this was obviously a Community-related issue, interest centred mainly upon the domestic political implications of the row.

The prominent role played by national parties in the European election campaign further reinforced the weight accorded to domestic issues. During the 1970s, three European transnational party federations were established as umbrella organizations to coordinate the extra-parliamentary activities of the three largest party groups in the European Parliament— the Confederation of Socialist Parties of the Community (established in 1976), and the (Christian Democratic) European People's Party (established in 1976). Since 1979, the federations have sought to direct the European election strategies of the constituent national parties by producing common manifestos, distributing leaflets, badges and posters, and arranging public speakers. However, this year's elections confirmed the extent to which European elections remain dominated by national party organizations, which continue to receive the bulk of the Community funds provided for the election and which produce their own electoral propaganda. In the United Kingdom, for example, it was noticeable that the Labour Party, which had expressed reservations about some aspects of the Socialist Confederation manifesto, scarcely referred to it at all during the campaign.

Whereas some leading national politicians in the past have tended to ignore the Euroelections, several leading party figures played a prominent role in this year's campaign. In the United Kingdom, television election broadcasts invariably featured well-known national politicians rather than Euro-candidates. Leading politicians also featured prominently on party lists. In France, for example, the Socialist Party list was headed by Laurent Fabius, President of the National Assembly and former Prime Minister, while the right-wing opposition RPR-UDF list was presided over by Valéry Giscard d'Estaing, former President of the Republic. Similarly, in Italy the leader of the Socialist Party and former Primer Minister, Bettino Craxi, headed the Socialist Party list in no less than three of the five constituencies (an example followed by Achille Occhetto, leader of the Italian Communist Party).

The interest shown by national politicians in the Euro-election campaign should not, however, be interpreted as an indication of their desire to become MEPs. Indeed, Laurent Fabius made clear during the election campaign that he had no intention of giving up his national mandate in order to take up a seat in the Strasbourg assembly.* For most national politicians the European elections provide, above all else, an opportunity to debate publicly national political issues. For Euro-candidates—most of whom are unknown to the electorate— the presence and support of well-known political figures is usually an electoral asset (though several UK Conservative candidates were keen this time to distance themselves from Mrs Thatcher's hostility towards the Community). The attitude of most leading national politicians towards the Euro-elections is thus an ambivalent one: they are prepared to 'front' the Euro-campaign, not because they personally wish to be elected to the European Parliament, but as a means of furthering their national political ambitions.

A.3   THE ELECTION RESULTS

When analysing the results of the European election results we should begin by asking how seriously the elections were regarded by the voters. One way of measuring this is to look at the turnout levels. As illustrated in Table A.2, turnout levels varied considerably between the member-states. At the bottom of the scale was the United Kingdom where only 37 per cent of the electorate actually voted, while in Italy, 82 per cent of the electorate voted. In Luxembourg and Belgium, where voting is compulsory, the figures were not surprisingly even higher. The significant increase in the turnout level in Ireland from 48 per cent in 1984 to 68

---

* Legislation introduced in 1985 means that it is no longer possible for an individual to combine a national mandate with a European one.

Table A.2   Turnout levels in 1989 Euro-elections

Country	Turnout (% electorate)		
	1979	1984	1989
Belgium	91	92	91
Denmark	48	52	46
France	61	57	49
Germany	66	57	61
Greece	79	77	79
Ireland	64	48	68
Italy	85	83	82
Luxembourg	89	89	88
Netherlands	58	51	47
Portugal	–	73*	51
Spain	–	69*	55
United Kingdom	32	33	37

* European elections held in 1987 in Spain and Portugal.
Source: Elections 1989: Results and Members (European Parliament, Publications and Briefing Division, June 1989).

per cent in 1989 is almost certainly due to the fact that the Euro-elections were held on the same day as the national election. To the consternation of some Europeanists, turnout levels were slightly lower in most countries than in 1984. The overall turnout level fell from 61 per cent in 1984 to 58.5 per cent in 1989. This decline prompted immediate calls from MEPs for an increase in the Parliament's powers, on the grounds that only then will voters take the Euro-elections seriously. Certainly turnout levels for the European elections remain, generally speaking, lower than those for national elections in the member-states, indicating that voters consider them to be 'second order' elections.

The 1989 European elections prompted a slight shift to the left in the Parliament (as shown in Figure A.1 and Table A.3), following a slight increase in support for social-democratic parties in several member-states and a decline in support for traditional right-wing parties, notably in the United Kingdom and Denmark. However, left-wing parties in several countries lost votes to Green parties, which experienced a surge of support in most states. In consequence, the size of the Rainbow (Green) Group has increased from 20 to 39 members. This figure would have been even higher had it not been for the use of the first-past-the-post system in the United Kingdom: the UK Green Party polled 14 per cent of the votes, but in the absence of proportional representation, won no seats. The number of extreme right-wing MEPs in the European right has also been increased from 16 to 22 as a result of increased support in Germany and France. The other interesting change in the political composition of the Parliament is the virtual collapse of the European Democratic Group. This group formerly comprised the 45 UK Conservative MEPs, 17 representatives of the Spanish Popular Party, and two Danish conservatives. The disastrous performance of the UK Conservatives in the elections (who lost 15 seats to the Labour Party) combined with the defection of the 15 newly elected Spanish Popular Party MEPs to the Christian Democratic group has left the remaining UK Conservative MEPs isolated within the Parliament.

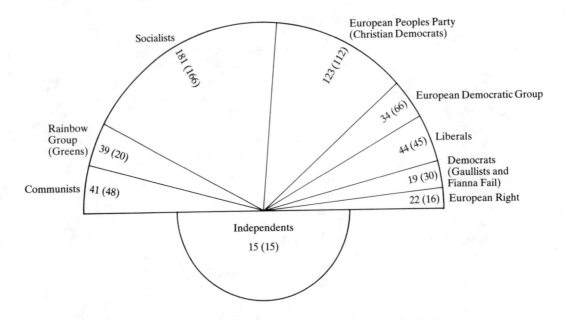

Figure A.1   Political composition of the European Parliament following 1989 European Elections. The numbers in parentheses are the seats held in the 1984–89 Parliament.

The Spanish Socialist MEP M. Enrique Baron de Crespo was elected as President of the new Parliament with the support of Communist, Socialist, Green, and Christian Democratic representatives. At its first meeting the new Parliament declared that it would concentrate its efforts on three policy areas: the promotion of the social dimension of 1992; institutional reform of the Community to strengthen further the powers of the Parliament; and implementation of the internal market.

A.4   CONCLUSION: THE EUROPEAN PARLIAMENT—MORE THAN A SUM OF ITS PARTS?

The key question, of course, is what do these changes amount to? How should we interpret the European elections? One view is that the 1989 European elections were, in fact, no more than a series of disparate national elections in which national issues played the determining role. According to this view, in casting their vote, voters were, first and foremost, registering their support for, or opposition to, the government of the day. In consequence, it is argued, it makes little sense to search for European-wide political trends or to interpret the results as a judgement on the performance of the European Parliament. There are some convincing grounds for accepting this view. Increased support in France and Germany for extreme right-wing parties, for example, is probably best explained as a protest vote against national immigration policies and the recent influx of East German refugees. Indeed, it is clear that national politics do play an important role in determining the outcome of European election results. One French opinion poll revealed that 29 per cent of French voters wanted 'to give a warning to the government' when they voted in European elections. National party leaders throughout the Community were also quick to point out the national political significance of

Table A.3 1989 European election results

	Seats	%		Seats	%
Belgium			**Italy**		
Socialists	8 (9)	27 (30)	CD	27 (26)	33 (33)
CD	7 (6)	30 (27)	Communists	22 (27)	28 (33)
Liberals	4 (5)	18 (18)	Socialists†	14 (12)	18 (15)
Greens	3 (2)	14 (8)	Lib. Rep.	4 (5)	4 (6)
Others	2 (2)	11 (17)	Ex. Right	4 (5)	6 (7)
Denmark			Greens	5 (0)	6 (0)
Soc. Dem.	4 (3)	23 (19)	**Luxembourg**		
Anti EC	4 (4)	19 (21)	Socialists	2 (2)	27 (30)
Liberals	3 (2)	17 (13)	CD	3 (3)	33 (35)
Conservative	2 (4)	13 (21)	Liberals	1 (1)	17 (22)
Others	3 (3)	17 (16)	Others	0 (0)	23 (13)
France			**Netherlands**		
Socialists	22 (20)	24 (21)	Labour	8 (9)	31 (34)
Centre/Right*	33 (41)	36 (42)	CD	10 (8)	35 (30)
Communists	7 (10)	8 (11)	Liberals	3 (5)	14 (19)
Ex. Right	10 (10)	12 (11)	Rainbow	2 (2)	7 (6)
Greens	10 (0)	11 (3)	Others	2 (1)	13 (11)
Germany			**Portugal**		
Soc. Dem.	31 (33)	37 (37)	Soc. Dem.	9 (10)	33 (37)
CD	32 (41)	38 (46)	Socialists	8 (6)	29 (23)
Liberals	4 (0)	6 (5)	Communists	4 (3)	14 (12)
Greens	8 (7)	9 (8)	CD	3 (4)	14 (15)
Ex. Right	6 (0)	8 (0)	Others	0 (1)	10 (13)
Greece			**Spain**		
Socialists	9 (10)	35 (42)	Socialists	27 (28)	40 (39)
New Dem.	10 (9)	42 (38)	Popular Party	15 (17)	21 (25)
Communists	3 (4)	14 (15)	Soc. Dem.	5 (7)	7 (10)
Others	2 (1)	9 (5)	Communists	4 (3)	6 (5)
			Others	9 (5)	26 (21)
Ireland			**UK**		
Fianna Fail	5 (8)	31 (39)	Labour	45 (32)	40 (35)
Fine Gael	4 (6)	22 (32)	Conservatives	32 (45)	35 (39)
Labour	2 (0)	10 (8)	Dem./Alliance	0 (0)	6 (19)
Prog. Dem.	1 (0)	12 (0)	Greens	0 (0)	14 (0)
Others	3 (1)	25 (21)	Others	4 (4)	5 (7)

* Includes both the Giscard and Weil lists.
† Includes Social Democrats (two seats and 3 per cent of the vote).
CD, Christian Democratic Party; Soc. Dem., Social Democratic Party; Ex. Right, Extreme Right. The numbers in parentheses are the seats held in 1984–89 Parliament.

the European election results. In the United Kingdom, for example, where the Conservative Party experienced their first defeat in a national election since coming to power in 1979, the results were widely interpreted as a protest vote against the Conservative government rather than as a vote for or against Community policies. On the other hand, there does seem to be a clear trend throughout Europe in favour of Green parties, reflecting widespread concern about the environment. Similarly, these elections also confirmed a falling off in support for neo-liberal right-wing parties and policies in several member-states and a shift towards centrist and social-democratic parties.

Realistically, it is difficult to imagine how the European elections, dominated as they are by national political parties and politicians, could ever be totally insulated from national politics. The anomalous constitutional position of the European Parliament (outlined in Chapter 2) further reinforces the tendency for the elections to become 'nationalized'. In contrast to national parliaments, the European Parliament does not sustain a government or implement an election programme. In consequence, there is no incentive for Euro-candidates to present a coherent European election programme or to defend their party's European parliamentary record. Since people vote on the basis of different electoral programmes, it is extremely difficult to detect European-wide electoral swings. Finally, the use of different electoral systems for the European election also fragments the Euro-election; it is, for instance, extremely difficult for the media to cover the elections in a comparative sense.

Does this mean that the Parliament cannot be more than a sum of its parts? An underlying theme of this book is the interrelationship between national and Community politics and policy-making pressures and the dynamic nature of that relationship. The development of the European Parliament should perhaps be viewed in the same context. Future reforms may strengthen the powers of the Parliament or introduce a common electoral system for European elections, but European elections and politics will almost certainly remain (as do local and regional elections and politics) closely intermeshed with national political trends.

EC RELATIONS WITH THE THIRD WORLD: THE LOMÉ CONVENTIONS

B.1 INTRODUCTION

The fourth Lomé Convention between the Community and a select group of developing countries in Africa, the Caribbean, and the Pacific was signed on 15 December 1989. This has brought into focus an aspect of EC policy that is of central importance: the way in which the Community deals with the Third World. This, in the long run, may arguably become of even greater significance than the way in which the Community deals with the current tumultuous events in Eastern Europe.

European policy towards development in the Third World broadly consists of the usual combination of trade concessions and aid which are granted to certain less developed countries (LDCs), especially the former colonies of the major European nation-states. Most of the policy is conducted at the national level. The vast majority of aid, for example, is dispensed by EC states through bilateral agreements with the recipients. In the trade field, the Community of course plays a much more important role. At present the intervention that does occur at the Community level is conducted through a number of different channels, principally the Generalized System of Preferences (GSP), the so-called 'Global Mediteranean Policy' (GMP), agreements with certain countries in South America and Asia, food aid, and, above all, the Lomé Conventions. Here we shall give some brief consideration to some aspects of the first four, but we shall concentrate on examining the Lomé agreements as the principal instrument of Community policy towards the Third World.

Like all industrialized countries, the Community operates a GSP in favour of LDCs who are members of the United Nations' group of 77. This was introduced in 1971 and is variable in its generosity, covering a limited range of industrial and agricultural products, and incorporating tight rules of origin and quotas and exceptions for important goods such as textiles and agricultural products covered by the CAP. Furthermore, under the GSP it is possible for the Community to withdraw preferential access, which it has done at various times of perceived threat from imports from the newly industrialized countries (NICs). The main beneficiaries from the Community's GSP have been Yugoslavia, Malaysia, Hong Kong, South Korea, and Brazil, although the overall impact of the system has in all probability been rather limited (see Hine, 1985).

The Community's GMP in fact consists of a series of preferential trade agreements that have been concluded at various times with all of the countries in the Mediterranean basin, with the not altogether surprising exceptions of Libya and Albania. The agreements therefore cover such diverse countries as Tunisia, Algeria, and Morocco (the Mahgreb countries), Egypt, Lebanon, Syria, and Jordan (the Mashrequ countries), Malta, Cyprus, Israel, and Turkey. Spain and Greece had cooperation agreements with the Community prior to their accession. The GMP agreements are considerably more generous than the GSP, and what evidence there is tentatively suggests that their impact on the recipient countries has been rather more favourable, in terms of export expansion, export diversification, and foreign investment effects (Yannopoulos, 1986). A small financial aid programme is also included in the GMP agreements. Aid to Latin American and Asian countries includes an extension of the STABEX system (see below) to certain of these countries from 1987, the sum allocated for this purpose during the first five years of the scheme's operation (1987–91) is 50 million ECUs.

The Community's food aid interventions have of course been the source of considerable controversy in recent years with the famines in Africa, and the likes of Bob Geldof exposing the paradox of world hunger amid the surpluses of the CAP. The Community, however, is the second largest source of food aid in the world, providing around 15 per cent of the global total. The current budgetary cost of the Community's non-Lomé Third World policies is shown in Table B.1. It should be noted that these are financed directly from the Community budget, whereas Lomé expenditures are financed directly by member-states and do not form part of the EC budget.

Table B.1 EC cooperation with developing countries and non-member countries

(million ECU)	1989 budget				1990 preliminary draft *			
	Commit-ments	%*	Payments	%*	Commit-ments	%*	Payments	%*
Food aid	473.400	38.16	469.400	44.63	500.950	35.88	508.700	44.57
Latin America and Asia	359.900	29.01	247.100	23.95	396.900	28.43	271.350	23.78
Mediterranean countries	197.000	15.88	139.000	13.47	267.500	19.16	156.600	13.72
Other	210.207	16.95	185.130	17.95	230.882	16.53	204.582	17.93
Total†	1 240.507	100.00	1 031.630	100.00	1 396.232	100.00	1 141.232	100.00

* Percentages are calculated without European Development Fund (EDF) expenditure.
† The appropriations for cooperation with the 66 countries signatory to the Lomé Conventions are not at present entered in the budget. They are covered by the operations of the EDF.
Source: see Table 6.1

B.2 THE LOMÉ CONVENTIONS

The most important and systematic part of the Community's Third World policy has, however, been conducted through the Lomé Conventions, named after the capital city of Togo in which they were signed. The Conventions are trade and aid agreements that the Community has concluded with a large and increasing number of LDCs, all of them, it is important to note, former colonies of the member-states. There have been four Lomé Conventions, the first three each covering a period of five years, while the latest one is due to run for 10 years from 1 March 1990. They were preceded by two similar agreements, known as the Yaoundé Conventions. The agreements have been based on four principles: security, since they last for five years and are legally enforceable; equality between the EC states and the Africa–Caribbean–Pacific (ACP) countries; a wide spread of measures to ensure all participants benefit; and consultation through institutions such as the EC-ACP Centre for Industrial Development. One must regard some at least of these principles with a certain amount of scepticism—how equal are France and Vanuatu, for example? The time-scale of the various agreements has been as follows:

Yoaundé I	1964–70
Yaoundé II	1971–75
Lomé I	1975–80
Lomé II	1980–85
Lomé III	1985–89
Lomé IV	1990–2000

The number of ACP states has increased substantially from 18 under Yaoundé I to 66 in Lomé III, and now 69 in Lomé IV—Haiti, the Dominican Republic, and Namibia being the latest additions. The signatories of Lomé IV are shown in Table B.2.

Table B.2 The ACP states involved in Lomé IV

Angola	Haiti	St Lucia
Antigua and Barbuda	Gambia	St Vincent and
Bahamas	Ghana	the Grenadines
Barbados	Grenada	São Tomé and
Belize	Guinea	Príncipe
Benin	Guinea Bissau	Senegal
Botswana	Guyana	Seychelles
Burkina Faso	Jamaica	Sierra Leone
Burundi	Kenya	Solomon Islands
Cameroon	Kiribati	Somalia
Cape Verde	Lesotho	Sudan
Central African	Liberia	Suriname
Republic	Madagascar	Swaziland
Chad	Malawi	Tanzania
Comoros	Mali	Togo
Congo	Mauritania	Tonga
Côte d'Ivoire	Mauritius	Trinidad and Tobago
Djibouti	Mozambique	Tuvalu
Dominica	Namibia	Uganda
Dominican Republic	Niger	Western Samoa
Equatorial Guinea	Nigeria	Vanuatu
Ethiopia	Papua New Guinea	Zaire
Fiji	Rwanda	Zambia
Gabon	St Christoper and Nevis	Zimbabwe

B.3   TRADE PROVISIONS

The trade concessions offered under the Lomé agreements have been, on the face of it at least, quite liberal. Almost all ACP industrial products (99.5 per cent, as the Community repeatedly emphasizes) are allowed to enter the Community without tariffs or quotas, and there are no reciprocity requirements. The concessions for agricultural products have been less favourable, with restrictions on products that compete with EC ones, such as sugar, beef, and strawberries. Critics of the Lomé trade concessions point out, however, that they have tended to be liberal only where this was compatible with Community interests. The regime for industrial products is put into perspective, for example, when one realizes that most ACP countries are in no position to take advantage of these concessions, since they do not have industrial products that can compete with those of the Community. When a competitive threat is posed, the Community has tended to negotiate 'voluntary' export restraint agreements to limit trade (Stevens, 1984). It is also pointed out that something like 75 per cent of ACP goods would enter the Community free of restriction anyway under the most-favoured nation rule of the GATT, and that, as primary products that are complementary to those that the EC countries tend to produce, they would be imported anyway. This means that Lomé gives ACP countries an advantage, but only at the expense of other world producers. In any case this advantage has been gradually eroded as the Community has reduced its tariffs in successive rounds of negotiations under the GATT, including the current Uruguay round which is due to be completed some time in 1990. Additionally, although the trade agreements are legally binding, they have contained a safeguard clause that has allowed them to be circumvented when EC interests are threatened. Furthermore, they have been governed by strict rules of origin, which the ACP countries have consistently claimed make it difficult for them to export processed goods to the Community, and also hinder their ability to attract Japanese and American direct investment, and to diversify their productive structures. A revealing statistic in this context is that over the period 1973–86, the ACP countries' share of total EC non-oil imports from developing countries has fallen from just under 25 per cent to around 13 per cent. From 1975 to 1986, however, the proportion of ACP non-oil exports to the Community has remained constant at around 75 per cent (McQueen, 1989). This is an indication both of the imbalanced relationship between the two blocs, and of the extent to which ACP exports are being squeezed out of EC markets, despite the Lomé trade concessions.

Lomé IV seems to have left the existing trade regime to all intents and purposes broadly unchanged, though access provisions for some forty agricultural products, notably sorghum, millet, yams, rice, molasses, strawberries, tomatoes, and citrus fruits, have been improved, while beef, veal, and rum are now subject to separate protocols that improve the conditions under which they are allowed entry into the Community. Additionally, the protocol on rules of origin has been made marginally more liberal, and there is now a chapter in the Convention covering trade in services, providing for more negotiation when the outcome of the Uruguay round of GATT is known.

B.4   AID PROVISIONS

The aid granted to ACP countries under Lomé is disbursed mainly through the European Development Fund (EDF), with some of it also taking the form of soft loans granted by the European Investment Bank (EIB). Under Yaoundé I, the aid package for the 18 members amounted to 666 million units of account (UA) from the EDF and 64 million UA from the

EIB. With Yaoundé II, this increased to 828 million from the EDF and 90 million from the EIB. By the time of Lomé III, the aid available for the 66 members had risen to a monetary value of 7400 million ECUs from the EDF and 1100 million ECUs from the EIB. In the negotiations for Lomé IV, the ACP states asked for a substantial increase in the dimensions of the aid package, claiming that they are part of the social dimension of the 1992 single market (Buchan, 1989). The result was a renewable five-year financial protocol, which for the first half of the new Convention will provide 12 000 million ECUs, 10 800 million ECUs of which will be disbursed through the EDF, the EIB handling the remaining 1200 million ECUs. This marks a shift in emphasis, for the size of the EDF has been increased by 25 per cent in real terms (46 per cent nominally), while the EIB's own resource financing has seen a nominal increase of a mere 9 per cent. Thus there has been an attempt to make aid more concessional. Henceforth all EDF aid will take the form of grants rather than special loans. The overall increase in the aid budget may not be substantial in real per capita terms, and is clearly inadequate compared with the scale of the needs to be met, but, as the Community is quick to point out, the increase is greater than that granted recently through any other official development assistance budget.

The most interesting and innovative aspect of the Lomé aid regime has been the introduction of the STABEX and SYSMIN schemes. These are trade-related aid schemes designed to stabilize the earnings that ACP countries derive from the export of commodities and minerals, respectively. STABEX was introduced under Lomé I, to be followed by SYSMIN under Lomé II; they represent creative attempts to tackle one of the central problems that LOCs have to contend with—heavy reliance on export earnings from a limited range of primary products, the international prices of which tend to be subject to wide fluctuation.

In essence STABEX provides compensation payments to exporters of a limited range of commodities when both a dependence requirement and a trigger requirement are satisfied. The dependence requirement relates to the significance of a commodity to a country's export earnings, i.e. the proportion of total exports for which a particular commodity accounts. This was set at 6 per cent under Lomé III, with a special rate of 1.5 per cent for the poorest ACP countries, and has been reduced to 5 per cent for most commodities and 1 per cent for the least developed, landlocked, and island countries (LDLICs) under Lomé IV. The trigger requirement, or fluctuation threshold, is the price fall needed to render a country eligible for compensation—the threshold was set at 6 per cent, with a special rate of 1.5 per cent under Lomé III, and has been replaced by an 'excess clause' of 4.5 per cent, with a special rate of 1 per cent under Lomé IV. Innovative and praiseworthy these schemes may be, but in practice they suffer from both limited coverage and serious underfunding. The funds available for STABEX under Lomé III were 925 million ECUs (10.9 per cent of the total aid budget), for example, but 'justified' claims on the fund amounted to 920 million ECUs in 1987 alone, with the result that only around half of them could be met in that year (Buchan, 1989). Lomé IV has increased the STABEX budget by 62 per cent to 1500 million ECUs, as well as revamping some aspects of its operation and adding three new products—octopus, essential oils, and primary cocoa products—to its coverage, but it remains to be seen whether this will be sufficient really to tackle the problems that the system has experienced during the 1980s. With SYSMIN, which is funded to the extent of 480 million ECUs under Lomé IV (up from 415 million ECUs under Lomé III), the difference between claims and available funds has been even more pronounced. Lomé IV has added two new products—uranium and gold—to its coverage, and has marginally reformed the way it is operated—not sufficient, in all probability, significantly to improve its performance.

The Lomé aid régime has been criticized on a number of counts. The size of the EDF is the most obvious source of controversy. The size of the EDF under Lomé III was less in real per capita terms than that of its predecessor, which in turn was some 25 per cent lower than the EDF for Lomé I (Hewitt, 1984). Lomé IV, as we have seen, has not resulted in any major changes in the overall situation. The problems this has created for specific schemes such as STABEX have been discussed above. Nevertheless, aid has to be funded, and one must bear in mind political realities when assessing the dimensions of the EDF. Community countries have, for example, spent more on development aid through the EDFs than they have on EC regional or social policy through the central budget. Secondly, what aid has been available has typically been allocated and disbursed in a slow and inefficient manner. Although the situation seems to have been improved with reforms introduced under Lomé III and Lomé IV, none of the previous EDFs had been fully committed, let alone spent, by the end of their official lives. For example, by March 1984, 80 per cent through its duration, EDF V for Lomé II had only managed to spend 20 per cent and comit 50 per cent of the funds available (Hewitt, 1984). Finally, and perhaps predictably, the effectiveness of the aid that has been disbursed has been frequently called into question. Lomé IV contains clauses on monitoring and evaluation, the effectiveness of which remain to be seen.

B.5   PROSPECTS FOR LOMÉ IV

The new 10-year Convention will come into operation against a background of economic difficulty for most ACP states, which are suffering from low growth rates, declining commodity prices, and high levels of indebtedness. The negotiations were, as usual, difficult. On the aid front, the ACP states pushed for a large increase in the size of the EDF, arguing, as we have seen, that they should be regarded as part of the social aspect of '1992'. The EC countries were, of course, wary of this, and attempted to make some aid tied to factors such as the adoption by the ACP of Community ideas on environmental issues and economic management. There was, however, agreement that part of the EDF VII should be dedicated to the structural adjustment that both parties agree is necessary for ACP economies to undergo. There was also agreement that EDF VII should cover a period of more than five years. The end result was the aid package described above, which includes provisions on support for policies of structural adjustment to be financed with a special additional allocation of 1150 million ECUs within the EDF. Lomé IV also contains some provisions for environmental protection, e.g. a ban on the movement of hazardous and radioactive waste between EC and ACP states, as well as (largely) rhetoric on issues such as cultural and social cooperation, regional cooperation, and debt, the latter warranting a whole new chapter.

As far as trade is concerned, the EC position is that the preferential treatment already afforded to the ACP states is very generous, and that everything possible has thus already been done by the Community. The ACP's declining share of EC markets is essentially their own fault, to be cured by dismantling protectionism, making economies more market orientated, and encouraging diversification. The ACP states not surprisingly disagreed with this perception, and would have liked the Community to, among other things, guarantee to buy an agreed proportion of their non-oil exports, liberalize rules of origin, compensate them for losses in preferences as a result of the Uruguay round of the GATT, and increase the quotas of sugar that it buys. The end result was the largely unchanged set of provisions outlined above.

How, then, are we to evaluate the EC's policy towards developing countries? The first point to note here is that it is not in fact a true Third World policy to the extent that it only covers countries that are or were in the spheres of influence of EC member-countries, or are of obvious strategic importance to the Community. Many LDCs are thus excluded, and much of the policy could, perhaps unfairly, be construed as being motivated by self-interest. If we specifically look at the Lomé Conventions, then according to the preamble to Lomé III, the stated objective is to make 'a significant contribution to the economic development and social progress of the ACP states and to the greater well being of their populations'. On the face of it at least, this objective would not appear to have been met. The economic gap between the Community and most of the ACP countries has, as we have seen, widened, and their share of EC markets has dropped. There is a view that the Lomé Conventions have frozen the ACP countries into a neo-colonialist form of dependency, by hindering diversification and discouraging extra-Community foreign direct investment. This view is probably a little unfair. For one thing the Lomé arrangements have considerably less political strings attached to them than the models adopted by other parts of the developed world, such as the United States, the Soviet Union, and Japan. Furthermore the generosity of their aid packages should be seen in the context of other aid that individual EC states disburse on a bilateral basis, and in the light of what it is politically realistic to expect in the present state of the world.

SUMMARY

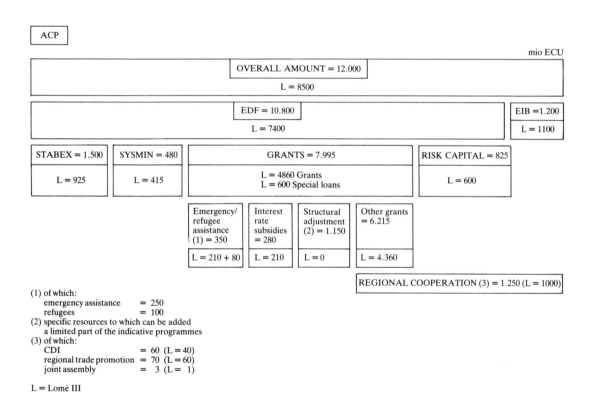

Figure B.1   From Lomé III to Lomé IV: summary of financial arrangements. (*Source:* EC Commission (1989).

REFERENCES/FURTHER READING

Buchan, D. (1989), 'EC, Lomé negotiate new trade-and-aid agreement', *Europe*, March.

EC Commission (1989), Information. 'The Fourth Lomé Convention', Brussels, 13 December.

Eussner, A. (1986), 'Agro-industrial co-operation between the EC and the ACP countries', *Journal of Common Market Studies*, **XXV**, September, 51–74.

Hewitt, A. (1984), 'The Lomé Conventions: entering a second decade', *Journal of Common Market Studies*, **XXIII**, December, 95–116.

Hine, R.C. (1985), *The Political Economy of European Trade*, Wheatsheaf, Brighton.

McQueen, M. (1989), 'Lomé IV negotiations', *European Access*, June.

Stevens, C. (1984), 'The new Lomé Convention: implications for Europe's Third World policy', *CEPS Papers*, no. 11, Brussels.

Yannopoulos, G. (1986), 'Patterns of response to EC tariff preferences: an empirical investigation of selected non-ACP associates', *Journal of Common Market Studies*, **XXV**, September, 51–74.

FURTHER READING

In addition to the detailed references provided at the end of each chapter, the following books provide useful further reading:

Allen, P.R. and Kenen, P. (1980), *Asset Markets, Exchange Rates and Economic Integration*, Cambridge University Press, Cambridge.

Balassa, B. (1975) *European Economic Integration*, North Holland, Amsterdam.

Begg, D., Fischer, S. and Dornbusch, R., (1987), *Economics*, 2nd Edn, McGraw-Hill, London.

Brown, L.N. and Jacobs, F.G. (1983), *The Court of Justice of the European Communities*, 2nd Edn, Sweet and Maxwell, London.

Budd, S.A. and Jones, A. (1989), *The European Community: a Guide to the Maze*, 3rd Edn, Kogan Page, London.

Bulmer, S. and Paterson, W. (1987), *The Federal Republic of Germany and European Integration*, George Allen & Unwin, London.

Burgess, M. (1989), *Federalism and European Union*, Routledge, London.

Butt P.A. (1985), *Pressure Groups in the European Community*, University Association for Contemporary European Studies, London, Occasional Paper no. 2.

Casson, M. (Ed.) (1985), *Multinationals and World Trade*, George Allen & Unwin, London.

Coffey, P. (Ed.) (1983), *Main Economic Policy Areas of the EEC*, Martinus Nijhoff, The Hague.

Cohen, C.D. (Ed.) (1983), *The Common Market—Ten Years After*, Philip Allan, Deddington.

Corden, W.M. (1974), *Trade Policy and Economic Welfare*, Clarendon Press, Oxford.

Corden, W.M. (1985), *Inflation Exchange Rates and the World Economy*, 3rd Edn, Clarendon Press, Oxford.

Cosgrove-Twitchett, C. (1981), *A Framework for Development?: the EEC and the AC*, George Allen & Unwin, London.

Daltrop, A. (1986), *Politics and the European Community*, 2nd Edn, Longman, London.

Dunning, J.H. (Ed.) (1985), *Multinational Enterprises, Economic Structure and International Competitiveness*, Wiley, Chichester.

El-Agraa, A.M. (Ed.) (1983), *Britain Within the European Community: the Way Forward*, Macmillan, London.

El-Agraa, A.M. (Ed.) (1985), *The Economics of the European Community*, 2nd Edn., Philip Allan, Deddington.

Featherstone, K. (1988), *Socialist Parties and European Integration: a Comparative History*, Manchester University Press, Manchester.

Fennell, R. (1979), *The Common Agricultural Policy of the Community*, Granada, London.

George, S. (1985), *Politics and Policy in the European Community*, Clarendon Press, Oxford.

George, S. (1990), *An Awkward Partner: Britain in the European Community*, Oxford University Press, Oxford.

Haas, E. (1968), *The Uniting of Europe*, 2nd Edn, Stanford University Press, Stanford.

Harrop, J. (1989), *The Political Economy of Integration in the European Community*, Edward Elgar, London.

Hartley, T.C. (1988), *The Foundations of Community Law*, 2nd Edn, Clarendon Press, Oxford.

Hill, B.E. (1984), *The Common Agricultural Policy: Past, Present and Future*, Methuen, London.

Hine, R.C. (1985), *The Political Economy of European Trade*, Wheatsheaf, Brighton.

Hitiris, T. (1988), *European Community Economics*, Wheatsheaf, London.

Holland, S. (1980), *Uncommon Market: Capital, Class and Power in the European Community*, Macmillan, London.

Hu Yao Su (1981), *Europe Under Stress*, Butterworths, London.

Jenkins, R. (Ed.) (1983), *Britain and the EEC*, Macmillan, London.

Keating, M. and Jones, B. (1985), *The Regions in the European Community*, Clarendon Press, Oxford.

Kirchner, E. and Schwaiger, K. *The Role of Interest Groups in the European Community*, Gower, London.

Klassen, L.H. and Molle, W.T. (1983), *Industrial Mobility and Migration in the EC*, Gower, London.

Kruse, D.C. (1980), *Monetary Integration in Western Europe: EMU, EMS and Beyond*, Butterworths, London.

Lasok, D. and Bridge, J.W. (1987), *Law and Institutions of the European Communities*, Butterworths, London.

Lewenhak, S. (1982), *The Role of the European Investment Bank*, Croom Helm, London.

Lindberg, L. (1963), *The Political Dynamics of European Economic Integration*, Stanford University Press, Stanford.

Lodge, J. (1983), *The Institutions and Policies of the European Community*, Frances Pinter, London.

Lodge, J. (Ed.) (1986), *European Union: the European Community in Search of a Future*, Macmillan, London.

Lodge, J. (Ed.), (1989), *The European Community and the Challenge of the Future*, Frances Pinter, London.

Long, F. (Ed.) (1980), *The Political Economy of EEC Relations with African, Caribbean and Pacific States*, Pergamon Press, Oxford.

Ludlow, P. (1982), *The Making of the European Monetary System*, Butterworths, London.

McQueen, M. (1987), *Britain, the EEC and the Developing World*, Heinemann, London.

Malcolm, N. (1989), *Soviet Policy Perspectives on Western Europe*, Routledge, London.

Marques Mendes, A.J. (1987), *Economic Integration and Growth in Europe*, Croom Helm, London.

Marsh, J.S. and Swanney, P.J. (1980), *Agriculture and the European Community*, George Allen & Unwin, London.

Mathijsen, P.S.R.F. (1985), *A Guide to European Community Law*, Sweet & Maxwell, London.

Myrdal, G. (1957), *The Theory of Underdeveloped Regions*, Duckworth, London.

Nicholson, E. and East, R. (1987), *From the Six to the Twelve: the Enlargement of the European Communities*, Longman, London.

Newman, M. (1983), *Socialism and European Unity*, C. Hurst, London.

Nugent, N. (1989), *The Government and Politics of the European Community*, Macmillan, London.

Oates, W. (1972) *Fiscal Federalism*, Harcourt, Brace, Jovanovich, New York.

Owen, N. (1983), *Economies of Scale, Competitiveness and Trade Patterns Within the European Community*, Oxford University Press, Oxford.

Owen, R. and Dynes, M. (1989), *The Times Guide to 1992*, Times Books, London.

Padoa-Schioppa, T. (1984), *Money, Economic Policy and Europe*, EC Commission, Luxembourg.

Palmer, J. (1987), *Europe without America? The Crisis in Atlantic Relations*, Oxford University Press, Oxford.

Palmer, J. (1988), *Trading Places: the Future of the European Community*, Radius, London.

Pearce, J. and Sutton, J. (1986), *Protection and Industrial Policy in Europe*, Routledge, London.

Pelkmans, J. (1984), *Market Integration in the EC*, Martinus Nijhoff, The Hague.

Pomfret, R. (1986), *The Mediterranean Policy of the European Community*, Macmillan, London.

Pryce, R. (Ed.) (1987), *The Dynamics of European Union*, Croom Helm, London.

Robertson, D. (1972), *International Trade Policy*, Macmillan, London.

Robson, P. (1987), *The Economics of International Integration*, 3rd Edn, Allen & Unwin, London.

Seers, D. and Vaitsos, S. (1980), *Integration and Unequal Development*, Macmillan, London.

Shanks, M. (1987), *European Social Policy Today and Tomorrow*, Pergamon Press, Oxford.

Sharp, M. (Ed.) (1985), *Europe and New Technologies*, Frances Pinter, London.

Shonfield, A. (1973), *Europe: Journey to an Unknown Destination*, Penguin, London.

Sodersten, B. (1980), *International Economics*, 2nd Edn, Macmillan, London.

Swann, D. (1983), *Competition and Industrial Policy in the European Community*, Methuen, London.

Swann, D. (1988), *The Economics of the Common Market*, 6th Edn, Penguin, London.

Taylor, P. (1983), *The Limits of European Integration*, Croom Helm, London.

Tsoulakis, L. (Ed.) (1981), *The European Community and its Mediterranean Enlargement*, Allen & Unwin, London.

Tsoulakis, L. (Ed.) (1986), *Europe, America and the World Economy*, Basil Blackwell, Oxford.

Tugendhadt, C. (1987), *Making Sense of Europe*, Penguin, London.

Vanhove, N. and Klassen, N.H. (1980), *Regional Policy: A European Approach*, Saxon House, Farnborough.

Wallace, W., Wallace, H. and Webb, C. (1983), *Policy-Making in the European Community*, 2nd Edn, Wiley, London.

Wallace, W., Wallace, H. and Webb, C. (1983), *Policy-Making in the European Community* 2nd Edn., Wiley, London.

Wallace, H. (1985), *The Challenge of Diversity*, Routledge, London.

Whitby, M. (Ed.) (1979), *The Net Cost and Benefit of EEC Membership*, Wye College, Kent.

Wistrich, E. (1989), *After 1992: the United States of Europe*, Routledge, London.

Yannopoulos, G. (1988), *Customs Unions and Trade Conflicts, the Enlargement of the EC*, Croom Helm, London.

Yannopoulos, G. (Ed.) (1986), *Greece and the EEC*, Macmillan, London.

Ypersele, J. and Koeune, J.C. (1985), *The European Monetary System*, Woodhead-Faulkner, Cambridge.

INDEX

Adenauer, K., 3, 4
Andreotti, G., 23
Article 119, 112–114, 117–118

Barre Plan, 61
Basle/Nyborg Agreement, 64, 66
Belgium, 2, 3, 4, 13, 14, 15, 46, 120, 165
Blum, L., 3
Briand, A., 2
Budget, xii, 9, 72–93, 103, 150–151
   European Parliament's powers, 15–16
   UK budget rebate crisis, 82–85, 150–151

Cecchini Report, 43, 44, 45, 46, 125
Churchill, W., 3, 5
Commission of the European Communities, 6,
   12–13, 15, 16, 19, 20–27, 74, 81, 88–91, 103, 109,
   115, 122
Committee of Permanent Representatives
   (COREPER), 6, 13, 88, 160
Common Agricultural Policy, xiii, 6, 8–9, 14, 16,
   72, 78, 82, 91, 94–109, 149, 174
Common Assembly, 5, 6
Common External Tariff, 6, 30, 31, 42, 75, 95
Common Market, xii, 5, 6, 20, 30–41, 56, 59, 60,
   114, 141
   theory of, 38–40
   1992 programme, xi, xii, 10, 11, 48–54, 69, 111,
   122
Community Programme in Education and
   Training for Technology (COMETT), 80, 123
Competition Policy, 50, 153
Conservative Party (UK), 5, 10, 55, 69, 107, 125,
   146–147, 154, 159, 163
Consultative Committee, 5
Cooperation Procedure, 16, 24–26
Co-responsibility Levy, 106, 109
Council of Europe, 3, 4
Council of Ministers, 5–6, 12, 13–15, 16, 19, 20–
   26, 48, 64, 72, 81, 85, 94, 109, 115, 165
   and budget, 87–91
Customs Duties, 76–77
Customs Union, xii, 5, 30–41, 52
   dynamic theory of, 37–40
   non-tariff barriers, 43–47, 51, 60
   practice of, 42–54
   static theory of, 31–37
   trade creation, 31–32, 36, 43
   trade diversion, 32–33, 38, 43, 101

Delors, J., 10, 21, 28, 111, 122, 124
Delors Plan, 62, 69, 70, 159
Denmark, 3, 13, 14, 15, 21, 23, 42, 47, 52, 101,
   107, 120, 165
Dooge Committee, 22
Draft Treaty on European Union, 2, 16, 22, 27

Economic and Social Committee, 9, 13, 16, 17,
   81, 119
Electoral system, 165–166
d'Estaing, Valéry G., 15, 21, 168
Euratom, 5, 6, 74, 112
Euro-groups, 9
European Action Scheme for the Mobility of
   University Students (ERASMUS), 50, 80, 124
European Agricultural Guidance and Guarantee
   Fund (EAGGF), 13, 16, 79, 80, 81, 90, 103, 109
European Centre for the development of
   vocational training (CEDEFOP), 117
European Coal and Steel Community (ECSC),
   4, 5, 6, 7, 8, 9, 74, 111
European Company Statute, 120, 139
European Council (summits), 15, 21, 156
European Court of Justice, 5, 6, 13, 16, 17–18, 51,
   81, 91, 125, 141, 155
European Currency Unit (ECU), 56, 61–62, 67
European Defence Community (EDC), 3–4
European Development Fund (EDF), 6, 13, 16,
   81, 176–178
European Economic Community (EEC), 6, 9,
   112, 129
European elections, 165–172
European Free Trade Association (EFTA), 28,
   30, 129
European integration, 1, 2, 4, 7–8, 10, 11, 13, 19,
   20, 27, 53, 55, 60, 61, 73, 85, 86–87, 92, 94, 95,
   98, 100, 103, 106, 107, 114, 167
European Investment Bank (EIB), 6, 65, 176–177
European Monetary Cooperation Fund, 64
European Monetary Fund, 64, 69, 70
European Monetary System, xii, 47, 48, 55, 57,
   60, 61–70, 162
European Parliament, 9, 10, 12, 13, 19, 72, 81, 85
   budgetary powers, 87–91
   Cooperation Procedure, 24–26
   powers, 15–17
European Political Community, 3–4, 18
European Political Cooperation, 9, 10, 18–19
European Regional Development Fund

(ERDF), 13, 16, 80, 81
European Social Fund (ESF), 6, 13, 16, 80, 81, 112, 113, 115–116
European union, 3, 11, 12, 16, 20–27, 122
Exchange controls, 47, 49, 152
Exchange Rate Mechanism (of the EMS), xii, 55, 61, 62–65, 66, 67, 68
Exchange rates, 56–60, 62
Export restitution, 95

Factor mobility, 38–39, 47–49, 112–113, 125
Federalism, 1–3, 10–11, 20–22, 167
Federalists:
   evolutionary, 2
   functional, 2, 27
   radical, 2
Fontainebleau Agreement, 85, 150
France, 2, 3, 4, 9, 12, 14, 15, 19, 23, 45, 47, 61, 66, 67, 82, 83, 105, 107, 120, 131, 142, 152, 165, 168
Frontier formalities, 46, 49
Functionalist theory, 7–8, 15
   neo-functionalist theory, 9–11

de Gasperi, A., 3
de Gaulle, C., 10, 19
General Agreement on Trade and Tariffs (GATT), 31, 36, 103, 132, 155, 177, 178
Generalized System of Preferences, 173
Germany, 3, 4, 9, 13, 14, 15, 20, 22, 45, 47, 52, 57, 66, 82, 83, 85, 101, 105, 120, 131, 152, 165
Global Mediterranean Policy, 173
Gonzales, F., 14, 167
Greece, 14, 15, 20, 21, 23, 42, 47, 82, 101, 107, 119, 167
Green Exchange Rate, 103

Haas, E., 5, 7, 8, 10
Hallstein, W., 19
Hague Congress, 3
Heath, E., 147, 167
High Authority, 4, 5, 6, 8
Howe, G., 14, 152
Hymer, S., 130–131

Inflation, 56–58
   impact of EMS on, 66–70
Institutional Reform, 12, 19–25
Interinstitutional Agreement, 91
Interest groups, 7–8, 9, 17, 52, 69, 90, 107, 120
Intergovernmentalism, 19–20
Internal Market, see Common Market
Intervention price, 95–96
Ireland, 13, 14, 15, 21, 42, 52, 61, 75, 82, 101, 107, 120, 165, 167
Italy, 2, 3, 4, 12, 14, 15, 20, 22, 23, 45, 46, 47, 52,

61, 67, 82, 83, 101, 105, 107, 119, 165, 167

Köhl, H., 66, 167

Labour Party (UK), 5, 68, 146, 149, 153, 159, 162, 163
Less developed countries (LDCs), 102, 173, 179
Lindberg, L., 7, 8–10
Lomé Conventions, 80, 103, 173–180
Louvre Accord, 66
Luxembourg, 2, 3, 4, 13, 14, 15, 59, 152, 167
Luxembourg Compromise, 10, 12, 19–21, 27, 156, 159

MacDougall Report, 87
Major, J., 14
Mansholt Plan, 94
Merger controls, 128, 140–142
Messina Conference, 5, 6
Mitrany, D., 7
Mitterrand, F., 10, 14, 21, 22, 59, 122
Monetary Compensation Amount (MCA), 46, 49, 103
Monetary integration, 55–71, 167
   theory of, 55–60
Monetary Union, 8, 9, 10, 27, 31, 55–60, 153, 162
Monnet, J., 4, 5, 6, 7, 11
Multinational Enterprises (MNE), xiii, 36, 40, 120, 128–145
Mutual recognition principle, 49

National interests, xii, xiii, 4, 10, 11, 14, 20, 58–59, 61, 92, 107, 117, 147, 156
Netherlands, 3, 4, 13, 14, 15, 45, 59, 107, 120, 152, 165

Own resources, 75

Papandreos, A., 14, 167
Parlimentary (UK) Scrutiny Committees, 158–161
Political parties, 8, 9, 10, 69, 165–169
Portugal, 13, 14, 15, 20, 42, 75, 91, 122, 167
Price support mechanism, 94, 95
Protectionism, 37, 47, 51, 53
   and CAP, 101
Public procurement, 43–44, 50

Regional policy, 40, 58, 80
Rome Treaties, 5, 6, 12–15, 42, 46–48, 65, 111, 121, 141, 153, 156

Scheme for Mineral Products (SYSMIN), 177
Schiller Plan, 61
Schmidt, H., 61

Schuman Plan, 4
Schuman, R., 4, 7, 11
Single Administrative Document, 49
Single currency, 56, 60
Single European Act, 9, 11, 12, 16, 18, 21, 65,
    122, 156, 159, 163
    and EC policy-making, 23–27
    and 1992 programme, 42–53
Social Charter, 14, 28, 48, 51, 111, 124, 150, 162,
    167
Social dialogue, 119–120, 122, 124
Social dimension, *see* Social policy
Social dumping, 126
Social policy, 9, 10, 111–127
Solemn Declaration on European Union, 22
Sovereignty, 2, 18, 20, 26, 27, 30, 52, 53, 64–68, 70,
    73, 106, 125, 146, 147
    economic, 58–59
    parliamentary (UK), 154–161
Spaak, H., 3, 5
Spain, 2, 12, 14, 15, 20, 42, 45, 91, 107, 122, 165,
    167
Spillover, 8, 9
Spinelli, A., 2, 136
Spinelli Initiative, 22
Stabilization of Export Earnings Scheme
    (STABEX), 174, 177
State subsidies, 46, 51, 154, 155–156

Supranationalism, 2, 5, 7, 9, 20–27, 64, 73, 125,
    156, 163

Target price, 95
Thatcher, M., 10, 13, 14, 20, 23, 27, 52, 55, 66, 69,
    85, 122, 124–125, 147, 156, 162, 167, 168
Tindemans Report, 21
Transnational party groupings, 168
Trevi Group, 49

United Kingdom, 4–5, 12, 14, 15, 18, 20, 42, 45,
    48, 52, 57, 59, 61, 70, 75, 98, 101, 105, 107
    and EC budget row, 82–87
    and ERM membership, 68–69
    impact of EC membership, 146–163
United States, 4, 9, 58, 59, 87, 103, 106, 125, 129,
    131–133, 152

Value added tax (VAT), 44, 46, 50, 75–76, 85, 150
Variable Levy, 30, 75, 95
Vredeling Directive, 120

Welfare effect, 58, 60, 96, 99
    of CAP, 99–101
    of customs union, 31–40
Werner Plan, 61

Yaoundé Convention, 175